RESTORATION

A Call for Pure and Simple Christianity

F. LaGARD SMITH

Copyright 2001

Published By

Cotswold

PUBLISHING

Cover design by Amy Allison

RADICAL RESTORATION
Copyright © 2001 by F. LaGard Smith
Published by Cotswold Publishing
50 Brookhill Circle
Nashville, TN 37215

ISBN 0-9660060-3-8

Library of Congress Control Number: 2001129254

Printed in the United States of America

WITH APPRECIATION

Given a subject as sensitive as this one, I felt a special need to seek out a wide spectrum of viewpoints to review my work before the book took final form. With appreciation for their thoughtfulness and forthright candor, I wish to thank Randy Bouldin, Dee Bowman, Tony Coffey, Peter Dahlstrom, Kerstin Dahlstrom, Earl Edwards, Eric Hedden, Cecil May, Jr., Clarence McDowell, John Parker, Jack Reese, Jim Woodroof, and Tim Woodroof. Although we are not in agreement on every point, we continue to be united by cords of Christian love.

Special gratitude goes to my wife, Ruth, whose sensitive heart has softened many a phrase, and whose persistent sense of practicality time after time has forced me out of the ivory tower.

My thanks to Fort Guinn for calling my attention to *Flatland*. Gratitude, as well, to Barry Brewer and the entire staff at 21st Century Christian for their work in the distribution of this book; to Cathy Brown for the arduous task of typesetting; and to Amy Allison for going the extra mile in designing the cover.

Finally, I wish to express my appreciation to those of you in the Nashville area who first met to consider how we might better achieve "pure and simple Christianity." And also all of you who have shared your hearts and minds in response to my "going public" about radical restoration last fall at York College and Lubbock Christian University. And especially to those of you who asked probing questions during the Lipscomb Bible Lectures, or who have corresponded with me since. Through your study, prayers, and many thoughtful suggestions, radical restoration's call for a more involved "mutual participation" has already taken wing!

DEDICATION

To my brothers and sisters in the Lord,
both in America and abroad,
whose faith will be sorely tested
in a world which radically changed
with the tragic events of September 11, 2001.

CONTENTS

PREFACE

This book has been almost forty years in the making. Even as a teenager, I began to question differences between what I read in Scripture about the New Testament church, and the Church of Christ of the 1950's and '60's, defined with doctrinal precision in our Sunday-school book, aptly (or inaptly) titled, *The New Testament Church*.

I'll never forget the first dawning of disillusionment, which came in the chapter on "Church Finances." Certainly, I was not surprised when the study guide cited 1 Corinthians 16:1-2 (along with Matthew 5:42 and Luke 6:38!) as authority for the proposition that we are commanded to make a "contribution" each Lord's Day as part of the divine plan for financing the church. I had heard this text referenced for that purpose for as long as I could remember. But this time, looking more closely at the text, I could find no such "command," only Paul's practical instructions about how to handle a special contribution which the Corinthian brethren themselves had initiated.

On high alert from that point forward, I was troubled repeatedly by what seemed to me to be variances between the first-century church and what we claimed was *fully-restored* primitive Christianity. Could we possibly have gotten it so wrong? It wasn't just the obvious contextual damage done by our careless proof-texting. Far more serious, I began to see significant differences in how we functioned as a body of believers—in organization, worship ritual, and—all too often—in spirit.

Throughout my college years and on into law school, my concerns only deepened. (For better or for worse, my harrowing experience with the notorious Socratic method used in law school only exacerbated my fierce cross-examination of our usual interpretations of the text.) During that time, endless discussions with those whom I held in highest regard did little to assuage my fears that, as a church, we were not practicing the restoration theology we were preaching. While never once wavering from the idea of restoration (if perhaps never terribly obsessed with the Restoration Movement itself), I was increasingly convinced that our attempts at replicating the early church had fallen far short.

By the mid-1970's, I was a man in search of a fellowship. Associated at that time with the so-called "non-institutional" congregations among whom I had grown up, I began to look for others who might share my concerns. I even mailed a cautious appeal to the members of six different "non-institutional" congregations in my vicinity, explaining that I was "in search of a less denominational and more meaningful church of Christ." There was virtually no response.

Since then, my spiritual quest has taken me into the more mainstream "Churches of Christ," in which I have found both renewed life and fresh frustrations. Actually, *old* frustrations. Indeed, the *same* old frustrations...the same life-long concerns about how distanced I believe we all are from the scriptural pattern we so boldly profess.

In the meantime, I, along with you, have witnessed increasing tension between "conservatives" and "liberals" (theologically speaking) and, even more so, between "traditional" and "contemporary" congregations (ritually speaking). The latter divisions have resulted principally from the so-called "worship wars" in which everything from clapping and hand raising to contemporary music and praise teams have been points of controversy.

Somewhere along the line, it occurred to me that, as important as those battles may be, they pale in comparison to the single overarching issue which we've all persistently ignored. The way ahead, it seems to me, is neither "conservative" nor "liberal"; neither "traditional" nor "contemporary." Rather, it's a "third way." A way which, almost unknowingly, I've been trying to articulate for myself over these many years. In short (as revealed in the title of this book), it's what I've lately come to call *radical restoration*.

Over a year ago now, I briefly sketched out a "white paper" which served as a discussion piece for a number of brothers and sisters who had begun to express similar concerns. Not long afterwards, I "went public" for the first time in back-to-back lectures at York College and Lubbock Christian University. As it happened, the text of my informal chapel talk at York made its way into cyberspace, and—further still, so it seems—into more hearts and minds than I ever would have guessed.

Prompted by the many positive responses I received (and already thinking of expanding the "white paper" into book form), I set out to do something I'd never done in quite the same way through all those years. As much as I suspected where such a project would lead, nevertheless I sequestered myself in my usual writing spot in England and simply opened my Bible (a virtually new one, without previous underlining and scribbled marginal notes). I wanted to read afresh—as if I had never read a word of it—what Luke and the other New Testament writers tell us about the early church. Not just about their worship ritual, but about what attracted people to Christ in the first place; what motivated their continuing fervor; what kind of lives they lived in the midst of an alien culture; what hope they shared as they were met with persistent persecution.

The picture which gradually emerged was both intimately familiar and strangely foreign, as if I had never even glimpsed it before. While many of the thoughts which had occurred to me over the years were clearly reinforced, others had to be modified as I put the pieces of the puzzle back together with greater clarity. And there were almost breathtaking insights I'd never before considered.

To say that my understanding of the text has never been influenced by others along the way would surely be presumptuous. I owe a great debt to scholars and fellow writers who have contributed so richly from their vast knowledge and insight. Yet, I can't remember reading anything in particular which might have prompted some of the specific ideas which follow in this book. Unlike Paul, of course, I did not "receive it by revelation." Yet, together with Paul, I can say that—at least consciously—"I neither received it from any man, nor was I taught it."

That said, since beginning this process I've been surprised—and in a sense relieved—to learn how many others (including at least two high-profile leaders in the church) are independently beginning to think aloud about a more intense restoration experience. In the case of one of these well-known leaders, in particular, I suppose it's fair to say that we've not exactly been on the same page regarding various significant issues. And yet, with but few exceptions, one of his recent articles could well be a summary of this book!

Although obviously it would be premature to speak of anything like a groundswell, it does seem that something extraordinary is taking place along a broad front. Where it will lead, I, for one, am not sure. What I've attempted to do in the pages of this book is simply to facilitate the dialogue. To report as objectively as possible what the New Testament tells us about first-century faith and practice. To be brutally frank about our own 21st-century version of that pattern. And, finally, to frame the hard questions which must be asked about whatever discrepancies we discover. (If perhaps not always easy, it is certainly a simple enough process, which I encourage you to experience for yourself.)

I must warn some of you in advance that this book may not be comfortable reading. It challenges many of our most fundamental assumptions and confronts some of us with issues having potentially serious personal repercussions. As one might predict from my use of the word *radical*, the case I'm presenting takes us all the way to the outer perimeters and back again. At the extreme edges, the view is dizzying, to say the least. Then again, hasn't that always been the case whenever God's truth has broken through to challenge our human thinking and experience? Are we to be spared painful self-scrutiny any more than the religious establishment of Jesus' day, or even the first-century church itself?

In the pages ahead, I have found myself walking a fine line between, on one hand, advocating a non-negotiable Kingdom radicalism (on the premise that it appears to be God's own radicalism), and, on the other hand, suggesting certain "half-measures" in the likely event we are chased off by some of the more frightening aspects of extreme restoration. Although that may smack of playing politics with God, I would hope that even half-measures would be a step in the right direction, and might just open avenues of trust for our going still further.

On the other hand, I remain convinced that anything less than full and complete restoration of the Spirit-inspired, apostle-led primitive church will never reap the full benefits which God intends for his people. Compromises and half-measures rob not only God, but ourselves as well.

As you read further, I hope you will forgive any perceived disparagement in the certitude of my tone or the toughness of my words. As I am wont to say (along with many others, I'm sure), I'm often wrong, but never in doubt! (And, indeed, I may well have "gone off the track," as someone recently put it, at some point along the line.) But my prayer is that you will listen most closely to my heart. It may not always be apparent, but no book I have written has come from the depths of my soul quite like this one. For I believe that much is at stake in every way: My life. Yours. Our families. Our congregations. The whole church. Perhaps our world. And certainly eternal life.

The worst part about writing a book of this nature is that I have raised the bar higher than I would prefer even for myself. After years of quiet ferment, and now months of intense study and reflection, I'm not sure what's more daunting: not being able to see the way as clearly as I would have liked over the years; or finally seeing the mist rise from the path ahead, only to discover it's a more challenging road than I ever wanted to travel. A few chapters from now, I think you'll understand what I mean.

That is, if you get that far in your reading! I think I should alert you now to a rather unusual opening chapter. Without scaring you away, I have to confess that some of my reviewers found the original draft of Chapter 1 tough going. Hopefully, I've simplified it considerably in the final draft, but it remains a rather protracted analogy based upon what is essentially a mathematical concept. If you are like me, math is a universe apart. The irony is that this exquisite analogy itself is meant to help us see a radically different universe, or at least to think from a radically different perspective. So bear with me for the first dozen pages or so, and I promise you less heavy-going from there on out.

In Part One, we will explore the idea itself of Restoration. As people linked historically to the Restoration Movement, we are increasingly being asked to revisit the most basic assumptions underlying our call to restore New Testament Christianity. For example, is it true, as we claim, that we are neither Catholic nor Protestant but the fully-restored primitive body of Christ? Was restoration ever the right idea? In our attempts to restore the faith and practice of the early disciples, have we focused on primitive forms to the exclusion of intended functions? What role, if any, is "pattern" to play in our thinking?

In Part Two, we will focus more closely on a number of particular areas of worship and congregational functioning which seem (to me) to be out of sync with the New Testament pattern we claim to follow. Do we, for example, observe the Lord's Supper in the same way as the early disciples? Are our assemblies anything like house-church worship in the first century? Have we veered from the pattern in maintaining the traditional roles played by elders and preachers? What would it be like today if we really and truly radically restored primitive Christian faith and practice?

In order to advance the dialogue about these crucial issues, I have included at the end of the book what I call "Dissenting Opinions" and "Concurring Opinions." In these two sections, you will see many of the comments of my reviewers, both positive and negative. They likely will reflect some of your own reactions, pointing as they do to both strengths and weaknesses in the case which I am presenting for radical restoration. What matters for the moment is not whether we all agree on every point, but whether we have seriously considered the matters at hand.

In the long run, of course, we don't have the luxury of merely engaging in an interesting discussion. What is at stake is nothing less than being the kind of people God has called us to be. If we agree on nothing else, surely on that fundamental proposition we find ourselves on common ground.

PART I

THE RESTORATION IDEAL

Restore us to yourself, O LORD, that we may return;
renew our days as of old unless you have utterly rejected us
and are angry with us beyond measure.

LAMENTATIONS 5:21-22

CHAPTER ONE

WHEN FLATLAND IS THE HEARTLAND

O wad some Pow'r the giftie gie us
To see oursels as others see us.
It wad frae mony a blunder free us,
And foolish notion.

ROBERT BURNS

A s we begin our quest for radical restoration of first-century faith and practice, I would like to share with you just a brief summary of a most wonderful little book which has stretched my own thinking recently. While it seems to come from right out of left field, I believe it can open up a dramatic new way of looking at ourselves as God's people. It's all about radical thinking. About intellectual honesty. About personal courage in the face of the obvious...and the not-so-obvious.

At times, the little book can be tough-sledding, but I assure you it's well worth the ride. Once you grasp its message, your familiar comfort zone may never quite be so comfortable again.

It was over a century ago when Edwin Abbott, head principal of an English school, presented the world with his delightful masterpiece of satirical science-fiction titled simply *Flatland*. Trained in the classics, with a keen interest in literature and theology, Abbott was a man ahead of his time. While Einstein was a mere child, and theories of relativity and the fourth dimension of space-time were only then being discussed in the abstract by mathematicians and physicists, Abbott broke through barriers of traditional thinking to suggest dimensions which had occurred to very few people on the globe.

Abbott's genius was to create a fantasy, two-dimensional world called Flatland, which is inhabited by geometric figures who think, feel, and speak very much the same as we humans do, but who have no appreciation of three-dimensional space. To better understand the world of Flatland, imagine yourself looking down at a triangle cut out of cardboard lying on top of a table. As you lean over it, naturally it looks precisely like the triangle it is. But if you draw back to the edge of the table and gradually lower your eye, the triangle will begin to take on a slightly elongated appearance. Lower your eye even further to the edge of the table, and the triangle (now with one of the sides facing you) will suddenly appear as nothing but a straight line. At that point, you, yourself, will have entered Flatland—a world of length and breadth but not height.

Now imagine a broad sheet of paper on which triangles, squares, pentagons, hexagons, and other geometric figures move about performing normal human activities. With great difficulty, they are even able to distinguish one type of geometric "citizen" from another. (The lower classes—Triangles, Squares, Pentagons, and Hexagons—detect each other's angles by "feel." The upper class Polygons are sufficiently educated in "sight recognition" so that they are able to know the shapes of their fellow citizens without having to physically grope them.)

Because the citizens of Flatland can never rise above, nor sink below, the surface of the paper, their worldview is exclusively two-dimensional. They can never perceive of their existence from any other perspective. In fact, the world of Flatland has the four points of the compass—North, South, East, and West—just as we have, but there is nothing higher or lower than the surface itself. Therefore, "North" is part of Flatland's vocabulary, but, importantly, not "up" or "upward."

To be sure, there are those in Flatland who dream of some other dimension, and even speak quietly about the prospect of such a universe. Yet, since Flatland is all-too-human, it is illegal to suggest that there might be some dimension other than the orthodox dimensions of length and breadth. Any heretical Square or Octagon who might go around advocating the existence of a Third Dimension is locked up or even "painlessly and mercifully consumed."

As an inhabitant of Flatland, Abbott (writing under the pseudonym of "A. Square") finds himself contemplating the unthinkable when, suddenly, he senses "a Presence." The stranger turns out to be a Sphere from Spaceland, who has come to spread the Gospel of the Third Dimension. By "feeling" the Sphere, Abbott knows the stranger has no angles, and therefore concludes he must be a circle. But the Sphere explains that he is a collection of larger and smaller circles stacked on top of one another, and that Abbott sees only one section at a time.

To demonstrate what he means, the Sphere begins to rise above, and then dip below, the surface of Flatland. To Abbott's amazement, the "length" of each of the circle's "lines" gets longer or shorter with every movement—a phenomenon he has never before experienced!

There follows an exchange in which the Sphere invites Abbott to imagine a flat Square moving parallel to itself upward—an exercise designed to present the idea, first of a Cube, then of a Solid. But Abbott is baffled by the unknown word *upward*. "What? Northward?" he asks, perplexed. The Sphere's response becomes, both then and later, the punch line of the entire book: "No, not Northward; upward; out of Flatland altogether."

Abbott is not so much unconvinced as stupefied. So the Sphere proceeds to demonstrate the reality of three-dimensional space by looking down on Flatland and telling Abbott everything that is happening all across Flatland at the same moment. With that, Abbott is "almost persuaded," but only almost.

In desperation, the Sphere finally yanks Abbott away from Flatland and flings him kicking and screaming into Spaceland. Looking down on Flatland, Abbott is astonished: "I looked, and, behold, a new world!" There was simply no denying it: Spaceland was real, and there was a third dimension after all!

But Abbott's exhilarating experience in Spaceland is short-lived. Hardly a day passes before he reluctantly finds himself once again in Flatland, and is faced with the greatest dilemma of his life: *to tell* or *not to tell*. Telling, of course, means certain arrest and punishment. Not telling is...well, simply impossible. When at last he can contain himself no longer, Abbott spills out his heresy and pays the predictable price of perpetual imprisonment. All that, and not one convert! To this day, the citizens of Flatland remain in a world of their own, certain that there is simply no other way to look at life. At the very least, they are certain that they will not risk the danger of even contemplating so radical a thought.

Flatland In Jesus' Day

As one reads *Flatland*, it is difficult not to think of the many parallels with events in Scripture. Principally, of course, there is the coming of Christ (Sphere-like) into our three-dimensional physical world, pointing to a spiritual dimension which defies the natural, earth-bound mind-set of even the most enlightened. Among Israel's religious leaders, for example, who more than Nicodemus ought to have understood what Jesus meant when he talked about being born again of water and the Spirit? But the highly-respected, well-educated (and apparently sincere) Nicodemus was as mystified about the Spiritual Dimension as Abbott was about the Third Dimension.

"Surely a man cannot enter a second time into his mother's womb...?" Nicodemus asked, incredulously. ("What?

Northward?") It was all beyond the conceptual grasp of this devout, commandment-keeping, righteous man of God. When it came to understanding the nature of heaven, eternal life, and the deepest matters of the soul, Nicodemus might just as well have been a citizen of Flatland. Despite the fact that, unlike Abbott, Nicodemus' frame of reference was already three-dimensional, he had an equally difficult challenge rising above that perspective to fully appreciate the radically different dimension of which Jesus was speaking.

What can be said of Nicodemus, however, is that at least he was open to thinking about his faith in ways which were not strictly orthodox to the conventions of his day. Why else seek out Jesus? And *at night*?

From what we are told later of his courageous part in the burial of Jesus, it seems clear that Nicodemus eventually understood Jesus' own version of the message, "not Northward, but upward." Not more of what you already know, but something you've never before contemplated. Not business-as-usual in worship and religious practice, but a whole new way of viewing one's relationship with God. Not decades, or even centuries, of innovative religious tradition based upon a merely human perspective, but patterns of faith and practice revealed by the divine "Sphere" who came down into our world to lift us up to that "higher plane" about which we so often sing.

The world into which Jesus came was as dimensionally-challenged as Abbott's Flatland. And as closed-minded. Certainly, it was also as resolute to ban any prophet or mad man who would dare suggest the possibility of any perspective other than that which was uniformly held. Indeed, Jesus would have fared better in Flatland, where at least he would have been "painlessly and mercifully" consumed.

By Flatland standards, the Gospel of the Third Dimension was radical thinking of the highest order. For Israel's religious establishment, the gospel according to Jesus was equally radical.

Indeed, it was not "good news" at all. The divine Son of God had not left heaven merely to redecorate the temple or synagogue. The incarnate Son of Man had not come simply to tweak the system a bit and make it more efficient. Rather, the bold, unmistakable oracle of Jesus was that Israel's religious institutions (as they had come to be) and her most hallowed traditions were fundamentally flawed from top to bottom.

It was as if, in a multi-dimensional spiritual universe, Israel was doggedly (even arrogantly) groping its way along in a stultifying religious Flatland. Its compass points, more fixed in tradition than in stone tablets, were Rules, Ritual, Rank, and Rhetoric. When Jesus responded, saying, "Not Rules, but righteousness," it was a call to radical living. When he said, "Not Ritual, but spiritual," he was pointing toward a radical relationship with God. What further need be said of Rank and Rhetoric? For Israel's power-obsessed religious leaders—indeed, even for Jesus' closest disciples—servant leadership was as radical a thought as Abbott's Spaceland. And the pure, unadulterated doctrine of Christ was as radical a departure from the rabbis' vaunted rhetoric as cubes and solids are from squares.

Living In A Denominational Flatland

All of which brings us to our own religious world and to the institutions and traditions which we ourselves hold most dear. Is it possible that we, too, live in Flatland? Or, perhaps more to the point: Is it possible for any of us *not* to live in Flatland? Given the human tendency to see only what we are accustomed to seeing, how will we ever escape our own religious Flatland unless we permit ourselves to openly and honestly entertain fundamental challenges to our faith and practice?

Such a process will not be easy, of course. Nor, if we truly begin to think in radical terms, will it allow us peaceful rest through the night. Speaking personally, I would rather not think about it at all. Already, I have had far too many sleepless nights,

pangs of conscience, and alternating bouts of unrequited ideal-
ism and frustrating cynicism.

For, among Flatlanders, I am chief. I myself am a fifth-
generation Flatlander. My father was a Flatland preacher, as was
his grandfather, and his father, and his. As a young man, I
attended Flatland College. For some thirty years now, I have
taught at two Flatland universities. Over the years, I have
preached from innumerable Flatland pulpits. And most personal of all—had my wife not also been a Flatlander, the odds of our
having met and married would have been slim indeed.

The "Flatland" of which I speak, of course, is the Church
of Christ; or, as variously referred to: the "Churches of Christ"
(or even "churches of Christ"). Insistence on the latter terminol-
ogy is most often an effort to reinforce one of the principal dog-
mas of our particular Flatland—that we are not a "denomination" like the denominations around us.

Lay aside for the moment the crucial doctrinal differences
which would separate us from the crowd. To the extent that
there are thought to be other fundamental, substantive differences between our fellowship and "the denominations," we find
ourselves "circles" in a world of "squares" and "triangles." By
groping others doctrinally, we sense that everyone else has
unauthorized angles, while we are the only legitimate geometri-
cal figure.

However, our adamant insistence that we are non-
denominational is not alone a matter of perceived differences in
doctrine. Aided by our own Flatland rhetoric, we have declared
that we simply cannot be a denomination, because Christ's
church—as known through Scripture—is not a denomination.
Having made a deft, if not entirely plausible, linkage between
the first-century model of *Christ's church* and the 21st-century
Church of Christ as we know it, the argument seems unassailable.

Yet, one need only take a trip into the Scriptures and,
from there, look back on our particular Flatland to see the vast

difference between the universal church of Christ we claim to be
and the particularized Church of Christ we are in fact. Certainly,
were time travel possible, there is little doubt but that first-century Christians would hardly recognize what we today call the
"Churches of Christ."

Beginning with the least significant of all the differences,
I suspect they would recoil in horror at our use of "Church of
Christ" as an adjective, such as in "Church of Christ school" or
"Church of Christ minister." More shocking still would be the
various linguistic equivalents of the "Church-of-Christ Church."
("What are you religiously?" someone asks; and the oft-heard
response is "Church of Christ.")

In the world of first-century Christianity, it would have
been unthinkable to speak of "the Jerusalem Church of Christ,"
or the "Appian Way Church of Christ," as we today so naturally speak of, say, "the Twelfth and Main Street Church of Christ."
We must not be tempted to think that the Christians in Rome
would have attached the same connotation to Paul's greeting,
"The churches of Christ salute you," in anything like the same
institutionalized, bumper-sticker way as we do today. Nor
would they have been bothered in the least, as would we, to be
called the "church of God."

When the apostles walked the earth, neither the "Church
of God" (Pentecostal) nor the "Church of Christ" (non-
Pentecostal except for Acts 2:38) were ever designations used in
our current denominational sense. The church of God at Corinth
was simply the collective group of God's called-out people in
that city. With equal correctness, the early disciples were known
as the "church of the firstborn," but never the "Church of
Christ" nor even the "Churches of Christ," in the sectarian sense
in which we use it.

Our stubborn Flatland insistence that we are non-denominational is easily betrayed by the simplest of methods. Open
any Yellow Pages, for example, and you will quickly find that

we have voluntarily joined the denominational ranks. Along with the Baptists, Methodists, and Presbyterians, there we are—for all the world to see—clumped under the heading of "Church of Christ." In our own Nashville Yellow Pages, no fewer than 65 congregations fall under that listing (including two or three which, despite their familiar name, would not be doctrinally aligned). With some irony, there are 36 listings exclusively under the heading, "Non-denominational" (as distinct from "Interdenominational"), and not one of them is part of the "Churches of Christ."

Our denominational nomenclature is only the most immediate and striking difference that would be noted by time-traveling Christians from the first century. Even allowing for revolutionary technological, economic, and cultural differences, they undoubtedly would find our organizational structure, manner of worship, and personal lifestyles strangely foreign. More important to the present discussion, it is unlikely that—apart from crucial doctrinal distinctions—these time-travelers from another world would readily detect a great deal of difference between ourselves and "the denominations." As they function, so we function. As they live, so we live.

It's the old story about the duck. If you look like a duck, quack like a duck, and waddle like a duck, is it possible that you just might be one?

Without question, those *today* who look at us from the outside invariably regard us as simply one denomination among many; and, given the way we think and act, they have every reason for doing so. To resolutely maintain the pretense that we are somehow uniquely non-denominational surely places us in the very heart of Flatland. Admittedly, we may not be sophisticated Polygons like the Catholics, Anglicans, or Episcopalians, with their intricate teachings and rituals. Maybe not even Pentagons like the Pentecosts, or Squares like the Foursquares. But we definitely have our own distinct form, easily recognized as denominational by everyone who comes close enough to grope us in the manner of Flatland.

Happy Campers in Denominationland

There are, of course, a growing number of Flatlanders among us who have tasted somewhat of "Spaceland's" new perspective, and now readily acknowledge that the "Churches of Christ" are seriously denominational. The surprise, however (if one understands them correctly), is that they appear to be completely comfortable with that thought. Emancipated from the head-in-sand delusions of their former Flatland, they seem to feel enlightened and liberated. Having acknowledged that we are, in fact, a denomination, they no longer feel burdened with defending the indefensible, and are now free to concentrate on changing and shaping our denomination in ever-progressive ways.

It's hard to say which is more disturbing: those who refuse to admit that we live in Flatland and are denominational, or those who have embraced the denominational community and are already rushing headlong to be *interdenominational*.

What possible benefit comes from discovering that we are merely one among many denominations, if, despite that epiphany, we remain content to remain denominational? Are some among us so embarrassed by our former exclusivism that they will do anything to be included in the larger community? Are they really so desperate to be "groped" in Christian fellowship and found acceptable?

Paraphrasing from Paul's letter to the Galatians (4:9)...Once we finally recognize how very denominational we have become, how can we possibly turn back to those weak and miserable principles of denominational thought and practice? Do we wish to be enslaved by them all over again?

Abbott doesn't mention it in *Flatland*, but I get the distinct feeling that Flatland has as powerful a gravitational pull as the

Earth's. Tearing ourselves wholly away from a century of denominational thinking may be one of the most difficult things we do in a lifetime. Merely consider those bitter critics of the church who disagree with even its most fundamental doctrines yet never launch away toward more doctrinally-friendly shores. Their continuing denominational allegiance in the face of doctrinal disenchantment is all the more remarkable given the increasing availability of broad-minded "community churches," which typically are more genuinely independent and non-denominational than ourselves.

Flatland gravity: Never underestimate its pull!

In the pages to come, the call for radical restoration is a call for greater trust in a dimension beyond our own intuitive, pragmatic knowing. It is a call to throw off the denominational thinking which obscures our historic commitment to biblical restoration, and to consider how wonderfully revitalizing true restoration might be. Indeed, it is an appeal, not just to a different dimension, but to a higher dimension.

"What? Northward?"

No, not Northward; upward.

CHAPTER TWO

"RADICAL" SOUNDS TERRIBLY RADICAL!

There are a thousand hacking at the branches of evil to
one who is striking at the roots.

HENRY DAVID THOREAU

When I discovered our little cottage in the English Cotswolds some fifteen years ago, one of the first things to catch my eye was the garden, and especially the beautiful roses. Not exactly an expert on flowers, I had no idea what particular variety they were. All I knew is that they were lovely red, cream, and yellow roses which, over the years, have given great delight to all who pass by. No one seems to know who first planted the bushes, nor how old they might be. Given the age of the cottage, I suspect they've been around quite a long time.

Until I met Ruth—my lovely bride and now Head Gardener—I can assure you that the roses received no special attention. As a keen gardener, Ruth knows just when to prune and precisely where along the stem to make the cut. And then there's all that tedious "dead-heading" with which I could never be bothered. To me, the fine art of gardening is as arcane as a Mason's secret handshake. Under Ruth's tender care, fortunately, the roses have not only survived their former neglect but actually flourished.

Yet not even Ruth was prepared for the extraordinary beauty with which we were greeted last summer. During our time away in the States the previous autumn, the young man whom we left in charge of the garden had done some pruning of his own...with a vengeance! Returning to the cottage before Ruth in early January, I was horrified to find the rose bushes virtually destroyed. Or so I thought. As spring turned into summer, and the bushes awakened to the pulses of the seasons, we were presented with the most wonderful bouquet of roses we had ever seen in our garden. Longer stems. Vigorous new growth. Not a trace of disease to be found. Only a bounty of resplendent roses permeating the air with their delightful fragrance.

And all because of radical pruning.

But should that be surprising? If you think about it, "radical pruning" is Nature's way of bringing out the best in God's Creation. Merely consider the raging wild fires out west which ravage whole forests, only to make way for new growth and even greater beauty. Or the devastating seasonal floods in some parts of the world, which despite their immediate havoc make possible the optimum environment for thriving crops. And if a short, sharp frost or two helps keep the pesky insect population under control, then I'm all for short, sharp frosts, whatever other damage they may do to overly-eager fruit blossoms in the early spring.

The same goes for human nature. If perhaps the wisdom of "Spare the rod, and spoil the child" is momentarily lost on the young miscreant whose bottom is still stinging from a little "radical pruning," one day he'll better appreciate the cost-benefit analysis involved. Of course, discipline comes in all sorts of packages. Those of us with a bit of experience under our belts can vouch for the many blessings which have come our way by means of the "radical pruning" of life's unexpected tragedies and disappointments. Our greatest periods of personal growth seem to have followed hard on the heels of our greatest losses.

None More Radical Than God

As with Nature and human nature, it is also the nature of God to bring about his purposes through radical pruning. In Jesus' own words, "...every branch that bears fruit he prunes, that it may bear more fruit" (John 15:2 NKJV). Throughout history, God's "pruning" has taken on many forms. As even the young ones among us all know, when the inclinations and thoughts of man's heart were continually evil, "the rains came down and the floods came up." Only that time, it wasn't just the foolish man's house that fell flat. Except for eight righteous souls and a boat-load of animals, a flood of catastrophic proportions wiped the earth completely clean. The time for rainbows and restoration would come, but not before a destructive deluge so radical that God vowed never to repeat it.

When God's chosen bride committed spiritual adultery with detestable idols, and filled the land with empty worship and the stench of injustice, God pleaded, begged, entreated, and implored in vain before finally putting Israel away. In the mouths of prophets like Jeremiah, Spirit-revealed words of restoration were inextricably tied with words of warning. Yes, "the days are coming when I will bring my people back from captivity and restore to them the land I gave to their forefathers" (30:3). But first, "disaster will be poured out on all who live in the land" (1:14).

Repeatedly, God raised up leaders to restore Israel's worship, which had either been neglected or become corrupt. In each instance, the spiritual cleansing was abrupt, far-reaching, and complete. Merely consider, for example, the way God worked through Hezekiah, who rebuked the priests and Levites, saying, "Listen to me, Levites! Consecrate yourselves now and consecrate the temple of the Lord.... Remove all [the pagan] defilement from the sanctuary" (2 Chronicles 29:4-5). Immediately, they set to work and brought out into the temple courtyard everything unclean which they found inside. "So the temple of the Lord was reestablished," and "Hezekiah and all the people rejoiced at what God had brought about for his people, because it was done so quickly" (29:35-36)

God's crusade against idolatrous practices was particularly harsh in the early reign of the young king Josiah. "In his twelfth year, he began to purge Judah and Jerusalem of high places, Asherah poles, carved idols and cast images.... The altars of the Baals were torn down.... These he broke to pieces and scattered over the graves of those who had sacrificed to them. He burned the bones of the priests on their altars, and so he purged Judah and Jerusalem" (2 Chronicles 34:3-5). No half-measures here. No slight, mid-course corrections.

Ten years later, when Josiah sent workers to repair the temple, the workers discovered the Book of the Law. Amazingly, it had been decades since God's Book had played an important role in the religious life of Israel. Upon news of the discovery, Josiah was so distraught that he tore his robes and lamented: "Great is the Lord's anger that is poured out on us because our fathers have not kept the word of the Lord; they have not acted in accordance with all that is written in this book" (2 Chronicles 34:21).

Do we simply dismiss this part of Israel's history as interesting but irrelevant? Is it so inconceivable that *we ourselves* have not acted in accordance with all that is written? Given the materialism, immodesty, immorality, unauthorized divorce and remarriage, and shallow spirituality which has become endemic among us, can we assert with assurance that we have no need, as an entire family of God, to let the words of his Book rebuke us? As God's covenant people, do we not, even now, need to renew our covenant to follow the Lord? A naive church that stood for misguided orthodoxy but still "lived the life" would be different from an arrogant church that has joined the world.

Never was Israel's national restoration more radical than when Ezra called the people to account for intermarrying with heathens. While Ezra was "praying and confessing, and weeping and throwing himself down before the house of God" (Ezra 10:1-4), the people themselves gathered around and wept bitterly. Then came the call for them to separate themselves from their foreign wives, and "the whole assembly responded with a loud voice: 'You are right! We must do as you say'" (10:12).

Unlike our present controversies, these prohibited marriages had nothing to do with scattered incidents of unauthorized divorce and remarriage. The issue here had to do with purifying the "whole church," as it were, and nothing short of radical action would bring about radical restoration.

Their question becomes ours: What are we willing to put away—as a fellowship of Christians—to ensure that we are wholly obedient before God?

With drastic action having been required to purge Israel of its inclination toward idolatry, whoever could have believed that a similar apostasy would be repeated? But as we know, Nehemiah, too, was faced with yet another round of intermarriages when he returned to Jerusalem to rebuild its walls. Our modern sensitivities are disturbed when we read that Nehemiah not only rebuked those who had married heathen wives, and called curses down upon them (Nehemiah 13:23-25), but he also "beat some of the men and pulled out their hair!" If that seems less than politically correct, think of his furious assault as if it were a parable. This wasn't simply an incensed religious leader losing his temper. This was an angry God pulling out Israel's idolatry by its roots.

To miss the *method* is to miss the *message*: If God's restoration is radical, dare ours be anything less? You can be sure that no one today would dare pull out the hair of those who have led us into denominational thinking and practice. But what's more disturbing is that so few of us, if any, seem to be pulling out our own hair in dismay at how far we have strayed from pure, apostolic Kingdom fervor and practice.

Us, Fundamentally Flawed?

It's been suggested to me that we are so little disturbed because we are so little convinced that the system is fundamentally flawed...or even flawed at all. Many congregations seem to be thriving more than ever, and most others seem to be humming along quite nicely, thank you. Thus comes the familiar response: "If it ain't broke, don't fix it!" Or, "Why get so worked up about being radical when we're not convinced there's anything wrong to begin with?"

Perhaps an illustration would be helpful. Suppose the President's energy czar goes on television and tells the nation that our whole energy system is fundamentally flawed because it is based on fossil fuels. The present system needs to be completely overhauled, he says, so as to include conservation strategies, and solar, geothermal, and wind technologies. In such a scenario, the energy czar would not be telling us that fossil fuels don't "work" in a technical sense. Indeed, cars are running more efficiently than ever and industry shows no signs of fuel-based decline. His message, of course, is that fossil fuels are fundamentally flawed because they have inherent, unavoidable problems—such as pollution, depletion of resources, and, most serious of all, health risks.

Similarly, just because what we do in the church today sort of "works" doesn't necessarily mean that we are completely and fully New Testament Christians. (The Catholic Church has "worked" for centuries. Indeed, the Jewish system at the time of Christ could not have appeared to be more alive and well.) The point is that to whatever extent we are, in fact, significantly different from the church described in the New Testament, to that extent we are "fundamentally flawed." To that extent, too, we have been deprived of the blessings which otherwise would flow our way, and unknowingly have become vulnerable to a host of spin-off consequences.

Beating Spears Into Pruning Hooks

Sometimes the consequences of being "fundamentally flawed" manifest themselves only as subtle changes in priorities, or perhaps attitudes—not necessarily in specific worship forms or practices. One wonders, for example, whether the historical priority we have given to doing doctrinal battle, as compared with the lesser attention typically given to personal spiritual discipline and development, is one such consequence. Is it possible that our priorities have become skewed because, given the very nature of our movement, we have viewed ourselves as *Restorationists* almost as much as *Christians*? (By and large, this only applies to those of us who are older. For the most part, the younger generation has pendulum-swung to the opposite extreme.) Whereas *Christians* seek sanctification, purity, and spiritual growth, *Restorationists* are reformers, crusaders, warriors.

Have you ever noticed the juxtaposition of images used by the prophets of old in referring to pruning hooks? Isaiah and Micah, of course, give us that wonderful vision of Israel's restoration—a time when, "They will beat their swords into plowshares and their spears into pruning hooks." But Joel's version (3:10) is just the reverse. When the time comes for God's wrath to be poured out upon Israel's enemies, the word goes out to Israel: "Beat your plowshares into swords and your pruning hooks into spears."

Not to read too much into these simple images, one does sense that there is a time for pruning hooks and a time for swords and spears. The history of our movement is replete, of course, with spiritual battles of all types, in which our enemies have been as much within our own ranks as outside our borders. Perhaps we love the taste of battle because, as in every war, we can all reassure ourselves that "God is on our side." As long as everyone else is wrong, we *must be* right!

Yet, constantly pointing fingers at everyone else has an insidious way of distracting us from our own failings. In order to reform others, we ourselves must be reformed. In order to restore, we must be restored. Imagine what a difference it would make if those outside the Lord's body could look with envy upon a fellowship of believers who obviously "walk the walk" of a radically-restored people. ("God's new society," to quote John Stott.) No longer would we have to convert them at the point of a sword. Imagine, too, how different even the Lord's body would be if restoration were not just a theological debate but a living reality.

If spiritual wars are inevitable (indeed, *because* spiritual wars are inevitable) surely there are times to pause in the middle of the fight and turn our belligerent, enemy-targeted spears back into pruning hooks of brutal self-censure. Who knows, then, but that we might require far fewer spears...and perhaps no more self-deluding swords.

Is There No Other Way?

Whenever I've shared my thoughts about radical restoration with others, I'm most often asked the question: "But isn't it possible to work *within the system* to bring about any necessary changes?" I accept that the question arises partly out of a responsible sense of prudence and caution. It was George Bernard Shaw who said that "reformers have the idea that change can be achieved by brute sanity." Yet, I suspect the question also reflects a sense of lingering institutional loyalty, apprehension about potential church conflicts, and misgivings about where we will end up once we head down a different path. I freely confess that I share each of those same fears. Whether we wish it or not, we are all joined at the hip with a heritage which is, if not genetic, at least for most of us deeply and stubbornly ingrained.

As much as I would like to think it were possible to partially reform rather than to radically restore, my every instinct says it is not. Certainly, of course, there are things about our worship which we could change significantly within the present context. For example, we could throw away the clock and truly "take time to be holy" without altering anything else at all. But the kind of rudimentary concerns which we will discuss in the next several chapters simply cannot be resolved without radically restructuring the church as it presently functions. Indeed, not so much *restructuring* it, but actually *dismantling* it by means of recapturing its original definition and meaning.

Before real progress can be made, we will have to undergo a pivotal paradigm shift in the way we perceive even the notion of "church" itself. The word "church," as used in our common parlance and practice—denoting a religious body complete with rules and rituals—has little in common with the "body of called-out-ones" (or even the "called-together" assembly) contemplated by *ekklesia* in the original text. Our concept of the church typically tends to suggest *organization*, complete with hierarchy and dogma. By contrast, the early church (while by no means disorganized) was far closer to being an *organism*—less dependent upon formal structure and more spontaneous in action.

Without question, the church which Christ came to establish falls within the broad definition of an institution. Yet the intended dynamics of that blood-bought body couldn't be further from what we normally think of as an "institution." Perhaps you've heard the old joke about marriage being a wonderful institution...but who wants to live in an institution! That double-entendre illustrates how the word *institution* can have altogether different meanings, depending upon its use. As used in this book, *institution* denotes an organized religious body whose doctrinal and organizational superstructure has overshadowed the more sublime purposes for which it was established.

It would be a great advance if only we could begin to think of the church more as *they* or *we* rather than *it*. In England, where I am writing, I still find it jarring when I hear on the evening news that "Ford *are* laying off 2,000 workers"; or that

"Manchester United [the soccer team] *are* on top of the league tables." Shouldn't that be "Ford *is* laying off..." and "Manchester United *is* on top..."? Yet, by British usage, these collective nouns contemplate, not the organization itself, but the people—individually and collectively—within the organization.

To use another British expression, we've all been "snookered" by the fairly universal translation of *ekklesia* as "church" into thinking of the Lord's body principally as a corporate organization, not altogether different from Ford or Manchester United. That is, thinking of the *institution* for which Christ died, rather than thinking of the *collective body of people* for whom Christ died. That, in turn, has allowed us to slide all too easily from thinking of "church" in a scriptural sense to thinking of "church" in a denominational sense.

A denominational church is one in which our identity is described most often in terms of institutional membership. (For example, "I became a member of the church of Christ after I was married"; or "We've placed our membership at the Seventh Avenue Church of Christ.") Listen to our language. It's not so much, "She's a Christian," but rather "She's a member of the church." How we talk betrays how unwittingly denominational we have become. In this and in most other respects, the so-called "non-institutional" brethren are just as institutionally-minded as those whom they call "institutional." The sad truth is that, with few exceptions, we are pervasively and intractably institutional.

More crucial still is how we view ourselves personally. Because of our denominational mind-set, we are more likely to think of ourselves as having been *baptized* (been there, done that, satisfied the church's entry requirements) than having been *sanctified* (spiritually regenerated and set apart for a lifetime of radical Christian living). Lamentably, our denominational-style membership is easily maintained by little more than dutiful attendance, minimal financial contributions, and sufficiently-circumspect moral conduct. If perhaps higher expectations are exhorted, rarely is anything more demanded. Before you know it, such token institutional participation is equated with "being a Christian." The quantum-leap, night-and-day difference is lost on most members—because, first and foremost, we are "members"!

Make no mistake. This is not just a matter of semantics or word games. Before we can begin to think in radically spiritual ways, we have to quit thinking in familiar, worldly ways.

The very nature of radical restoration is such that the act of demolition is as vital as the act of creation. Invariably, wrecking crews must raze the old structure before they can begin to build anew. It's the ancient question revisited: is it possible to pour new wine into old wineskins? One answer keeps coming back: Before God could lovingly restore Israel, he had to put her away. In like fashion, for Christ to enter into a new covenant, the old covenant had to be done away.

Think not, then, that the plea of this book is just one more instance of progressive "change agents" trying to be innovative by introducing contemporary forms of worship at odds with our tradition. That is the work of perhaps well-intentioned but ineffectual quick-fix artists who deal only with the symptoms of our malaise, not the root causes. Their palliatives might serve temporarily to mask more basic problems, and even—for a time—to breathe fresh life into one's limping spiritual walk. But still the fundamental flaws remain. Ironically, the more exciting new programs a church plugs into, the more likely it is that there's a lifeless body being kept alive on artificial life support. We keep thinking that if we just stick a few more tubes into the body, no one will notice that the patient is virtually dead.

Whether consciously or unconsciously, most of our innovations—from joy buses, to youth ministries, to marriage and family seminars, to church-growth theories, to contemporary music and worship teams—are borrowed, bag and baggage, from the denominations. Injecting innovations while running breathlessly to "keep up with everybody else" is not at all the idea. Purposeful restoration of God's patterned people is the idea.

Repentance, The Perfect Parable

Let me shift gears for a moment. To this point, we've been talking mostly about the collective body of believers we know as "the church" and about how that body might be radically restored. However, looking from a more personal viewpoint, we could just as well talk about radical repentance...if that's not redundant. True repentance is always radical, for to repent is to have a radical change of heart and mind. Indeed, more heart than mind, for the demons believed and trembled; and, even now, millions have been immersed without ever having been converted. So many of us have been persuaded, but not permeated; taught, but not transformed.

I say *us*, not *they*, as if we could more easily point fingers at others. Despite so closely associating our collective identity with Acts 2:38, we nevertheless tend to slice our corporate-logo verse neatly in half. Preaching mostly the tie between baptism and forgiveness, we have remained ominously silent about the connection between repentance and receiving the gift of the Holy Spirit. But if there is no such thing as an unbaptized Christian—and there is not—by the same force of argument, there is no such thing as an unrepentant, Spirit-less Christian.

In theory, of course, we all agree about the need for repentance. After all, repentance is one of the time-honored "five steps to salvation," and an indispensable digit in our five-fingered outline. Yet, sadly, I fear that many of us (beginning with myself) are greatly distanced from the meaning of true repentance. Those of us who "grew up in the church" and were immersed at an early age are particularly vulnerable to the possibility that we have never once experienced the radical change of heart that sustains faith, deepens commitment, and makes it virtually impossible *not* to tell others about the dramatic difference which that transformation of heart has made in our lives.

At the moment of our faith commitment, most of us could not have related to those among our Corinthian brothers and sisters who, prior to being washed in the blood, were "fornicators, idolaters, adulterers, effeminate, abusers of themselves with mankind, thieves, covetous, drunkards, revilers, and extortioners" (1 Corinthians 6:9-11). Nor, I dare say, were any of us on a conscious par with the reprehensible "tax collectors and sinners" associated with Matthew Levi (Luke 5:27-32). At the point of our adolescent baptisms, surely few of us regarded ourselves as sinners in the same bone-wearying, soul-wrenching way as the conscience-stricken tax collectors and despairing prostitutes who eagerly received John's preaching of repentance. Before one toe had been covered by the waters of their immersion, they had fully committed themselves to a radical turning of their lives before God (Matthew 21:28-32).

Unlike baptism, which is a disarmingly simple physical act, repentance is a matter of the heart demanding—where necessary—ourageous, extreme reversals of former habits, lifestyles, and attitudes. In such cases, nothing short of total, radical spiritual restoration will suffice for true repentance. If you think about it, genuinely penitent people have always been "a bunch of radicals," known not for what they demonstrated *against*, but for the radically-changed lives which they demonstrated.

Those of us who were immersed more out of studied obedience and idealistic commitment than the desperate hope of emancipation from sin's captive chains have some catching up to do in understanding the dynamics of radical restoration on a personal level. For many of us, only a shameful falling-away from those youthful ideals has given us any glimpse at all of the harsh realities demanded by genuine repentance.

The pernicious effects of a spiritual body composed mostly of second-generation Christians whose early-youth baptisms
were, in the main, more convention than conversion are more
spiritually devastating than we might ever imagine. Why are we
not more evangelistic? Because we ourselves were never radically converted. Why do spiritual matters not hold center place
in our busy, work-a-day lives? Because a merely *"mentalized"*
faith can too easily become a *compartmentalized* faith. Why are we
just as materialistic, worldly, and secular as our irreligious (or
religious!) next-door neighbors? Because we have been duly initiated into a worldly church, but never properly introduced to
an other-worldly Kingdom.

If only we had the luxury, I too would vote for reform
over revolution. But how can we possibly bring about reform
"within the system" when the system itself—precisely because it
is *perceived* to be a system, as opposed to a dynamic organism of
faith-prompted, grace-driven, Spirit-filled believers—is fundamentally flawed from its very inception? Certainly, organization, doctrine, rule, and ritual all have their place. Call them collectively a "system" if you will. But a church that is not radically reformed individual by individual, soul by soul, mind by
mind, and heart by heart, is a church that will never know true
spiritual restoration, radical or otherwise.

Radical People, Radical Body

The irony is that if, in fact, we were all radically changed
as individuals, then automatically we would be a radically-
changed collective body of Christ, and a book of this nature likely would never be necessary. If the discussion within even these
pages seems to focus on organization and ritual, let it not be forgotten that no radical restoration is more important than our
own: one by one. Christian by Christian. If we, ourselves, were
truly transformed in faith and life, most of the problems of "the
church" would take care of themselves. Without doubt, the sin-

gle, underlying, bedrock cause of most church problems is our hopelessly misconstrued concept of "church" itself.

Look how convoluted the system easily becomes. When even passionately penitent believers begin to think of themselves as an institutionalized church instead of simply being God's sanctified people, they no longer produce other passionately penitent people who can perpetuate that spiritual body. Instead, they produce people who are wet but not warmed—people for whom mere attendance suffices for fervent participation, and pre-packaged ritual (whether traditional or contemporary) is assumed to be synonymous with things spiritual. Loyalty to God is measured by loyalty to the church.

When that happens, the time has come for a top-to-bottom spring cleaning. One can almost see our Lord striding through the temple courts with a determined glint in his eyes and a talis cord wrapped tightly in his right hand as he begins to knock over tables and animal pens—sending coins, merchants, and doves flying! It was not a time for just a little tidying up here and there. Jesus wasn't merely concerned about the corruption of the moneylenders, or the irreverence of wide-open commercialism in the temple courts. From the priests to the rabbis to ordinary Jews, God's people had lost all sight of true religion.

Over time, temple practices which were meant to encourage meaningful spiritual worship had evolved into a highly-structured political, social, and economic system that more often served to obscure faith rather than to promote it. Yet if you had asked virtually anyone in Israel, they would have insisted that their religious system was definitely of God. They could even (in today's terms) quote book, chapter, and verse. Every point of doctrine was certified; every practice justified; every questionable assumption conveniently rationalized.

Through the lenses of Christian thought and comfortable hindsight, of course, we immediately recognize how deluded the Jews were in their ritualistic concept of worship. We even heap scorn on them for their Pharisaical exclusivism and legalism. But to possibly think that we could be equally deluded is unthinkable! Surely, Jesus would never walk into one of our congregations and create a scene....

Are we absolutely certain about that? Is it so unreasonable to think that if our Lord suddenly appeared among us he might begin knocking over lecterns, and smashing communion cups, and ripping down basketball nets in our family life centers? If what we are about as a fellowship of believers is not of God, then we dare not take comfort in the fact that the Lord is no longer on the earth to literally overturn our tables. Instead, we ourselves must manifest divine outrage and cleanse the temple of its impurity.

If this somehow seems a terribly radical thing to do, should it not give us pause to consider that the alternative could be more radical yet? John hints of it in his Revelation letters:

> To Ephesus—"If you do not repent, I will remove your lampstand from its place."
> To Sardis—"If you do not wake up, I will come like a thief...."
> To Laodicea—"I am about to spit you out of my mouth."

At the Resurrection of the living and the dead, will we not also be judged for our unfaithfulness? If Spirit-led, apostolic faith and practice is ever to be recaptured, it can't wait for Forever. Surely, the time for being radical is now.

CHAPTER THREE

NEITHER CATHOLIC NOR PROTESTANT?

He was of the faith chiefly in the sense that the
Church he currently did not attend was Catholic.

KINGSLEY AMIS

It has been just short of 500 years since the religious world was turned on its head by the courageous protests of a relatively unknown German monk who dared to take on the most powerfully-organized religious institution in human history. When Martin Luther nailed his heretical ninety-five theses to the door of the Castle Church in Wittenberg, hardly anyone noticed. In fact, not one soul took up his challenge to debate the controversial propositions at the appointed hour the following day. Yet, Luther had set in motion an ecclesiastical conflagration that would sweep from Wittenberg all the way to Rome and eventually throughout the whole Western world. Not only was the Roman Catholic Church itself largely cleansed of its worse dross, but Luther's "Protestant" thinking resulted in an unprecedented religious revolution of which we, ourselves, are heirs.

One can almost see the seeds of revolution being sown early in Luther's life. Luther's father was a well-respected mine owner and civic councilor, but at home he was a strict disciplinarian, dispensing corporal punishment with vigor. Luther's mother and teachers weren't far behind, sparing him few rods during his early training. What we might view as perverted cruelty was seen then as a taste of God's own terrible judgment. In

Luther's day, the devil was real. (On one occasion, Luther even hurled his ink bottle at him.) But if the devil didn't get you, Christ would! For Christ himself was viewed as a harsh judge, just waiting to pounce on sinners.

Haunted by thoughts of his abject sinfulness before a grimacing God, Luther eschewed the study of law (to the great disappointment of his father) and, instead, took the vows of the Augustinian order. Luther immersed himself fully in the monastic life, torturing himself with prayers, fasting, vigils, and freezing. He would later recall, "If I could have got to heaven by fasting, I would have merited that twenty years ago."

Luther's piety was matched only by his dedicated scholarship. Reading widely in philosophy, ethics, Latin, Hebrew, and Greek, Luther eventually earned a doctor of theology degree and spent his life teaching at the university in Wittenberg. But it was when he discovered his first copy of the Bible, chained to the monastery pulpit, that Luther's life was forever changed. The more he read, the more he began to see that the biblical Christ was a Christ of grace and mercy who had come to bring forgiveness to sinful man. There was judgment, to be sure, but there was also a divine love Luther had never known.

No passage caught Luther's attention more than Romans 1:17. When he read Paul's words, "The just shall live by faith," Luther began to see that the onerous system of "good works" demanded by the Roman church was not at all the type of good works which flow naturally from fervent faith. Slowly, it was dawning on Luther that the endless deprivations and exhausting acts of penance demanded by the Church were aimed at pleasing the Church rather than receiving God's forgiveness—a thought which eventually would open doors of doubt Luther never knew existed.

The Bubble Begins to Burst

Luther's growing disillusionment only intensified as he began to observe widespread corruption throughout the Church. Sent as an emissary on a brief trip to Rome, Luther was shocked by the luxurious, even immoral, lifestyle of the Renaissance monasteries along the way. In the Vatican itself, he observed Church officials openly accepting bribes to grant the annulment of marriages, or to legitimize children born out of wedlock, or to remove obstacles to marriage. Luther could hardly believe his ears when he heard priests in Rome making an outright mockery of the Eucharist. Instead of reciting the words which (by Catholic doctrine) are spoken as the bread and wine are changed into the literal flesh and blood of Christ, some of the priests dared to say, "Bread you are, and bread you shall remain; wine you are and wine you shall remain."

Yet despite what he had witnessed in Rome, Luther's loyalty to the Church as the custodian of truth on earth was undiminished as he journeyed homeward. It was not long, however, before his loyalty was severely put to the test once again. In Luther's own backyard, the Dominican monk, John Tetzel, began selling papal indulgences, guaranteeing renewal of the spiritual state which the people enjoyed at the point of their baptisms—which is to say, sinless perfection! For yet more money, indulgences could also be bought to free the souls of loved ones from their anguished torture in the fiery inferno of purgatory. "At the very instant the money rattles at the bottom of the chest," Tetzel promised brazenly, "the soul escapes from purgatory, and flies liberated to heaven." And who makes that possible? "The Lord our God no longer reigns," came Tetzel's breathtaking response. "He has given all power to the pope!"

Tetzel's blasphemy led directly to the posting of the ninety-five theses in which Luther challenged the whole system of indulgences, together with the sanctioned avarice which lay behind it. Even more important was his challenge to the pope's authority to remit guilt from sin. Without knowing it, Luther was edging closer and closer to a fundamental break with Rome.

It was not long before Luther was taking issue with the Church's veneration of holy relics, Church festivals, and the devotion and invocation of Mary and the saints. With rapid-fire speed, Luther's concern quickly moved beyond corrupt practices and human innovations to more substantial matters of faith and doctrine. In the end, the battle was over the ultimate source of spiritual authority. The pope's insistence that he, and not Scripture, was the highest religious authority finally compelled Luther to condemn the pope as the antichrist.

Not Just Reform, But Radical Reform

As we look back from our comfortable vantage point on Luther's extraordinary accomplishments, what we first must appreciate is how radical Luther's reforms were for his day and time. Things we take for granted—such as scriptural authority, the priesthood of all believers, and something as simple as being able to take both the bread *and* the wine at communion—were quite unthinkable. And for priests and nuns to marry was absolutely scandalous. (Luther's own belated marriage to a former nun raised more than a few eyebrows.)

Although Luther had risen in protest against abuse within a system, inexorably he realized that much about the system itself had to be radically changed. Reaction from the Church, of course, was recrimination, excommunication, book-burnings, and threats of execution. And just that quickly, the revolution had begun. Luther's militant cadre of emerging Protestants were the radicals of their day, joining together in a leap of new-found faith from the secure arms of the Mother Church.

Addressing others who were more hesitant to take that final, bold leap away from much of Catholic orthodoxy, Luther himself looked back on the early days of protest, saying, "Learn from me how difficult a thing it is to throw off errors confirmed by the example of the world, and which, through long habit, have become second nature to us."

Half a millennium on, I fear it is a lesson we, too, must learn.

Not Just a Reformer, But a Restorationist

One of the hidden (to me) surprises about Luther's experience is how very much it was, in fact, a miniaturized *restoration* movement, not merely "the Reformation," as it is usually known. Having recently re-read books about Luther's life and ministry, I've come to the conclusion that I've been wrong in thinking that Luther was only a reformer. The truth is, his plea for scriptural authority in all matters of faith and doctrine could not be more restorationist. When it came to specific doctrines and particular practices (for example, the legitimacy of monastic vows), his first and last question was: "What does Scripture say?" He might just as well have said, "We will speak where the Bible speaks and be silent where the Bible is silent"!

More remarkable yet is how much stock Luther put in the binding precedent of New Testament pattern. For a restorationist fellowship whose historic commitment to scriptural pattern (now derisively referred to as "patternism") is under increasing fire, it is instructive to note the crucial role that "pattern" played in Luther's thinking.

For instance, when struggling to determine which of Catholicism's seven sacraments were legitimate, Luther was adamant that no sacrament was valid if it could not find justification in the New Testament. On that basis, he ruled out confirmation, holy orders, extreme unction, and the doctrine that marriages are valid only when Church-sanctioned. For Luther, only "baptism" and the Eucharist (and possibly penance, as it might relate to genuine repentance) were consistent with the New Testament pattern.

On the issue of whether the clergy could marry, Luther made a direct "pattern" appeal to 1 Timothy 3:2—"A bishop must be the husband of one wife." That very verse, interestingly enough, was later to indicate the full strength of Luther's commitment to primitive pattern in a rather more bizarre case. The issue arose when Philip of Hesse sought Luther's advice about his loveless marriage to a woman with whom he had not cohabited for years. The question was, Could Philip marry a young woman of the Leipzig court without dissolving his first marriage?

In Europe at that time, the question of a man's having two wives was somewhat open, especially in cases where the wife was stricken with leprosy or insanity. (In fact, Cardinal Campeggio had suggested this solution to Pope Clement in the discussions which swirled around Henry VIII's request for a divorce.) Luther firmly believed that the Church had a right to authorize such marriages in special cases, not only for the protection of morals and character, but also because (presumably from at least one possible inference in 1 Timothy 3:2) *it was a practice of the ancient church.*

Certainly, Luther's strange judgment, if even remotely correct, would bring to an end all the head-scratching that continues to this day about the intended implications of that mysterious passage! But even if he was dead wrong in his textual interpretation, the obvious point must not be overlooked: Luther was a dyed-in-the-wool "patternist."

No Detail Too Small

Lest anyone think that Luther sought to honor only primitive Christian *functions*, as opposed to explicit first-century *forms*, consider Luther's carefully-chosen words in the confession of faith which he wrote on the occasion of his discussion with the Swiss reformer, Ulrich Zwingli:

We believe with regards the Lord's Supper, that it ought to be celebrated in both kinds [i.e., that the congregation should partake of both bread and wine] according to the manner in which it was instituted in the early church.

Do the words "according to the manner" have a familiar ring? Are they not but a paraphrase of the biblical injunction to do everything "according to the pattern?" Of more immediate concern, one could hardly apply the pattern principle with greater attention to the specific details of first-century apostolic practice. Whereas Catholic tradition had always considered the communicant's taking of the bread alone as sufficiently symbolic of the Eucharistic *function*, for Luther, primitive apostolic *form* was equally crucial.

At times, certainly, Luther pressed his passion for precedent to a fault, as seen, for example, in his split with Zwingli over the doctrine of the Real Presence, which Luther defended. In the midst of their heated discussion at Marburg, Luther took a piece of chalk and defiantly wrote on the velvet table cloth, *"Hoc est corpus Meum"* (Jesus' own words, "This is my body"). How could anyone not see that Jesus meant it *literally*? It was Luther's version of the familiar debate line: "It says what it means, and means what it says!" Yet, even in this doctrinal miscue, we see Luther as committed to scriptural authority—and even to New Testament pattern—as are we.

If perhaps Luther might never have regarded himself as a "restorationist," as we understand that term, nevertheless his instincts were clearly those with which we are intimately familiar. But for the grace of God, one simply has to wonder whether, without Luther's trail-blazing Reformation, the Restoration Movement of the nineteenth century ever would have happened.

Once A Catholic, Always A Catholic

Given the vehemence of his protests against the Roman Church, the great surprise is that Martin Luther died a practicing Catholic, not even a separated "Lutheran." The church which bears his name came into being against his will. Despite his heroic ground-breaking efforts to reform the Church which he loved, and to foster its return to scriptural authority, Luther died believing in numerous doctrines and practices which we find to be patently unscriptural.

Luther, for instance, was "Calvinist" before Calvin's name became associated with such teaching. In fact, regarding original sin, predestination, and irresistible grace for the elect, Luther followed in the steps of Augustine; and Calvin in the steps of Luther. Among the words which Luther inscribed on the tomb of his young daughter, Lena, were David's lament: "In sin and trespass was I born." (For Luther, it was yet another instance of taking literally what was meant to be figurative; or, in the case of David's lament, hyperbole.)

However, Luther was not in the least concerned about Lena's eternal security; for, like himself and virtually everyone he knew, Lena had been "baptized" as an infant. The fact that adult, faith-prompted immersion was the exclusive mode of baptism practiced by the early church was lost on Luther, despite his strongly intimating to the contrary in one perplexing sermon.

As it happens, the issue of believer's baptism was forcibly raised by a group of Anabaptist zealots from Zwickau who declared that infant baptism was the invention of Satan, and that everyone ought to be baptized again (by them) in order to enter the true church. Unfortunately, Luther had every reason to dismiss their plea out of hand. It seems their leader was a weaver, named Storch, who not only claimed to have had a vision in which the angel Gabriel announced that Storch would sit on his throne, but also dared to say that his teachings were coming directly from the Holy Spirit. Without ever specifically addressing Storch's challenge of infant baptism, Luther simply preached on the finality of scriptural authority. About that, he was right; about infants, he was wrong.

As a dissenting Catholic, Luther also continued the practice of the Mass, although no longer as a "re-sacrifice" of Christ. He even revitalized the Mass by overseeing its translation into German. And, despite his newfound belief in the priesthood of all believers, Luther did not dismantle the practical distinction between clergy and laity. Or, for that matter, give up his belief in Mary's own immaculate conception. Or reject Augustine's teaching that man has no free will.

Did Luther, then, really reform the Catholic Church? He certainly did. Did he reform it completely? Clearly not. Whatever his light, its brightness did not illuminate every darkened corner. This should be a sobering thought to all of us who follow in Luther's fallible footsteps. No matter how much we reform or restore, there seems always to be work left undone. It's one thing to say, along with Luther, "My conscience is captive to the Word of God.... Here I stand, I can do no other." It's another thing altogether to dare think there is absolutely nothing left to challenge our consciences in the revealed Word we so boldly profess.

From Reformation to Restoration

Luther's widespread influence would be felt long after his death, especially in northern Germany and Switzerland, and in Scandinavia and Scotland—also, in France and the Netherlands among the French Protestants and Huguenots. In England, anyone listening closely to John and Charles Wesley could hear tones of Luther ringing as loudly as village church bells.

The French theologian, John Calvin, was almost a direct prodigy of Luther, having been influenced by a Wittenberg teacher while learning New Testament Greek. Eventually, Calvin's Puritan theology would cross the Atlantic in tiny ships and walk ashore into a new land of hope and glory. Among Calvin's own proteges, meanwhile, was the Scottish leader John Knox, whose stern piety became the cornerstone of the Presbyterians. At that point the stage was set for "Reformation with a twist." From among those same Presbyterians would emerge a father and son, Thomas and Alexander Campbell, whose names are familiar (or used to be) to every person associated with our Restoration heritage.

The links from Martin Luther to Alexander Campbell—indeed, even to ourselves—are surprisingly few. In one sense, we are but fifth-generation descendants of Luther. We may not be Calvinists, Puritans, Presbyterians, or Campbellites, but we can hardly deny our religious roots or escape the family tree.

Our unique heritage becomes particularly important in two ways. First—on the positive side—is the almost genetic instinct which predisposes us toward scriptural authority and primitive Christian pattern. Wittingly or unwittingly, Protestant thinking has always borne within it the seeds of restoration thinking—ironically creating a never-ending cycle which invariably leads to its own undoing. When Christian practice, ritual, and hierarchy inevitably begin to ossify and deaden, Protestant instinct first attempts reform, then finally is forced to seek a more extreme restoration which, in time, once again begins to ossify and deaden. This process goes a long way toward explaining the work of Thomas and Alexander Campbell, whose inherited Protestant instincts ultimately clashed with their Presbyterian upbringing, which itself was the product of Protestant thinking!

We need merely look back at the period of the Judges to see that the cycle of departure, reform, and restoration is as ancient as it is modern, and as modern as ancient. The only question for each generation is, Which part of the cycle are we in?

In their generation, the Campbells (along with Barton W. Stone and the other nineteenth-century American restorationists) realized that departure was long past, and that attempts to reform were being received with little enthusiasm. The only thing left was restoration. Radical restoration!

In the Campbells' day, as now, Protestantism was hopelessly splintered into a multiplicity of denominations, each with its own unique creed, practices, and ritual. Troubled by a religious pluralism running counter to Jesus' prayer for unity among his disciples (John 17), the Campbells sought a return to the primitive Christian pattern. Was that not the one and only basis upon which all Christians could unite? (Little did they initially realize how far that novel approach would take them, especially concerning the thorny matter of who is actually contemplated within the meaning of all "Christians.")

Yet, the issue for Alexander Campbell was not solely one of Christian unity. Drawing particularly from his experience with European religious establishment, he was convinced that institutional Christianity of all stripes was pervasively apostate, certainly beginning with the historic departures of Catholicism, but even continuing under the leadership of Luther, Calvin, and Wesley. In his call for "A Restoration of the Ancient Order of Things," he minced no words, boldly proclaiming: "The Christian religion has been for ages interred in the rubbish of human invention and tradition."

Heady with the hubris of all great reformers, Campbell confidently asserted that "there is not one voice heard in all the world outside of the boundaries of the present reformation, calling upon the people to return to the original gospel and order of things."

At first blush, his claim seems overly dismissive of the extent to which men like Luther had fought monumental battles of reform, armed with the same fundamental commitment to scriptural authority and primitive Christian pattern. However, if what he meant by that was the bulldozing away of every plank and stone of ecclesiastical rubble accumulated since the first century, and building once again upon the original, primitive foundations, then he probably was right. No single historical figure or group had ever made such a wide-sweeping plea.

From that perspective, what might be thought of as the "Grand Cycle" had moved from departure (in the apostasy of Catholicism) to reform (among the Protestants), but never to *conscious, systematic, philosophical, dogmatic, start-from-scratch Restoration*. Never before had there been an entire movement driven by the very concept of attempting to duplicate first-century Christianity.

No matter how radical the previous efforts at reform might have been in their own context, none could match the even more radical *idea itself* of total, complete restoration from the ground up. Whereas previous reformations periodically had stripped away multiple layers of paint in various spots around the table, as it were, the Restoration Movement would not be content until the entire table had been stripped right back to the grain to reveal its original beauty.

Genes Of A Perverted Spirit

Despite the positive role which Protestant thinking played in fostering the more sweeping concept of Restoration, even now its history of sectarianism continues to be felt in other, more negative, ways which few of us seem to realize. Merely consider, for example, the pugilistic style of doctrinal debate employed by Campbell and others in pressing the case for restoration. Even one of Campbell's most devoted supporters, John Rogers, commented at one point about Campbell's "sometimes terribly sarcastic pen." Anyone at all familiar with Restoration history is aware that Campbell's own hard style and biting sarcasm has been all too characteristic of the movement.

I suppose an argument could be made (especially by those of us who are restorationists!) that even our Lord was not above hurling personal epithets-referring to the Pharisees as

"You brood of vipers," and saying of Herod, "Go tell that fox...!" Certainly, the Apostle Paul didn't exactly pull any punches when he said of the circumcision-bound Judaizers, "As for those agitators, I wish they would go the whole way and emasculate themselves!" But Alexander Campbell was as likely to have inherited his bombastic style from Martin Luther as from Paul.

In a mostly-flattering report of Luther's celebrated debate with John Eck, Peter Mosellanus was critical of Luther in one aspect, saying, "He is blamed, however, for being more sarcastic, when he reproaches others, than is fitting for a theologian, especially when he is putting forward new ideas."

Perhaps it was just the tenor of the times. Of Luther's opponent, John Eck, it was said: "He gave one the idea of a man striving to overcome his opponent rather than of one striving to win a victory for the truth. There was as much sophistry as good reasoning in his arguments; he was continually misquoting his opponent's words or trying to give them a meaning they were not intended to convey." Unfortunately, much the same could also be said regarding far too many of Luther's own Protestant progeny in the innumerable debates which have dotted the Reformation landscape over the intervening centuries.

That we, as restorationists, should have inherited this harsh, combative style from our Protestant forebears has done little to advance the cause of Restoration, much less the cause of Christ. Jesus' "brood of vipers" statement notwithstanding, our Lord did not make *ad hominem* arguments, or employ deceptive sophistry, or misquote and misconstrue the words of his opponents—all tactics which are regularly employed still today by the most vociferous defenders of the Restoration Movement. If it should ever happen that radical restoration found itself on the brink of success with the exception of this lingering bitter spirit among brethren in Christ, then it would fail altogether.

By definition, the concept of restoration assumes—indeed, demands—an honest and open search for truth. To make use of slander, innuendo, and dishonest debate is to deface the Restoration ideal. Indeed, it was the Pharisees' use of just such tactics that earned them Jesus' stinging indictment: "You bunch of snakes!"

Far from being genuine restorationists, today's self-styled "defenders of the faith" who stoop to such unworthy methods are, by that fact alone, marked out to be the very ones most in need of radical reform. The further irony is that, if faced with the prospect of a more radical restoration than they themselves have ever experienced, these same proud "defenders of the faith" undoubtedly would be the most strident defenders of our denominational status quo. (Touch the patient's body closest to his ailing organ, and he will scream the loudest.)

The result, of course, is a self-serving double standard. Restoration is good for the Protestant goose, but the Restorationist gander doesn't want to hear about it. "Haven't we done that already?" some will ask. "Are we not already the New Testament church fully restored?"

As we will soon explore in more depth, the simple (if uncomfortable) answer is "no," neither in the nineteenth century nor in the 21st. Even beyond that, however, for restorationists the yellow caution flag must always be out. Inherent in the very fact that we are restorationists is the ever-looming reality that each day brings us closer to the next phase of the cycle...which, of course, is departure. (Would anyone today affirm that the "Churches of Christ" have remained unchanged in the last 200 years? Or that we have not become increasingly more static and institutional as we've made our way along the sect-to-denomination continuum?) Complacency, too, is a temptation. "So, if you think you are standing firm, be careful that you don't fall!"

Still Bound By Our Roots
All my life I have heard (and often repeated) that we are neither Catholic nor Protestant but the one true church of Christ

founded on the day of Pentecost in A.D. 33 (or thereabout). However, for much of my life, I've been confronted by the obvious questions. Where was the Lord's church between the end of the first century and the beginning of the nineteenth? Did it even exist? Were there always pockets of genuine faith and practice which, to historians, were unknown? Or did primitive Christianity become utterly extinct beneath a lava flow of Catholic apostasy?

Among non-Catholics, at least one group of believers raises particularly difficult questions. The Anabaptists (and perhaps unknown others before them) insisted, just as we do, upon adult, faith-prompted immersion. If that combination of faith and obedience adequately responds to God's grace in bestowing full salvation, then the body of Christ was indeed alive and well at various points throughout the intervening centuries.

Perhaps the Anabaptists' failure to completely recapture apostolic worship and practice becomes problematic, but to raise that problem is to focus the spotlight squarely on our own restoration shortcomings. To what extent is the verifiable existence of the Lord's church predicated upon complete and total restoration of primitive Christian practice as compared with simply being a collective body of Christians? If the former criterion is to be the acid test, then we ourselves stand in jeopardy. Our own initial salvation is no guarantee that we have been fully faithful to first-century apostolic practice.

What can be said with confidence is that there is no trace of anything like the nineteenth-century Restoration Movement in the long, dark centuries of Roman rule. Certainly, beyond all doubt, the "Churches of Christ" as we know them did not exist. But to say, therefore, that we are neither Catholic nor Protestant is a bridge too far. Just as Luther reformed—but not wholly—so too Campbell and Stone restored, but not completely. To this day, we ourselves perpetuate numerous vestigial remains which we have inherited from both Catholicism and Protestantism.

We should not be surprised that the melody has a way of lingering long after the song has ended. As we know, the first converts to Christ had great difficulty putting away their own centuries-old Jewish practices. To Paul's chagrin, they even tried to impose those forms on Gentile converts. Again and again, Paul had to remind Jewish Christians that circumcision was not required for those in Christ. Nor the festivals, nor the priesthood, nor the sacrifices. The very point of the letter to the Hebrews is that old habits die hard. It's a verity from which none of us seems to be exempt, not even the early Restorationists.

Much more will be said about our dubious religious legacy in the chapters ahead. For the moment, consider just four salient examples. There is, first of all, the seemingly irrepressible distinction between clergy and laity, initiated under Catholicism and maintained by Protestants. No matter how much we affirm the priesthood of all believers, or reject formal ordination, or even make use of what others would call "lay preachers" more than most fellowships, the truth is that our denominational-style "ministers" occupy a position of honor and responsibility not widely shared with the person in the pew. An *undeclared* clergy is still a clergy.

Similarly, our typical pattern for church organization and leadership closely follows the blueprint of both Catholic and Protestant ecclesiastical structure. Although our unique emphasis on congregational autonomy has spared us the elaborate hierarchy of the Catholic Church, and even the councils, conventions, and synods of the Protestants, nevertheless we have inherited their penchant for organization and administration even within our local congregations. We may not call our elders "bishops," as do the Catholics, or "presbyters," as do the Presbyterians, but—given the influence of our spiritual ancestors—our elders are likely to think and act mostly as administrators rather than as "pastors" or shepherds.

Then there is our ritualized, sacramental-like "communion," which is a direct descendant of Catholicism's highly formal Eucharist. Certainly, we have Luther to thank for being able to partake of both the bread and the wine; and Zwingli, for challenging Luther's continuing support of Christ's "presence" in the wine (even if Zwingli's own modern concept of "remembrance" might also be found lacking). Still, the formalized ceremony which we observe from week to week in celebrating the Lord's Supper bears far more resemblance to the Catholic Eucharist than to the *koinonia* fellowship meal with which the memorial of Christ was associated in primitive Christian practice.

Finally, we have our Catholic and Protestant heritage to thank for the highly-structured worship format which we typically follow. Compared with the intricacies of the Catholic Mass, of course, we are far from the "smells and bells" of high church observance. Even so, our own set-piece, traditional services (and, more lately, our slickly-managed, hi-tech contemporary worship productions) stand in sharp contrast to the spontaneous, mutually-participatory, and intimate worship of first-century believers.

Let's Be Honest

The truth, therefore, is that we are neither Catholic nor Protestant, *nor* the fully-restored first-century church. We are a hybrid of the three...at the very least. (There is also the influence of the Enlightenment and American culture to consider.) Our literature and sermons to the contrary notwithstanding, we are the offspring of religious history as well as the spiritual descendants of Peter, James, and Paul. When the Restoration Movement first took flight in the nineteenth century, Catholic and Protestant traditions were unnoticed stowaways. Had we realized they were on board, we might have kicked them off...in mid-air!

The grand irony is that now, nearly two centuries on, some of us absolutely love having our religious neighbors on board and almost insist that they share with us whatever denominational concepts and practices they're carrying in their bags. Instead of moving farther away from Protestant denominations, in particular, some of us are beginning to move closer to them. From all appearances, we like being up in First Class with them. We're tired of sitting back in Coach Class, cramped by narrow-minded, archaic notions of restoration. And even though flying First Class may cost more than we've bargained for, we're all too willing to part with the Restoration ideal if that's the price of the ticket.

For a fellowship claiming to be neither Catholic nor Protestant, it's been a stretch from the very beginning. And now, trade our Restoration ideal for the luxuries of First Class? Surely, even Martin Luther would be spinning in his grave!

Chapter Four

Restoration? The Very Idea!

Most of us spend too much time on the last twenty-four hours
and too little on the last six thousand years.

Will Durant

When our American friends wing their way across the Pond for a visit to England, one of the "must see" tourist sites is the lovely Stratford-Upon-Avon, a short jaunt north of us. With its Tudor-style architecture, meandering River Avon, and resplendent gardens, the charming town is quintessentially English. Who doesn't enjoy watching the brightly-colored narrow boats being raised and lowered in the lock of the canal, and shopping for souvenirs, and having an ice cream in the park? But you already know that none of this fully explains why the tour buses disgorge thousands of excited visitors there each month. Almost to the person, they've come from the farthest reaches of the globe for only one reason: to see the birthplace of the Stratford bard, William Shakespeare.

They don't seem to care (or know) that Shakespeare's actual birthplace is shrouded in speculation. As long as there is a building duly designated as the very site of his birth (conveniently provided, I'm sure, by the Chamber of Commerce), there will always be pilgrimages to "Mecca." They want to see it. They want to touch it. They want the T-shirt.

Even if they have never read a line of Shakespeare's sonnets or any of his many plays, these wanna-be Shakespeare groupies will stand patiently in orderly British queues and pay the high ticket prices necessary to see a performance at the riverfront Royal Shakespeare Theatre. After all, it's *Shakespeare* in Shakespeare's home town! What person of culture has ever gone a lifetime without at least rubbing elbows with "Romeo and Juliet," or "A Midsummer Night's Dream," or "Hamlet," or "King Lear?"

Imagine my surprise, then, when I opened my *Daily Telegraph* over breakfast and discovered that William Shakespeare was passè...or soon would be, if avant-guard educators in Britain had their way. It seems the Qualifications and Curriculum Authority (the principal body which advises the Government on what is taught in British schools) was proposing that the nation's major testing program drop altogether what teachers of English Literature call "the canon." That includes everything from Chaucer to Joyce and...incredibly...none other than The Bard himself! Suddenly, my heart sank. My mind reeled. William Shakespeare banished to exile from his own homeland? Say it ain't so!

By the universal rule of sloth, if a subject is not tested, then effectively it's not taught...or not taught effectively. This, of course, is merely the logical extension of typical student whimpering: "Why should I bother to learn this stuff if it's not going to be on the exam?" Why, indeed.

So what *is* to be tested, and thus taught? According to the Qualifications and Curriculum Authority, the two previously-compulsory Shakespeare plays would be replaced with an amorphous "drama," based mainly on Hollywood films, pop videos, and television "soaps." ("Romeo and Juliet" might just squeak by in film-script version, but not Shakespeare's brilliant tragedy upon which it is based.) Gone, too, would be any requirement to study poetry, blank verse, or any other rigorous literary form. All of that would be displaced by contemporary, *relevant* "media" studies: words on the Web, or in computer training manuals, commercials, current-events articles, or even product labels.

Hamlet was only joking when, upon being asked what he was reading, he responded, dryly: "Words, words, words." Now, the joke is on us. *Words* are all we have. Their syntax, beauty, meaning, and rich emotion seem not to matter in the least. Nor their message. Shakespeare was not just a master wordsmith, but one of history's most insightful observers of the human condition. Welling up from some fortuitous combination of genius and soul came an uncanny ability to articulate guilt, lust, irony, humor, power struggles, romance and interpersonal relations with a richness few others have ever achieved. Great themes of morality and divine justice are laced throughout both comedy and tragedy almost as overtly and powerfully as in Scripture itself.

And all this is to be replaced by banal psychobabble and commercial drivel?

To be fair, Britain is not alone in succumbing to the philistine forces of political correctness. Read again Bloom's *The Closing of the American Mind* and Bellow's *The Western Canon*. But Britain is sounding an alarm not heard since the air raid sirens of the wartime Blitz, warning of things to come even in America. If any theatre in England were to depend solely upon local audiences to support its Shakespeare productions, it quickly would go bankrupt. The younger Brits, in particular, don't flock to Stratford-Upon-Avon like the rest of the world. If one wonders why, it has little to do with "familiarity breeding contempt," or "around the world, but not in our own backyard." The unlikely culprit—a cynical regard for history—knows no geographical boundaries and will soon be just as socially destructive in the States as in England. Before that happens, Stratford's busy shopkeepers and ice cream vendors better save up while they can. Not even the Americans will be coming forever to the birthplace of The Bard.

What History Teaches Doesn't Matter Any More

In reaction to this outrageous literary vandalism, I'm tempted to say something like: History teaches us that the dumbing down of culture results in populist writers beginning sentences with conjunctions and using plebeian phrases like *dumbing down*! But the sad truth is that history doesn't teach us much anymore. Perhaps it never did. As Aldous Huxley put it: "That men do not learn very much from the lessons of history is the most important of all the lessons that History has to teach."

I suppose there are lots of reasons why we tend to repeat the mistakes so well documented in history, which have little or nothing to do with history itself or our attitude toward it. For the moment, however, I'm chiefly concerned about our *view* of history and where it fits into the scheme of Restoration thinking. For, if we dig down far enough, we will discover that Restoration thinking has two primary foundations—authority and history.

The decline of historical authority begins in our culture at large. Despite thriving museums, continuing sales of history books, and television's successful History Channel, we are increasingly ignorant of history. As playwright Simon Gray puts it, we have become "an Alzheimer's civilization—one with no past." More than ignorance, the problem is attitude.

Reflecting the "what's-happening-now" culture around us, we tend to operate somewhere between being merely ahistorical (unfazed one way or the other by the past) and being outright anti-historical (openly contemptuous of the past). Henry Ford gave us not only the Model T, but a modern, technologically-driven disdain for anything not contemporary, saying, "History is more or less bunk."

Why, then, should we be surprised that a new generation in the church has little affinity with the *notion itself* of restoration, and little actual knowledge of the Restoration Movement, or even the broader Reformation Movement? It's as if we were all hanging by "sky hooks," not standing on anyone else's shoulders who have gone before us. Little wonder, then, that appeals to biblical precedent are increasingly falling on deaf ears. Precedent is history; and now, history is irrelevant.

The good news about the Gospel is that, while it is undoubtedly historical, it is also timeless: Jesus Christ came into the world to save sinners! Although the current generation of Christians is irredeemably contemporary in music, dress, and cultural outlook, praise God that at least they can buy into the Gospel. Yet, try convincing them of the importance of doctrinal precedent based upon the actions of first-century Christians, and you've got an uphill battle on your hands. It hardly matters that Jesus of Nazareth was inextricably linked with the same first-century culture, or that history itself is the account of God's eternal plan for mankind...and thus was *His story* before it was ever *history*.

Certainly, Jesus fits nicely with the current generational focus on "relationship" (which by nature is contemporary), but we dare not press it too far. We must be careful not to point out that Jesus told his apostles he would send the Holy Spirit to guide them into all the truth; or that the history of the early church—and not just the teaching of Jesus—was obviously preserved for a reason. To insist on doing so changes the historical biblical landscape from something of possible passing interest (as if reading an historical novel) to something which has the force of authority. How, we are asked, can anything so ancient be binding on us today? Surely, times have changed. Surely, they didn't know then what we know now. If history proves anything, is it not that those who are stuck in the past are condemned never to live in the present?

Historical Battle Lines

Make no mistake. Both within and without the church today, a cultural and generational battle having endless implications is raging over the authority of history. It may not be headlined as the Great History Wars, and indeed few of the combatants would understand their involvement in those terms. Yet, undoubtedly, future historians will observe that the role of history itself was at risk during our lifetime.

The battle is being waged along many, seemingly-unrelated fronts by two powerful alliances. The chart below indicates the various assault points and beachheads currently being contested:

Historical		**Anti-historical**
The Past	vs.	The Present
Authoritative	vs.	Advisory
Hierarchy	vs.	Community
Deductive	vs.	Inductive
Rational	vs.	Intuitive
Traditional	vs.	Contemporary
Precedent	vs.	Pragmatism
Restoration	vs.	Innovation

As in any war, the battle lines often become blurred and indistinguishable. At times, even great alliances are not always as cohesive as they might appear. But, generally speaking, this map of the conflict is reasonably accurate...at least if carefully understood.

Over the past two decades, congregation after congregation has fallen victim in the midst of the fray without really ever knowing what ultimately was at stake. There has been much talk, of course, about "traditional" versus "contemporary" worship styles, but rarely have we appreciated how even that relatively small skirmish fits into the larger context. Changes in style can be upsetting, frustrating, and I suppose even maddening; yet, where skirmishes over worship style have led to division, it is not unusual that, behind the scenes, a wider struggle was taking place between the two competing alliances.

It is equally possible that what appears to be innovative worship style might actually be nothing more than an attempt to turn back the clock and restore a style of worship more in line with New Testament practice. (Further along in this book, we will explore several such changes.) In these instances, change *appears* to be innovative, simply because it is different from the way we've always worshiped. However, it is not "innovative" in the sense of rejecting scriptural precedent and introducing unauthorized worship. It is *corrective*, not *creative*. Or, put differently, it is *renovation*, not *innovation*.

If, for example, a congregation currently affiliated with the Christian Church were to abandon its use of instruments, the move to *a cappella* music might be seen by them as being somewhat innovative. However, if it were being done with the specific intent to honor New Testament precedent, then the change would be a matter of renovation, discarding what once had been an unauthorized innovation.

As that example illustrates, the battle between the two alliances of competing perspectives is not always as clear-cut as one could wish. Traditional worship (which, according to the chart, ought to fall neatly within the "Historical" alliance) might not be at all consistent with early Christian practice. When first introduced, it may well have been an unscriptural innovation itself. On the other hand, just because contemporary worship is different from established tradition (and therefore normally would be associated with the "Anti-historical" alliance), it might actually be more in line with primitive first-century practice.

One must also not assume that the two alliances are always, and in every case, mutually exclusive. For example, God himself has given us the ability to be both rational and intuitive; and to think deductively or inductively as is appropriate to the situation. Furthermore, having "community" doesn't automatically rule out having hierarchical structure within that community. Nor does recognizing scriptural precedent necessarily preclude our being pragmatic in the implementation of that precedent. So it is that there are few, if any, inviolable "no-fly zones" separating the two alliances.

Nor should we assume that association with either alliance automatically produces a predictable result. For example, anti-historical, forward-thinking theology may be a legitimate reaction to an unscriptural tradition in which we are mired—or, alternatively, the worst possible kind of backward thinking from God's perspective. On the other hand, backward-thinking, historical theology may be the most progressive thinking after all—or merely an excuse to maintain unscriptural traditions. "The web of our life is of a mingled yarn, good and ill together." (*All's Well...*, 4.3.74)

That said, we should not underestimate the crucial, fundamental differences between the two alliances and their overarching attitudes toward history...and thus toward Scripture. Because we are likely to get out of Scripture what we take to it, our particular perspective regarding things past and present is not just "much ado about nothing." It is pivotal to everything else we think and do.

How, then, resolve the impasse? And what are the rules of engagement? To employ a legal analogy, it used to be that the burden of proof was on anyone proposing an innovation inconsistent with first-century practice. Today, that burden of proof has shifted to anyone insisting that we follow New Testament precedent. Time-honored assumptions no longer apply. Almost as a matter of principle, it's out with the old and in with the new.

That is why this chapter undoubtedly is the most important in the book. If we can't agree on the very idea of restoration itself, then radical restoration will make no sense whatsoever. To restore, then, or not to restore—that is the question!

Re-digging Ancient Wells

The idea of restoration is as old as history itself. There is, for example, that fascinating account in Genesis 26 of Isaac coping with a famine reminiscent of the one which had earlier driven Abraham down into Egypt (Genesis 12). Something rings awfully familiar when Isaac lies to Abimelech about Rebekah, exactly as Abraham lied about Sarah, but this time the geographical setting is different. God had instructed Isaac not to go down to Egypt, as Abraham had done, but rather to "live in the land where I tell you to live." (That land was Philistine territory, ruled by Abimelech.)

Whether it was Abraham or Isaac—or David, Naaman, or Paul—God has not left his people without direction. For, "a man's life is not his own; it is not for man to direct his steps" (Jeremiah 10:23). And "there is a way that seems right to a man, but in the end it leads to death" (Proverbs 14:12).

As those passages suggest, Restoration's threshold assumption is that without God's guidance we are without hope. This initial premise is followed quickly by a second: that God is not silent, but has spoken...in such a way as to meet our every need. In light of those premises, God's instruction to Isaac becomes the very watchword for Restoration: *Live in the land where I tell you to live.*

That watchword vividly describes our responsibility in the face of God's having spoken, which is to be fully obedient to his leading. Yet, Isaac's lying about his wife is a striking reminder that we are all disobedient servants. We stray from the path. We go in our own direction. Perhaps, like Isaac, we prevaricate. More often, we simply innovate. In short, we fill in gaps where God has *not* spoken.

Which leads us to the rest of the story....

Abimelech, of course, is piqued not only by Isaac's deceit, but also by his threatening prosperity; and so he urges Isaac to move on. Isaac agrees, and settles in the Valley of Gerar where he "reopened the wells that had been dug in the time of his father Abraham, which the Philistines had stopped up after

Abraham died, and he gave them the same names his father had given them" (26:17-18).

Who knows why we are given these details, or, for that matter, all the other seemingly irrelevant details found throughout Scripture? (Unless, perhaps, we are being told that no detail escapes God's attention.) But there could hardly be a clearer picture of the process of restoration. Wells that were first dug by Abraham, then maliciously filled in by the resentful Philistines, now have to be re-dug by Isaac. Before life-giving water can flow, the wells must be restored. And when they are restored, even their names are restored.

Should it matter that he gave them the same names? Was it sheer nostalgia on Isaac's part? I have no idea. I just find it interesting that when God himself restores, he restores completely. Just ask Naaman. Or Jairus. Or Lazarus.

What I do know is that when wells get filled in, they have to be dug out—whatever the effort, whatever the cost. More often than not, restoration is the high price of obedience.

Restoring Fallen Walls

In the story of Nehemiah, the metaphor of restoration changes from wells to walls. Instead of digging down, it is a time for building up. Indeed, the rebuilding of Jerusalem's walls was itself a metaphor depicting God's spiritual restoration of Israel.

While still exiled in Susa's citadel, Nehemiah received news that the walls of Jerusalem were broken and in ruins. For days, Nehemiah mourned, and fasted, and prayed. On behalf of all Israel came this grief-stricken plea to God: "I confess the sins we Israelites, including myself and my father's house, have committed against you. We have acted very wickedly toward you. We have not obeyed the commands, decrees, and laws you gave your servant Moses" (1:5-7). If ever there was a need for restoration, it was then.

Yet even before Israel's descent into idolatry, God had promised that he would restore the nation. It is to this promise that Nehemiah appealed, pleading, "Oh Lord, remember the instruction you gave your servant Moses, saying, 'If you are unfaithful, I will scatter you among the nations, but if you return to me and obey my commands, then even if your exiled people are at the farthest horizon, I will gather them from there and bring them to the place I have chosen as a dwelling for my Name'" (1:8-9).

Are we to believe that Nehemiah's subsequent reconstruction of Jerusalem's crumbling walls was the point of the exercise? Not a chance! It was Israel herself who needed to be restored; and even now it is we who need to learn the same lesson of restoration. It is we who are repeating the sins of Israel in not seeking justice for the oppressed, or answering the desperate cry of those in need. Ironically, it is we who continue to worry more about whether we are doctrinally restored than about whether we are spiritually restored! "Day in and day out we may seek the Lord and seem eager to know his ways" (Isaiah 58:2), but Isaiah's call to Israel is our call as well: "If your people will rebuild the ancient ruins and will raise up the age-old foundations; you will be called Repairer of Broken Walls, Restorer of Streets with Dwellings" (58:12).

I'm aware, of course, that this use of Isaiah's prophecy in the context of the present discussion could have the whiff of bait-and-switch. After all, who among us would deny that, as a people of God, we stand perpetually convicted of our failure to do social justice, and therefore continually need to be restored? By contrast, the type of restoration we are primarily talking about in this book is of a wholly different kind...at least at first blush. Whereas every denomination in the nineteenth century would have agreed on the need for ongoing spiritual restoration, what became known as the Restoration Movement took particular aim at church doctrine, organization, and practice.

Yet, we should not be overly hasty in dismissing any connection between the two types of restoration. If, in fact, we are *not* doing social justice as we ought, there may be reasons for that, which themselves might well be associated with issues of doctrine, organization, and practice. Certainly, such was the case with Israel herself, which had evolved into a formalistic system of worship that eventually became a substitute for personal, individual acts of righteousness.

If, then, we truly wish to be Repairers and Restorers of the broken lives around us, we may need to reconsider our self-perception as God's people, and radically re-think how we are to function as a church in the midst of a hurting world. Doing business-as-usual as a church may be the very thing standing in our way of doing righteousness as never before as a called-out people.

A Patterned People

For those of us who grew up with words like "Restoration" ringing in our ears, it is nigh unto impossible to think of restoration without simultaneously thinking of the word "pattern." After all, how can you possibly restore something without having a pattern to follow? Restoration and pattern are like horse and carriage, love and marriage. You can't have one without the other. Yet, I am painfully conscious that this paired association of words and ideas is mostly lost on a younger generation. So, for those who've heard "the pattern sermon" a thousand times, please forgive the repetition. Within my own lifetime, familiar wells have caved in and are in dire need of re-digging.

The "pattern principle" emerges, first of all, from a number of passages in the Old and New Testaments where either the word "pattern" or some close equivalent is actually used. It is used most often in connection with the building of, first the tabernacle, then the temple. For example, the Lord said to Moses (Exodus 25:9): "Make this tabernacle and all its furnishings exactly like the pattern I will show you." What follows thereafter is incredible detail, right down to the "blue, purple, and scarlet yarn" (26:1), the "curtains of goat hair" (26:7), and "fifty bronze clasps" (26:11). God obviously had definite ideas about how he wanted things done.

And that, really, is the whole point. *If* God has given us detailed instructions or patterns of worship, then who are we to do things differently? (Naturally, that *"If"* is crucial to the discussion. But when we finally get to the point of *"Where* God has spoken...," then our duty is clear.)

Just to cite the full record, God repeats himself (in Exodus 25:40), saying, "See that you make them [the lampstand and the seven lamps] according to the pattern shown you on the mountain." And again (26:30): "Set up the tabernacle according to the plan shown you on the mountain." And yet again: "Make the altar hollow, out of boards...just as you were shown on the mountain" (27:8).

I particularly like the nice touch we get in 2 Chronicles 24 where we find both restoration and pattern explicitly linked together. When Joash sets about to restore the temple, the record tells us that, "They rebuilt the temple of God according to its original design and reinforced it" (24:13). That's what Restoration is all about: replicating the work and worship of the early church *according to its original design.*

The writer of Hebrews, of course, draws directly upon this pattern principle. Arguing that Christ was not just an earthly priest but our High Priest in heaven, the writer parenthetically notes that earthly priests serve in a sanctuary that is only a "copy and shadow" of what is in heaven. He immediately follows on with the intriguing statement: "This is why Moses was warned when he was about to build the tabernacle: 'See to it that you make everything according to the pattern shown you on the mountain.'" Why follow Christ? Because he is our High Priest (which is to say, *God!*), and what he has directed us to do on earth is but a preview of what it will be like in heaven. Get it wrong here, and we will have gotten it wrong for an eternity!

Indeed, Jesus Christ was himself a pattern. "Anyone who has seen me has seen the Father," Jesus said to the apostles on the night he was betrayed (John 14:9). No wonder he had said to them in the beginning, "Follow me," as if also to say, "I am the divine Pattern revealed in human likeness." He didn't simply mean, "Tag along after me," but "pattern your life after mine."

Nor did Jesus leave his apostles without guidance after his ascension. "I will ask the Father," he promised, "and he will give you another Counselor to be with you forever—the Spirit of truth" (14:16). "The Counselor, the Holy Spirit, whom the Father will send in my name, will teach you all things and will remind you of everything I have said to you" (14:25-26). "When he, the Spirit of truth, comes, he will guide you into all truth" (16:13). A truth that forms the divine pattern...about God...about us...about how we should live as followers of Christ...about how we should worship him...even about how we are to judge our fellow Christians.

Ironically, that judgment is to be based upon how faithful our fellow Christians are to the pattern. "Join with others in following my example," Paul admonished his Philippian brethren (3:17), "and take note of those who live according to the pattern we gave you." Or rather (as the context clearly implies), take note of those who *don't*.

And to Timothy, his young protégé, Paul wrote: "Follow the pattern of the sound words which you have heard from me...guard the truth that has been entrusted to you by the Holy Spirit who dwells within us" (2 Timothy 1:13-14, RSV). That Paul in both instances is referring to a theological pattern as compared with a specific pattern for church worship and practice does not detract from the principle of pattern itself. Even those who reject patterns of form quite happily regard themselves as "patternists" relative to theology and function.

Given this pervasive biblical emphasis on following divine pattern, whether it be for temple furnishings or core theology, is it so unreasonable to accept that apostolic practice in the years immediately following Jesus' ascension is our "best evidence" of what we are to be and to do as God's people? God has spoken not only through the Word-made-flesh, Jesus of Nazareth, but also through his Written Word, which reveals to us indirectly what the Holy Spirit revealed directly to first-century Christians. His pattern became theirs; their pattern has become ours.

Barring personal visions, how could our link to God's own mind possibly be any closer? Of necessity, anything beyond the New Testament record is only rumor, hearsay, conjecture, or innuendo. Or, more likely, human invention. One of the great unheeded lessons of history is Israel's repudiation of the warning: "Do not add to what I command you and do not subtract from it, but keep the commands of the Lord your God that I give you" (Deuteronomy 4:2). As long as the Israelites were faithful to the divine pattern, they were blessed. When they ignored the pattern, there was nothing but disaster.

Dare we scorn the hard lesson Israel learned when they moved the ark in an unauthorized manner? "It was because you, the Levites, did not bring it up the first time that the Lord our God broke out in anger against us," David lamented. "We did not inquire of him about how to do it in the prescribed way" (1 Chronicles 15:13).

Israel should have known better than to think that God is indifferent to how we live and move and worship in his presence. From the very beginning, Israel had been forewarned: "Be careful not to sacrifice your burnt offerings anywhere you please. Offer them only at the place the Lord will choose..." (Deuteronomy 13:13-14).

The lesson from history is clear: Not just any way we please, but the prescribed way. The patterned way. God's way.

Choose Your Pattern

That there should be (particularly from among ourselves) serious criticism of "pattern thinking" defies belief. But of one thing we can be certain: contrary to what some critics might lead us to think, the debate has nothing to do with *whether* we ought to follow a pattern, only *which*? For either we are following the pattern of primitive Christian practice or else we are following the "pattern of this world" (Romans 12:2). Everyone is following some pattern! If it is not God's pattern, then what's left?

I've purposely framed these two choices in terms of the starkest possible dichotomy, fully aware that current discussions about pattern are couched in far more thoughtful nuances. While I think I understand what is being presented in the debate over scriptural pattern and precedent, I nevertheless fear that even the most sincere arguments against pattern are prompted, at least in part, by a worldly pattern that stands in opposition to divine authority.

My own comfort zone with arguments critical of pattern would be increased considerably if only I could hear sharper distinctions being made between the *abuse* of pattern theology and the *use* of it. Unfortunately, much of the talk about *abuse* of pattern seems to be little more than a convenient rationalization for avoiding its *use*. Winning that game, of course, is a slam-dunk. It takes little imagination to parade forth all the abuses of pattern which can be observed within our fellowship. Too many times, we've made *pattern itself* our idol. For too many of us, meticulously following pattern has become a matter of works-righteousness. And too often we've turned pattern into an indiscriminate smorgasbord, picking and choosing with seeming abandon which examples we will follow and which we will not. So if you want to find pattern abuse (call *that* "patternism," if you will), it's on every tree and vine, ripe for the picking.

But this only begs the obvious plethora of questions: What are we to do in the *absence* of any such abuse? Suppose, for a moment, there simply weren't any. Now what pattern do we follow? How do we know what God desires and expects of us? If God's mind is not to be found in Scripture, then where? The direct leading of the Holy Spirit? In paths and directions quite unlike primitive Christianity? Different paths and directions for some, but not for all? One generation being led differently from another?

"That way madness lies!" (*King Lear*, 3. 4. 21)

Fortunately, no one I know is suggesting that we are simply left to our own devices, or to revelations capriciously received from the Holy Spirit. Everyone I know is pointing to Scripture as the basis for how we should live and worship as Christians. Therefore, the debate about pattern must surely be concerned with something other than the notion of pattern or precedent itself. Is not the question of the hour: *What* is the pattern? Or, perhaps: The pattern *for what*?

When we ask, "*What* is the pattern," inevitably we are led to a number of thorny issues. For instance, was a particular practice of first-century Christians (such as footwashing) actually meant to have the force of precedent? And how do we safely distinguish trustworthy apostolic doctrine from practices which were merely cultural? (Consider, for example, the wearing of veils.) And might there be some primitive practices (notably the charismatic gifts) which were set in place solely as "start-up" measures, but never intended to last beyond the apostolic era? Those difficult issues, and more, will be the subject of our discussion in the next several chapters. Nobody ever promised restoration would be easy!

In fact, complete candor compels acknowledgment that the pattern of first-century faith and practice is not nearly as clear-cut and straightforward as we've typically assumed. Unlike the minute details given for the construction of the tabernacle, we don't always have the luxury of explicit details regarding the early church. It's more a matter of reading between the lines, or piecing together a complicated puzzle. I take it that this is intentional on God's part, consistent with the broader pattern of minimizing externals under the new covenant, and allowing for necessary cultural adaptation throughout the centuries. Yet, to the extent that intended divine pattern can be determined with any reasonable assurance (admittedly always the fly in the ointment), then that must surely become the model which we commit ourselves to follow. Any other response—as virtually all of us agree—would be a blatant disregard of God's leading.

When we ask, on the other hand, "Pattern *for what*?" we turn our attention to exploring possible distinctions between form and function. Assuming we are meant to restore primitive Christianity, some are now asking whether that necessarily includes restoring identical first-century *forms*, or only the underlying *functions* which those forms were meant to advance?

More on this momentarily. The immediate point is that both of these questions—however we might answer them— bring us back full circle to pattern theology. Or apostolic practice. Or biblical Christianity. However you wish to put it, we simply have no other way to know the will of God but to follow in the footsteps of our Christ-centered, Spirit-led, apostle-taught forebears in the faith. That, in a nutshell, is the very idea of Restoration!

Restoring *Form* Or *Function*?

Before we leave this chapter, let me briefly share some further thoughts about the case now being put forward for the proposition that first-century forms are not really important as long as first-century function is achieved. A forceful argument for that position has been put forward in a recent book titled *A Church That Flies* by Tim Woodroof, who happens to be a much-loved cousin of mine.

We are never quite sure whether we should acknowledge that we are related!

Strange is it that our bloods,
Of colour, weight, and heat, poured all together,
Would quite confound distinction, yet stands off
In differences so mighty.

(*All's Well...*, 2. 3. 118)

I suppose only a cousin would dare say of his book, "While I applaud both Tim's heart and his vision, if his *Church That Flies* happens to crash and burn instead, his book will be the black box that explains what went wrong!" Not surprisingly, that recommendation never made it to the back cover!

Initially, I had hoped that Tim and I might respond to each other's books within this volume, but space simply did not permit. Hopefully, we will have opportunity for further dialogue in a future book. For now, however, let me briefly outline the issues involved.

I think it is fair to say that Tim and I are equally concerned about a stagnant, institutionalized church which no longer seems to "take off and soar." (Hence, the title for his book.) However, we could hardly be farther apart on the solution to the problem...or even its cause. In Tim's view, the villain of the piece is the church's rigid adherence to archaic first-century forms which, he believes, are a barrier to our reaching a vastly-different contemporary culture and generation. The solution he proposes is to move away from restoration of *form* and concentrate, instead, on restoration of *function*.

Whatever its merits, that perspective is hardly "Restorationist," as it is presented. ("Our desire is to remain firmly within the Restoration Heritage...") To the contrary, the argument for "function rather than form" rips the very heart out of the Restoration concept. While Restoration thinking never consciously elevated form itself over function (and would be wrong to do so), the essential, indispensable, non-negotiable crux of the Restoration idea is that first-century, apostolic *forms, themselves*, were ordained of God.

In that light, interestingly enough, Tim's major premise—that "form follows function"—actually works! For, having determined at the dawn of eternity which functions he desired for those who would become his chosen people, God specifically and purposely designed forms of worship, organization, and practice which best would achieve his eternal purpose. His forms were designed to function! Believing that those very forms were given to the early church by the Holy Spirit, we maintain that they represent our best hope for achieving the results which God intends. Divine *function* led to divine *form*, which even now leads us back to divine *function*.

Tim contends the exact opposite: 1) That many primitive Christian forms were a cultural and coincidental response to the Gospel, unique to their time and circumstance; 2) That New Testament "pattern" has little to do with form, and everything to do with "the seven eternal, immutable functions" of Worship, Holiness, Community, Maturation, Service, Witness, and Influence; and 3) That, as long as we are attempting to "restore" these same seven functions, then (with the exception of baptism and the Lord's Supper) the forms we happen to choose are a matter of indifference to God. ("In the end, we believe it is a functioning church that is important to God—whatever forms that church adopts.")

With that argument, of course, virtually all Christian denominations could agree. In fact, have always agreed! Had that been the "restoration" argument in the nineteenth century, there never would have been a Restoration Movement.

This explains, of course, why the denominations—despite their avowed commitment to Scripture—feel no compelling need to justify practices which significantly deviate from the New Testament pattern. (On a sliding scale, merely consider infant baptism, women in leadership, or instrumental music). Once the pattern principle is repudiated, any reference to first-century practice (unlinked to specific doctrinal teaching) becomes entirely moot. Paul's statement, "We have no other practice" (said regarding gender roles) simply no longer matters. And whatever mode of music was used by the early church (even if there is overwhelming evidence that it was non-instrumental) has now become immaterial.

By focusing on "form and function," doctrinal debate is won by sheer premise and conclusion—which is to say, by completely ignoring the issue. *If* (premise) function is all that matters, *then* (conclusion) primitive Christian practices simply aren't precedent. From that starting point, we can be as pragmatic, inductive, anti-historical, and contemporary as we wish to be in aid of what we perceive to be biblical functions.

No matter how well-intentioned, at its root this argument maintains that the ends justify the means—or, as Shakespeare titled it, *All's Well That Ends Well*. Indeed his famous play is a classic tale of form following function, which, in the end, justifies various and sundry dubious deeds done to bring about a legitimate purpose. When young Bertram runs off to war to avoid consummating his forced marriage to the lovely Helen, a resourceful Helen follows Bertram to Italy and tricks him into her bed under the ruse that he is seducing another woman. Confronted with the fact that he has unwittingly consummated his marriage, Bertram is shamed into acknowledging Helen as his wife.

Naturally, Helen rationalizes her cunning scheme ever so easily, saying:

> *Let us essay our plot, which if it speed*
> *Is wicked meaning in a lawful deed*
> *And lawful meaning in a wicked act,*
> *Where both not sin, and yet a sinful fact.*
> (3. 7. 44-47)

Yet, having acknowledged her own deception and Bertram's lustful intentions, Helen nevertheless points to the inherent lawfulness of their liaison to conclude that:

> *All's well that ends well; still the fine's the crown.*
> *Whate'er the course, the end is the renown.*
>
> (4. 4. 35-36)

Unlike Helen's connivance, of course, there is nothing impure in motive about worship forms and practices sincerely aimed at better achieving biblical functions. Even so, for us to rationalize innovative forms and practices on that basis alone does not preclude the possibility that, as Helen put it, they are "yet a sinful fact." When God himself has married together form and function, dare we divorce them for even the noblest of reasons?

Merely consider what surely must have been only a superficially happy ending for Bertram and Helen—finally wed but likely locked in a loveless marriage. Just when you think there could not be a better example of the lack of intended function justifying a change in form, we are brought face to face with the reality that choosing man's way (a seemingly merciful divorce) is not God's way at all. Indeed, the trouble came much earlier when God's way was unheeded in the first place. Surely, it is a vivid reminder that to dispense with divine form is, ultimately and inevitably, to invite the risk of compromising the divine function itself.

As it was in the beginning, so it is even today: It is not within man to direct his own steps...nor to dare presume that "all's well that ends well."

> *'Let me not live,' quoth he,*
> *'After my flame lacks oil, to be the snuff*
> *Of younger spirits, whose apprehensive senses*
> *All but new things disdain....'*
>
> (1. 2. 58-61)

CHAPTER FIVE

A FIRST-CENTURY MODEL OF PERFECTION

*Fewer things are harder to put up with than the annoyance
of a good example.*

MARK TWAIN

For almost a week, I had been wandering around the Old City of Jerusalem in search of various significant sites, only to get hopelessly lost, particularly in the Arab quarter with its complex maze of souks crowded with merchants and shoppers. Even when I was guided by my friend and resident expert, Joseph Shulam, I could hardly make sense of all the ruins he would show me: a wall from the time of Ezra, here; a column from the Byzantine era, there; a street built by Herod, over there. By the end of a week in the Old City, Jerusalem was beginning to look like little more than ruins and rubble.

How is a person ever supposed to get a feel for the reality of the first-century world of Jesus and the apostles when it lies mostly buried under layer upon layer of political and military conflict? Where does a person begin to get his bearings when one ancient wall has been replaced by a more modern one; and that one replaced by yet another?

You can imagine, then, how thrilling it was for me to find a true-to-life model of Jerusalem during the Second Temple period, constructed (next to the Holyland Hotel) under the direction of a team of archeological, literary, and biblical scholars. As far as possible, it is even constructed of the original materials used at the time, including marble, stone, wood, copper and iron. (Heim Perez, the man who actually built the model, proudly handed me a small piece of the marble to carry home.)

At last, it all made sense. At a scale of one to fifty, you could almost believe that you were hovering above the Old City in a helicopter. Look! There is Herod's Palace and Pilate's residence in the same luxurious complex. And over there is Caiaphas' house, where Jesus was first brought after being arrested. With but the slightest imagination, you can almost see Jesus as he is being led back and forth through the city during the long night of his arrest and trial.

For me, the highlight of the model was the Second Temple itself—the one built by Ezra and renovated by Herod. Despite reading about its construction and generally knowing its layout and dimensions, I still could never quite grasp what the temple must have looked like in the first century. Guided by literature alone, it was almost impossible to visualize the site of the temple as it relates, for example, to the City of David or to Mount Zion.

With each street, structure, and elevation clearly shown by the model, the biblical Jerusalem I had read about so many times finally came to life. Only when I looked over and saw a cat taking a drink from the Pool of Bethesda was I brought back to reality! It was, after all, only a model. But how very close it must be to the real thing.

Like first-century Jerusalem, first-century Christianity lies mostly buried under layer upon layer of religious and doctrinal alterations. It's back to ruin and rubble all over again. If only we had a model! Then we could restore "the real thing," the genuine article. No more added traditions. No more tawdry substitutes. That's the kind of Christianity I want. Just primitive Christianity at its very best!

The good news, of course, is that we *do* have a model, providentially preserved for us in the New Testament record of the early church. When carefully uncovered and dusted, there it lies in its original, unvarnished state, before the onslaught of ruinous innovations and apostasies. To be sure, the original church was flawed from the word go by the obstinance and frailties of human sin. But the divinely-inspired ideal itself, in all its pristine perfection, stands out in glistening beauty amid the ruin and rubble of man's imperfection. Hence, the net result: an imperfectly-modeled *model of perfection.*

A Model of Conversion

When one reads afresh Luke's stirring account of the acts of the apostles, and then the various epistles written to the early church, one is struck by how vastly different primitive Christian practice was compared with anything we have ever known. Over the past several weeks, I have plowed back through all of that familiar text, only to be surprised anew by a world of faith which seems absolutely foreign to my experience. To somehow be able to go back in time and share in those first heady decades of apostolic Christian faith and practice would be the most thrilling prospect this side of having walked and talked with our Lord himself!

Re-reading that fascinating history of the early church, I'm intrigued all over again by what drew people to become Christians in the first place. There seemed to be no single path. Some, of course, were bowled over by the miracles they witnessed. What else could they honestly conclude when they saw the crippled beggar healed at the temple gate; or Dorcas raised from the dead; or Aeneas healed of his paralysis—each time, in the name of Jesus? "All those who lived in Lydda and Sharon saw [Aeneas] and turned to the Lord" (Acts 9:35). How could they not!

For others, the experience was more cerebral. Knowledgeable Jews (in particular those who were eagerly anticipating the coming of the Messiah) were persuaded by sermon after sermon in which the apostles demonstrated how Jesus of Nazareth was the son of David by lineage and the promised Christ of prophecy. "Many who heard the message believed..." (4:4). And never did an intellectual message have greater emotional impact than when Peter, on Pentecost, convinced the Jews that they had been instrumental in crucifying the very son of God. "Brothers, what shall we do?" they cried out in guilt and despair. Can we begin to imagine ourselves in their shoes—remembering that, only weeks before, they had been part of a frenzied crowd baying for Jesus' blood!

For Gentile converts, the appeal seems to have been, not just the miracles (which certainly got their attention), but the clarion call to righteous living, which—in a sex-saturated, politically-corrupt, and crime-ridden culture—intuitively rang true. Or perhaps (as in Paul's sermon on Mars Hill) it was the revolutionary idea of an "unknown god" who was not just some *object* of Nature but rather the *Creator* of all Nature (17:22-31). Or, more particularly, it may have been Paul's concluding line: "He has given proof of this to all men by raising him from the dead" (17:31). Most of them scoffed at the seemingly preposterous idea of resurrection, but at least a few in the audience found it compelling. Indeed, for many more hearers in less philosophical settings, the good news of Jesus' resurrection irresistibly resonated with the hope of an eternal existence which God has put in the hearts of all men (Ecclesiastes 3:11).

Little wonder, then, that the early Christians were characterized repeatedly as being filled with joy. For expectant Jews who, as a nation, had waited centuries for the Messiah to appear, their Savior had finally come! For exhausted, meticulous keepers of every jot and tittle of the Law, there was enough freedom in Christ to make their heads swim! For God-fearing Gentiles, of course, there was a ray of hope that never before had existed. And for guilt-ridden sinners of all sorts, there was the unexpected, almost inconceivable, promise of divine grace and mercy. It was an exhilarating time in which multitudes of disciples came to share the experience of the Philippian jailer, who "was filled with joy because he had come to believe..." (16:34).

A Model of Christian Initiation

Another convert who went his way rejoicing was the Ethiopian eunuch, to whom the evangelist, Philip, had proclaimed the good news of Jesus. What the eunuch and the jailer had in common was not just the joy of their newfound faith, but an experience which was also common to all other first-century disciples—namely, immersion in water. "Then both Philip and the eunuch went down into the water and Philip baptized him" (8:36-38). There is no specific mention that Philip had taught the eunuch anything about baptism, but the text says that "as they traveled along the road, they came to some water and the eunuch said, 'Look, here is water. Why shouldn't I be baptized?'"

The same can be said of the jailer's experience. In answer to his compelling question, "Sirs, what must I do to be saved?" Paul and Silas replied, "Believe in the Lord Jesus, and you will be saved...." Again, there is no record of baptism being mentioned. But Luke does tells us that they "spoke the word of the Lord to him and to all the others in his house. At that hour of the night the jailer took them and washed their wounds; then immediately he and all his family were baptized" (16:25-34).

When you think about it, the act of getting one's body completely wet in conjunction with the moment of conversion is strange, to say the least. Certainly, it is not something that anyone likely would have thought about on his own; and the odds that every first-century convert would come up with exactly the same idea simply boggles the mind. If, as it appears, the Ethiopian was familiar with the Jewish faith (he was reading the book of Isaiah when Philip joined him in the chariot), then he likely would have been familiar with Jewish ceremonial cleansings (or *mikvehs*), and perhaps even reports of John's baptizing in the Jordan. But there must have been something significantly different about a baptism into Christ, because the eunuch couldn't wait to experience it!

The jailer in Philippi, on the other hand, was a Gentile in a Roman colony more used to idolatry and fortune-telling than baptisms. Yet, he also was immersed in the very same hour that he came to believe in Jesus. Surely, it's not mere coincidence that he was baptized just like the eunuch. Nor is there likely any coincidence in the fact that his question ("What must I do?") was the very question asked by the Jews on Pentecost, to whom the answer was given: "Repent and be baptized, every one of you, in the name of Jesus Christ for the forgiveness of your sins" (2:38).

Although not every account of first-century conversions happens to record an act of immersion, it is crystal clear that there was no such thing as an "unbaptized Christian." It is instructive, for example, that Paul mentions in his first letter to the Corinthians his having personally immersed Crispus and Gaius (1 Corinthians 1:14). In the actual account of Crispus' conversion (Acts 18:8), nothing is said about Crispus being immersed, only that he believed. ("Crispus, the synagogue ruler, and his entire household believed in the Lord....") Even from within that same text, however, the uniform practice of immersion is implied from the simple summary: "...and many of the Corinthians who heard him believed and were baptized."

In fact, it is their common experience of having been immersed into the name of Christ which Paul later references in rebuking those same Corinthians for their division into personality cults. "Is Christ divided? Was Paul crucified for you? Were you baptized into the name of Paul?" (1 Corinthians 1:13). It was a not-so-gentle reminder that (as he told the Ephesians) they, too, were to maintain the spirit of unity which comes from the fact that there is one Lord, one faith, and one baptism. What was that "one baptism?" It was the *one baptism* by which each of them had been "clothed with Christ" (Galatians 3:27); and the same one *baptism* which Peter told them "now saves you...as the pledge of a good conscience toward God" (1 Peter 3:21).

Indeed, it was more than a pledge; it was also a picture—a graphic reminder of the basis for their personal, spiritual identity with the One whose dramatic resurrection had made their own resurrection possible. Paul paints that picture in his Roman letter (6:3-6), saying, "Don't you know that all of us who were baptized into Christ Jesus were baptized into his death? We were therefore buried with him through baptism into death in order that, just as Christ was raised from the dead through the glory of the Father, we too may live a new life. If we have been united with him like this in his death, we will certainly also be united with him in his resurrection."

For the early disciples, immersion into Christ was both a present "washing away of sin" and a perfect picture of hope for the life to come.

Model Of A Purposed People

Of course, Christian immersion theoretically might have signaled little more than a token change in one's official religion (not unlike the immersion associated with Gentile proselytes who accepted the Jewish faith). But you certainly don't get that indication from the text. To the contrary, these joyful, dripping-wet disciples were quickly beginning to realize how their own obedient faith (as well as the inclusion of Gentiles along with Jews) was part of an eternal master-plan drawn up prior to the dawn of Creation. As Paul explained in his Ephesian letter, God in his omniscient foreknowledge had known from before their births exactly how each one of them would respond to the preaching of the gospel. Even then, he had predestined them for the good works that he would do through them.

Unlike the Jews, whose identity with the nation of Israel was by a passive, physical birth, these ardent followers of

Christ—both Jew and Gentile-had become God's *new* chosen people by their active, personal faith in his redeeming grace. "You were included in Christ when you heard the word of truth, the gospel of your salvation. Having believed, you were marked in him with a seal..." (Ephesians 1:13). Because *they* had chosen, they *were* chosen! And the good news is that every person who has ever glimpsed the light of truth has been given that same choice, for "He is patient...not wanting anyone to perish, but everyone to come to repentance" (2 Peter 3:9).

Naturally, Jewish Christians would have related more easily than Gentile Christians to the idea of "chosenness" and being God's "elect." Had not God chosen Abraham, Isaac, and Jacob through whom he would bless the world? Had he not, from among all the nations, elected Israel as his bride? But as Paul took pains to point out in his letter to the disciples at Ephesus, their chosenness in Christ was personal, not national. *Any and all* who put their faith in Christ became a part of God's elect; or, as Peter put it, became "a chosen people, a royal priest-hood, a holy nation, a people belonging to God" (1 Peter 2:9-10). *Once* they were not a people, but *now* they were. *Once* they had not received mercy, but *now* they had.

Our forebears in the faith had a keen sense of having been called—one by one and collectively. Having been justified and sanctified, they understood that their faith was involving them in something far greater than any idolatry, philosophy, or Jewish theocracy which may have been their former framework. As God's special people, they had become part of a predestined, foreordained mission from on high.

And so it was that, to these special people, God-breathed letters began to arrive, addressing them as chosen people:

To all in Rome who are loved by God and called to be saints.

To the church of God in Corinth, to those sanctified in Christ Jesus and called to be holy....

Paul, a servant of God and an apostle of Jesus Christ for the faith of God's elect...to Titus.

Peter, an apostle of Jesus Christ, To God's elect...who have been chosen according to the foreknowledge of God the Father, by the sanctifying work of the Spirit....

The elder [John], To the chosen lady and her children.

Jude, To those who have been called....

What a magnificent heritage was theirs! Being specially called into a personal relationship with God was more than simply a point of doctrine. It was meaning, purpose, significance, and destiny all wrapped up in one. Not just any calling, mind you, but a higher calling. Not just election, but direction. Not just foreordained, but *ordained*. These were people who had begun to grasp the hidden mystery of what they were about. And what they were about was increasingly the all-consuming focus of their existence—determining their values, ordering their priorities, and firming up their commitments. Given their calling, what else could they be but a people for whom sacrifice would become normative, evangelism imperative, and their response to persecution, simply courageous?

A Model of Radical Purity

Yet, it was not a calling to be taken for granted, as if once called, always called. Who more than Peter understood what it was like to plunge from the highest heights? No surprise, then, to hear his warning: "My brothers, be all the more eager to make your calling and election sure" (1 Peter 1:10-11). "Just as he who called you is holy, so be holy in all you do; for it is written: 'Be holy, because I am holy'" (1:15-16).

As Peter well knew, a return to sin was always possible, but never an option. Not for God's elect! Not for those who had been redeemed by the blood of the Lamb! Having experienced the light of Christ, how could they ever again live in darkness? As God's chosen people, they were made for finer things!

"I urge you, therefore, to live a life worthy of the calling you have received," came Paul's admonition (Ephesians 4:1). And again, "Be very careful, then, how you live..." (5:15). "There must not even be a hint of sexual immorality...or impurity...or obscenity, foolish talk, or coarse joking...for these are improper for God's holy people" (5:3-4). "Do not get drunk," but instead, "be filled with the Spirit" (5:18). "I also want women to dress modestly, with decency and propriety...appropriate for women who profess to worship God" (1 Timothy 2:9-10). Over and over came the reminder: You were foreordained for finer things!

Called people were to be cleansed people. People of scrupulous moral purity. Radically righteous people. People who kept themselves holy because they were *wholly* dedicated to God—body and soul. For those of us today who are battle-scarred from our struggle with this world's seductive passions, the uncompromising moral standards promulgated and wit-nessed among first-century Christians mark out a challenging, rebuking pattern of personal purity.

A Model Of Radical Piety

It is said that "cleanliness is next to godliness," and certainly that was true of the early church. For first-century Christians, moral purity was invariably twinned with godly piety. No, not just weekly worship, but daily spiritual exercise. As a people of prayer, first and foremost, they prayed in the Spirit "on all occasions with all kinds of prayers and requests" (Ephesians 6:18). They prayed alone. They prayed together. They prayed when they were happy.

They prayed when they were sad, lonely, or afraid. They prayed on their knees, and with outstretched hands. They prayed for healing, and for miracles, and for boldness in preaching the Word. And "after they prayed, the place where they were meeting was shaken" (Acts 4:31). First-century Christians not only believed in the power of prayer; they experienced it!

And with prayer sometimes came fasting. Although the Gospels refer more often to acts of individual fasting (such as Anna the prophetess who "never left the temple but worshiped night and day, fasting and praying," Luke 2:36-37), the practice seems to have continued in some form in the early church. For example, "While they were worshiping the Lord and fasting...," Barnabas and Saul were set apart by the Spirit for their work as evangelists (Acts 13:1-3). In this case, as well as when Paul and Barnabas themselves appointed elders in the region of Pisidia (14:21-23), fasting and prayer specifically seemed to accompany the laying on of hands. Although there is scant evidence in the New Testament record, it seems probable that private acts of spiritual fasting may also have been an ongoing practice among primitive Christians, following on from this centuries-old fixture of Jewish piety.

To whatever extent it was done, the purpose for fasting is revealed, oddly enough, in a kind of "sexual fasting" which was also associated with prayer. This curious form of piety was alluded to when Paul advised Corinthian couples not to deprive each other sexually, "except by mutual consent and for a time, so that you may devote yourselves to prayer" (1 Corinthians 7:5). Whether fasting from food or from sexual relations, the focus was on *getting focused.* It was a means of putting one's priorities into perspective. It was a tangible, dramatic way of reminding one's self about the difference between the fleeting hungers of this world and the eternal longings of the Spirit. But ours is a fast-paced world, not a "fast"-driven one. Whether it's because we've simply gotten out of the habit, or (more likely) because we live in an age of gluttonous over-indulgence, fasting for the soul has given way to fast food for the stomach.

Other forms of primitive piety are equally intriguing, including the mention of Paul's having his hair cut off at Cenchrea "because of a vow he had taken" (Acts 18:18). Perhaps the nature of the vow is more fully explained when, in Jerusalem at a later time, Paul joined four other men in their purification rites, "then went to the temple to give notice of the date when the days of purification would end and the offering would be made for each of them" (21:20-26). Even if these vows were taken to enable Paul to become "like one under the law...so as to win those under the law" (1 Corinthians 9:20), still, it indicates that personal acts of piety promoted under the Jewish system were not necessarily abandoned by Jewish converts who were now giving their allegiance to Christ.

In terms of Christian piety, much also could be said about case after case of uncommon generosity toward the benevolence of others. "No one claimed that any of his possessions was his own, but they shared everything they had" (Acts 4:32). Perhaps we too easily dismiss this extraordinary philanthropy by citing exceptional circumstances in the early days of the church. The fact remains that, "There were no needy persons among them. For from time to time those who owned lands or houses sold them," and the money "was distributed to anyone as he had a need" (4:34-35). Taken at face value, the New Testament pattern of Christian piety is far more costly than we might ever have expected.

Of course, Christian charity began at home, in the support of their own families, and then spiraled out to the support of those (particularly widows) who had no families to look after them (1 Timothy 3-10). Yet, even in the case of family obligations, sacrificial giving was not only a matter of meeting obvious needs. It was an act of piety denouncing trust in material goods and affirming, instead, one's dependence upon God.

From our perspective of unprecedented material afflu-ence—and the web of conspicuous, mad consumerism in which most of us are caught—this kind of piety seems not just radical but entirely out of the question. The more we have (especially compared with our first-century brothers and sisters), the less willing we are to part with it. Piety (even extraordinary gen-erosity from out of our abundance) is fine as long as we don't have to sacrifice our normal standard of living to pay for it! (Say I, writing from my *second* home.)

Yet another feature of the early church was the practice of hospitality—itself, a form of benevolence—in which the disci-ples regularly opened their homes and shared their tables with fellow believers. From the very beginning, they "broke bread in their homes and ate together with glad and sincere hearts..." (Acts 2:46). In fact, table fellowship played such a significant role in the first-century church that its withdrawal became one of the primary means of disciplining those who were unrepentantly immoral. "With such a man do not even eat," came Paul's com-mand (1 Corinthians 5:11), underscoring the importance which was placed upon hospitality in the early church.

Never was that table fellowship more significant than when it was practiced as part of the "love feasts" observed in connection with the Lord's Supper. More on that later. For the moment, it is important to understand that gathering around *the table* on the Lord's Day would have had little meaning for them were it not a natural extension of their gathering around *a table* from day to day throughout the week.

In short, then, first-century piety was an open heart in prayer, an open spirit in fasting, an open hand in benevolence, and an open home in hospitality.

A Model of Radical Relationships

Given what we have already seen, one would be justified in thinking that radical Christianity necessarily entails a radical change in relationships. Certainly, relationships are central to the gospel—whether between God and man, or between man and fellow man. But as we look at the model church, we are surprised at what did *not* change at the point of conversion.

In answer to questions put to him by new converts in Corinth, Paul said explicitly: "Each one should remain in the situation which he was in when God called him. Were you a slave when you were called? If you can gain your freedom, do so...[otherwise] don't let it trouble you" (1 Corinthians 7:20-21). True enough, Paul entreated Philemon to regard his runaway slave, Onesimus, as a brother in Christ and no longer as a slave (15-17), but nowhere does Paul issue a universal Emancipation Proclamation. For a slave to become a Christian meant only that he now had *two* masters to please instead of one!

There was a similar message regarding marriage and singleness (1 Corinthians 7:1-16). Clearly, a new convert who was single did not have to get married in order to become a disciple; and, clearer still, no married converts were compelled to separate from their spouses, nor certainly to get a divorce. In whatever state one found himself at the time of his conversion, the message remained the same: "Each one should retain the place in life that the Lord assigned to him and to which God has called him" (7:17).

Yet, there was definitely a sense in which all earthly relationships radically changed. In five separate letters (Romans 13:1-7; Ephesians 5:21-6:9; Colossians 3:18-4:1; 1 Timothy 6:1-2; and Titus 2:9-10), Paul enjoined a new attitude toward those in authority; or, rather, urged a greater motivation for submitting to their lead. "Everyone must submit himself to the governing authorities," said Paul, "for he who rebels against the authority is rebelling against what God has instituted." Of course, that's easy for us to say within the context of our intoxicatingly-free modern democracies, but consider the potential implications for the early Christians who were persecuted by that self-same

"God-ordained" Roman government. For them, submission to governmental authority was often a matter of life and death.

By the grace of God, we may never face that excruciating possibility, but most of us have experienced (or will) the family relationships which first-century disciples had to radically reconsider as a called-out people. Both Peter and Paul addressed these bedrock relationships, speaking to husbands and wives, as well as to parents and children, in passages which seem altogether familiar to us...if perhaps too familiar:

> *Husbands love your wives...*
> *Wives submit to your husbands...*
> *Children obey your parents...*
> *Fathers, do not embitter your children...*

For Jews, especially, there was nothing particularly revolutionary about these injunctions. It was the motivation behind them that became so uniquely compelling:

> Submit to one another *out of reverence for Christ.*
> Wives, submit to your husbands *as to the Lord.*
> The husband is the head of the wife, *as Christ is the head of the church.*
> Husbands, love your wives, *just as Christ loved the church.*

In view of Christ Jesus, all relationships were radically changed by an attitude reflecting his own—"who...being found in appearance as a man...humbled himself and became obedient to death-even death on a cross!" Given that divine model of submission, New Testament Christians were "predestined to be conformed to the likeness of his Son" in even the most difficult relationships and trying circumstances (Romans 8:29).

You mean, remain a slave? Stick it out in a dead-end marriage? Obey parents who don't have a clue where you're coming from? In the early church, hard questions received hard answers. But if you were to ask those early disciples how they managed to do it, their response would not be long in coming: "If we are out of our mind, it is for the sake of God...for Christ's love compels us" (2 Corinthians 5:13-14)!

A Model Response To Persecution

For most of us, I suspect, Christian martyrs seem a world apart—no more real than a historical footnote. But in the early church, the threat of persecution and martyrdom was a daily reality. As one might expect, the leaders in the church were the prime targets, which explains the brutal execution of James the apostle (Acts 12:1), and the death-by-stoning of Stephen the evangelist. In Acts 4, 5, and 12, we read that Peter himself only narrowly escaped execution, and was imprisoned at least three times, as well as being flogged along with the other apostles. Indeed, from Jesus' prediction in John 21, there is every reason to believe that Peter eventually came to a violent end for his defense of the faith. Paul, of course, was stripped and beaten (16:22); imprisoned (16:22-24); stoned and left for dead (14:19); and repeatedly kicked out of town (13:50).

Before we all breathe a collective sigh of relief that persecution touched only the apostles and other high-profile leaders, we'd do well to read more closely. On the very day that Stephen was murdered, "a great persecution broke out against the church at Jerusalem, and all except the apostles were scattered throughout Judea and Samaria" (8:1). The text further tells us that "Saul began to destroy the church. Going from house to house, he dragged off men and women and put them in prison" (8:3). No one was exempt from harassment, beatings, and imprisonment. Ordinary Christians were as likely to be persecuted as were their leaders.

Had you and I been numbered among the disciples in Jerusalem during those dark early days, surely "standing up for Jesus" would not just be familiar lyrics in a jaded hymn, but words having every potential for ending up in a funeral dirge. I suppose we should be thankful that, given the fortuity of 21st-century religious tolerance, we can only imagine what official persecution is like. Then again, our greatest potential for persecution is not physical persecution at the hand of outsiders. It's most often verbal persecution leveled by people who are our own brothers in Christ—brothers who slander and speak evil of us. Brothers who "kill" us with lies and distortion. Who knows but that a radical return to primitive Christian fervor might, in fact, generate even greater hostility from brethren wedded to traditions—and, yes, perhaps even official persecution as well?

How, really, could it be otherwise? Paul told Timothy in no uncertain terms (2 Timothy 3:12) that "everyone who wants to live a godly life in Christ Jesus *will be persecuted*!" Nor should we be misled when Peter says, "*If* you suffer as a Christian..." (1 Peter 4:16). It is obvious from the context that what he really means is "*When* you suffer as a Christian," clearly suggesting the inevitability of persecution in response to radical Christian faith and practice. Did not John write: "Do not be surprised, my brothers, if the world hates you" (1 John 3:13)?

Indeed, if we truly wish to model ourselves after the early church, we must not only come to expect persecution in some shape or form, but in a sense, actually welcome it as a bond between ourselves and the One who suffered all on our behalf. According to Paul (in Romans 8:17), it is only by sharing in Jesus' sufferings that we are co-heirs with Christ. Believe it or not, the prayer of first-century Christians was epitomized by Paul's own desire when he said: "I want to know Christ...and the fellowship of sharing in his sufferings" (Philippians 3:10).

Where does that leave us today if, in fact, one can't really know Christ *without* sharing in his suffering?

Little wonder, then, that we have Peter's message to the early church (in 1 Peter 4:13): "Rejoice that you participate in the sufferings of Christ, so that you may be overjoyed when his glory is revealed." Dare we pray the radical prayer: *Lord, send us suffering that we, too, might have true fellowship with you, and exceeding joy?*

A Model of Belief in the Supernatural

The success of the early disciples' response to persecution was based in large measure upon their unflinching acceptance of a supernatural world beyond their own. Belief in a supernatural dimension made it possible to endure suffering in a natural world. "Who," Paul asked rhetorically, "shall separate us from the love of Christ? Shall trouble or hardship or persecution or famine or nakedness or danger or sword?" "No," comes his resounding answer, for "in all these things we are more than conquerors through him who loved us. For I am convinced that neither death nor life, neither angels nor demons, neither the present nor the future, nor any powers...will be able to separate us from the love of God..." (Romans 8:35-39).

The first-century world was filled with angels and demons...and "powers." A fierce, cosmic spiritual battle was being waged between the powers of evil and the power of God. Hence Paul's stirring admonition: "Be strong in the Lord and in his mighty power. Put on the full armor of God so that you can take your stand against the devil's schemes. For our struggle is not against flesh and blood, but against the rulers, against the authorities, against the powers of this dark world and against the spiritual forces of evil in the heavenly realms" (Ephesians 6:10-12).

Angels, demons, spiritual forces of evil, and the devil.... For the early disciples, these other-worldly phenomena and personalities were as real as breathing. They saw them; they talked to them; they felt them.

Cornelius, for example, "distinctly saw an angel of God" (Acts 10:3)..."a man in shining clothes" (10:30)..."a holy angel who told him to have [Peter] come to his house" (10:22). It was also an angel who later released Peter from Herod's clutches, unlocking his chains and leading him out of the prison (Acts 12:1-11). When Herod himself refused to reject the people's adulation that he was a god, "an angel of the Lord struck him down..." (12:23). And it was an angel who stood beside Paul and spoke to him in the midst of the storm at sea (27:21-26). You say you don't believe in angels? The early disciples did!

They also believed that Satan was alive and well...at least for the moment. Certainly, God was going to crush Satan under their feet (Romans 16:20), but not before Paul was given "a thorn" in his flesh, "a messenger of Satan, to torment" him (2 Corinthians 12:8). Is it possible that Paul was referring to "Satan" as simply a figure of speech? Not likely. Paul told the Corinthians that he had forgiven them, "in order that Satan might not outwit us. For we are not unaware of his schemes" (2 Corinthians 2:10-11). Paul himself had been a victim of Satan's schemes, not only with the "thorn in his flesh," but also in his travel plans. "For we wanted to come to you—certainly I, Paul, did, again and again—but Satan stopped us" (1 Thessalonians 2:18). And it was Satan to whom false teachers were to be handed over (1 Timothy 1:20), as well as the man who was sleeping with his father's wife (1 Corinthians 5:4-5).

The devil of Scripture has a long and vivid history which first-century disciples, unlike ourselves, had not forgotten. Who among us, for example, would ever begin an argument, saying (as Jude did, in verse 9): "But even the archangel Michael, when he was disputing with the devil about the body of Moses, did not slander...?" Whatever may have been involved in this dispute over Moses' body (and I, for one, don't claim to know), the early Christians accepted with aplomb Jude's literal references to Michael and the devil. They also took it as fact that "the devil has been sinning from the beginning," and that "the reason the Son of God appeared was to destroy the devil's work" (1 John 3:20).

Satan, a metaphor for evil? Perhaps. But for the early Christians, that ancient serpent, the devil, was not simply a metaphor!

Nor were his legions of demons or the evil spirits, whom, we are told (in Acts 8:7), Philip cast out to the sounds of bone-chilling shrieks! In Ephesus, when people touched handkerchiefs and aprons which had been touched by Paul, "their illnesses were cured and the evil spirits left them" (Acts 19:12). Lest anyone think that those "evil spirits" were a euphemism for "illnesses," we are immediately given that incredible account in which an evil spirit rebukes some counterfeit exorcists and then jumps on them and overpowers them all (19:13-16). "He gave them such a beating that they ran out of the house naked and bleeding!"

Can we begin to imagine the impact on the early church when the news spread among the disciples about these extraordinary exorcisms? For Christians in the first century, evil was so real it could beat you up.

Visions, too, were genuine spiritual manifestations, not just imaginary dreaming. On the strength of a vision in which he spoke personally with the Lord, Ananias risked his life to take the gospel to Saul (9:10-16). Of course, both Cornelius and Peter had visions (Acts 10) which opened the doors to Gentile evangelism. And we know that Paul, having first been called through his famous "Macedonian vision" (16:9-10), remained longer in Corinth than good judgment might have dictated because of assurances given him in yet another vision (18:9-11). While I'm not suggesting we today can have similar visions, there are lessons to be learned for those of us so inextricably caught up in today's naturalistic worldview.

Both figuratively and literally, the model church was a visionary church. They didn't have today's trendy "vision statements;" they had *visions*! Theirs was a world of the supernatural in which these wondrous visual manifestations—together with the working of angels, demons, evil spirits, and the devil himself—provided assurance that a God outside themselves was working powerfully in them and through them. Whatever suffering they had to endure along the way was made bearable in view of a larger context in which the forces of Good would eventually triumph over the forces of Evil.

And, for first-century Christians, "eventually" was not that far away....

A Model of Radical Urgency

The more I reflect upon the nature of the primitive church, the more convinced I am that they lived (and often died the death of martyrs) with an expectancy of the Lord's Coming which is essentially unknown among ourselves. "The time is short!" Paul virtually screams at the Corinthians to get their attention (1 Corinthians 7:29-31). "From now on, those who have wives should live as if they had none; those who mourn, as if they did not...those who buy something, as if it were not theirs to keep; those who use the things of the world, as if not engrossed in them." Why? "For this world in its present form is passing away."

In the minds of first-century Christians, the prospect of that literally happening was clearly *sooner* rather than *later*. As in...their lifetime! As if there would be no second-century church, nor even conceivably a 21st-century church!

Hear the sense of urgency expressed over and over:

Let us encourage one another—*and all the more as you see the day approaching.* (Hebrews 10:25)

The God of peace will *soon* crush Satan under your feet. (Romans 16:20)

The revelation of Jesus Christ, which God gave him to show his servants what must *soon* take place. (Revelation 1:1)

Hold on to what you have, so that no one will take your crown.... I am coming *soon*. (Revelation 3:11)

It's always *soon, soon, soon!* Even the call to persevere in the face of suffering is predicated on time's being short. "I consider that our present sufferings are not worth comparing with the glory that will be revealed in us," Paul reckons (in Romans 8:18-19). "The creation waits in *eager expectation* for the sons of God to be revealed." Yet again, "Our citizenship is in heaven. And we *eagerly await* a Savior from there..." (Philippians 3:20). James joins the chorus of anticipation, saying, "Be patient and stand firm, because the Lord's coming is *near*...The Judge is standing at the door!" (James 5:8-9).

Beyond question, the early disciples believed that they were poised at the threshold of eternity. Had not Micah prophesied (4:1) that, "*In the last days* the mountain of the LORD's temple will be established as chief among the mountains..."? And had not Peter applied Joel's prophecy ("*In the last days*...I will pour out my Spirit on all people") to the events transpiring on Pentecost (Acts 2:17)? Were they not, therefore, living in *the last days*?

Indeed, they were...as are we. But they really believed it, and we really don't. In much the same way that "justice delayed is justice denied," so too for us Christ's Coming delayed is Christ's Coming denied! And in that denial, we are not alone. Peter spoke of such skepticism even among a few of the early disciples. "First of all," he warned, "you must understand that in the last days [right then!] scoffers will come.... They will say,

'Where is this "coming" he promised? Ever since our fathers died, everything goes on as it has since the beginning of creation'" (2 Peter 3:3-4). Is that not what we ourselves say, in effect, when day after day we are focused on living a materialistic life?

"But the day of the Lord will come like a thief," Peter assured them. "The heavens will disappear with a roar; the elements will be destroyed by fire, and the earth and everything in it will be laid bare." Then comes the punch line: "Since everything will be destroyed in this way, what kind of people ought you to be? You ought to live holy and godly lives as you look forward to the day of God and speed its coming" (2 Peter 3:10-12).

We know all too well that, with the Lord, "a day is like a thousand years and a thousand years like a day." But the plain fact is that *some day, one day*, will come *that day*! Instead of our pointing back over the past two millennia as proof that it isn't likely to happen in our own lifetime, surely we must face another cold fact: the more "the last days" have been prolonged, the more likely it is that the day of the Lord is nearer than ever!

If all that still seems too theoretical, perhaps we might begin to capture something of the urgency of first-century faith by thinking not of *that day* but about *our day*: the day when, if the Lord has not already come to us, we will certainly go to him. The disciples in the first century never saw "the day" they thought they would see; but not one of them missed their day of death that, looking back, we can see. Surely, there is a lesson here. Since we too will be "destroyed in this same way" (and *soon, very soon!*) what kind of people ought we to be, if not radically-thinking, radically-living, radically-loving disciples of Jesus Christ?

Are you surprised by this model of New Testament faith and practice? Do you not find it intriguing? Disturbing? Challenging? Rebuking? I confess I'm overwhelmed by it—simultaneously shamed and inspired. Just think what a vibrant, victorious church we could be if all of us together were radically pure, practicing radical piety and radical relationships, and

having a radical sense of being called as God's elect! Imagine
how our hearts would beat if we were sufficiently honored to
literally share in our Lord's suffering, and thereby to know—
really know—that our lives were being lived with meaning and
purpose in the eternal battle for men's souls! And, oh, what a
thought—that we might somehow recapture the hope of Christ's
imminent Coming, and therewith plunge ourselves with abandon into truly being his people!

THE CHURCH OF...THE SPIRIT!

*The Church of Christ is not an institution; it is a new life
with Christ and in Christ, guided by the Holy Spirit.*

SERGIUS BULGAKOV

In the blockbuster movie *Thirteen Days*, starring Kevin Costner, the gripping story is told of the thirteen days in October, 1962, in which America risked nuclear war in facing down the Soviet Union over the Cuban missile crisis. That story is plausibly and movingly told through the eyes of Costner's character, Kenneth O'Donnell, who in real life was a political adviser to the Kennedy brothers and served as White House appointments secretary.

As it turns out, the importance of his role as depicted in the movie bears no resemblance to historical truth. Absolutely no one familiar with the facts places O'Donnell anywhere near the vortex of the agonizing decision-making that was involved during the crisis. Regardless, Costner's role was recast so that O'Donnell, as an intimate insider, could become a credible narrator of the story, and particularly of the private conversations which ostensibly took place between the two Kennedys. In the end, this clever use of artistic license assured the film's box office success.

Never mind that more important historical facts were either glossed over or wildly distorted. According to Michael Nelson, professor of political science at Rhodes College, "Inflating O'Donnell's importance in the missile crisis is not the main problem with *Thirteen Days*. From a historical perspective, the film's main problems are that it inflates the role of White House political-staff members and portrays the military brass as cartoonish hawks." Deftly sorting out historical wheat from Hollywood chaff, Nelson then cites a long list of "facts" gleaned from the movie which simply never happened.

What most interests me about Professor Nelson's review of the film (and explains why I've used it as an unlikely introduction to this chapter) is this single, compelling observation: that "*Thirteen Days* is especially deserving of criticism on these large matters because it is so scrupulously accurate on the small ones." In other words, accurate details give undue credibility to an inaccurate story-line. The viewer automatically assumes that if the details ring true, then the story-line itself must certainly be true. Thus, the more correct the details, the more dangerous larger issues become when they are, in fact, distorted.

In the movie, as Nelson points out, "the thin ties and horn-rimmed glasses the actors wear, the tail-finned cars they drive, the physical gestures they make, even their rotary-dial phones and transistor radios are all dead-on perfect. Black-and-white establishing scenes and actual excerpts from Walter Cronkite's live television reports on the crisis further contribute to the movie's verisimilitude. This is the way it really was, the film-makers implicitly promise with those fine points: Just look at McNamara's slicked-back hair. It's all the more distressing, then, when we discover that in several important respects this isn't the way it was at all."

False Confidence From Accurate Details

Hopefully, you will already have drawn the connection. Even in the realm of faith, it is possible to get the details right, yet miss the story-line altogether—perhaps for the very reason that accuracy of detail has led us to assume the rest of the story *simply has to be right*. This, if anything, is the real problem with "patternism." (By contrast, most criticism of "patternism" is little more than a smokescreen for rejecting the authority of precedent itself.) It's not that the details don't matter. In God's eyes, the minutest details of his patterns have always mattered. Rather, it's that we can too easily convince ourselves that, because we've got some of the details right (or even many of them), therefore it must be true that we have fully restored New Testament Christianity.

This has been the danger, especially, of popular Sunday school workbooks that propose to demonstrate, in proof-text fashion, the organization, worship, and practice of the early church. Moving topic by topic and item by item, the "pattern" unfolds with apparent accuracy. And because a significant number of the "details" of the early church have really, truly, and legitimately been established, we simply assume that we have a perfect picture of first-century faith and practice. As with the movie, "It's all the more distressing, then, when we discover that in several important respects this isn't the way it was at all."

Few workbooks of that type, for example, ever paint a picture of the church anything like the first-century model described in the previous chapter. No matter how accurately they may depict certain organizational aspects of the early church, they never seem to capture the dynamic organism of the primitive body of Christ: what motivated it, what energized it, what sustained its faith in times of crisis. And so the picture that emerges is actually quite different from the historical model itself. Instead of achieving genuine expressions of "patterned worship," we've ended up worshiping a pattern that may be meticulously true in part, but misleading on the whole.

What, then, does the text really tell us about both "the details" and "the big picture" of the apostolic church? Hopefully, by leaving the details until after the story-line itself is written we can "walk out of the theater" with an equal sense of accuracy and exhilaration.

The Intimate Insiders

In the story of the early church, three apostles (Paul, Peter, and John), two of Jesus' own earthly brothers (James and Jude), and one of Paul's traveling companions (Luke) take on Kevin Costner's "Kenneth O'Donnell role" as the intimate insiders who narrate the events for us with credibility. Or, I should say, with "double credibility." Not only were they each (with the possible exception of Luke) eyewitnesses of our Lord, but they were also inspired by the Holy Spirit. "For prophecy never had its origin in the will of man, but men spoke from God as they were carried along by the Holy Spirit" (2 Peter 1:21). Just as with Old Testament scripture, the body of scripture which they addressed to the disciples in the first century was "God breathed" (2 Timothy 3:16-17).

If Paul is to be believed at all, God spoke directly to him, and thereby, through him, to the early disciples. "I want you to know, brothers, that the gospel I preached is not something that man made up. I did not receive it from any man, nor was I taught it; rather, I received it by revelation from Jesus Christ" (Galatians 1:11-12). Whether this was while he was in Arabia (1:17) or at later times, Paul tells the Corinthians that he spoke God's secret wisdom, "not in words taught us by human wisdom but in words taught by the Spirit, expressing spiritual truths in spiritual words" (1 Corinthians 2:6-13).

As perhaps the leading "intimate insider," therefore, Paul assured the disciples in Thessalonica that the story-line itself was trustworthy. "Our gospel came to you not simply with words, but also with power, with the Holy Spirit and with deep conviction" (1 Thessalonians 1:5). The advantage the Thessalonians had over us is that they, themselves, personally witnessed the work and power of the Holy Spirit. Indeed, in its work of revealing and verifying the story, the Holy Spirit *became* the story!

Lights, Action...Spirit!

If you were to think of New Testament Christianity as a blockbuster movie (I would challenge Hollywood to do it, but they could never get it right!), the opening scene would show the apostles reclining around a table in a house in Jerusalem celebrating the Feast of Weeks, or "Pentecost." However, this normally joyous harvest-time celebration is a subdued affair. It has been some seven weeks since the beginning of a roller coaster series of events which led, first to Jesus' horrendous crucifixion, then to his astonishing resurrection, and finally to his glorious ascension into heaven before their very eyes. Yet he had instructed them to wait in Jerusalem until they had "been clothed with power from on high." Virtually as his feet were leaving the earth, he had promised them: "You will receive power when the Holy Spirit comes on you...."

But that was many days ago, and still nothing has happened. And so we hear them asking one another around the table: "When will the power come?" "In what form?" "Did we misunderstand him?" "Have we been duped by our own egos?" Then, suddenly, the giant Dolby speakers fill the theater with tornado-like sounds of a violent wind, and, on screen, we see the walls of the house trembling, and what appear to be tongues of fire resting on each of the apostles. Overwhelmed with fear and excitement, they begin speaking in languages which they've never before spoken, creating such a commotion that a large crowd quickly gathers outside the house. To the amazement of everyone in this multinational crowd of festival pilgrims, they can each understand what the apostles are saying...in their own native tongues!

What follows in our hypothetical film is the familiar story of Acts chapter two, in which Peter and the other apostles stand before the crowd and proclaim that what they are witnessing is the fulfillment of Joel's prophecy. This was the day on which God was to pour out his Spirit on all people—on sons and daughters who would prophesy, on young men who would see visions, and on old men who would dream dreams. On men and women alike, the Spirit would be poured out!

And how would it be poured out? Not just in prophecy, and visions, and dreams, for those miraculous manifestations had been around for centuries. Nor was it simply the outpouring of tongues on the apostles, because Joel spoke of an outpouring "on all people." So it is that we know the answer from memory, if not by heart: "Repent and be baptized, every one of you, in the name of Jesus Christ for the forgiveness of your sins. *And you will receive the gift of the Holy Spirit.*"

At least we know the correct "detail." But do we really remember the story-line? Do we fully appreciate what a radical difference the active, working power of the Holy Spirit made in the life of the early disciples?

Immediately, "everyone was filled with awe, and many wonders and miraculous signs were done by the apostles" (Acts 2:43). True enough, the Lord had already been working through the apostles in this way before Pentecost, but the Holy Spirit was now to become the heart and soul of the fledgling church. "Encouraged by the Holy Spirit, it grew in numbers..." (Acts 9:31). In Antioch of Pisidia, the word of the Lord spread throughout the whole region, and "the disciples were filled with joy and with the Holy Spirit" (Acts 13:52). Everywhere you turn, the Holy Spirit is filling, speaking, moving, healing, and revealing.

In scene after scene, we begin to see a connection between being "filled" with the Spirit and being "bold in the word." There is Peter, who, "filled with the Holy Spirit," proclaimed and defended the gospel before the Sanhedrin (Acts 4:8). And also Stephen. We are told that his enemies "could not stand up against...the Spirit by whom he spoke" (Acts 6:9-10). Indeed, the whole church became instruments of proclamation when "the place where they were meeting was shaken...and they were all filled with the Holy Spirit and spoke the word of God boldly" (Acts 4:31).

There were also the seemingly endless miracles which came by the power of the Holy Spirit. They were so common among the early church that Paul uses them as an argument in teaching the disciples in Galatia the difference between law and faith. "Does God give you his Spirit and work miracles among you because you observe the law, or because you believe what you heard?" (Galatians 3:5).

Naturally, when we think of miracles, we tend to think of healings. In at least one instance, however, "Paul, filled with the Holy Spirit," actually blinded Elymas the sorcerer for his calumny in opposition to the gospel (Acts 13:6-12). And make your own association between Ananias and Sapphira "lying to the Holy Spirit" one minute and dropping dead the next (Acts 5:1-11)! If the power of the Holy Spirit could bring rejoicing, it could also be frightfully sobering. "Great fear seized the whole church and all who heard about these events." Even the scary bits in our film are about the Holy Spirit!

Both "Gift" and "Gifts"

Because the Holy Spirit played such a leading role in the primitive church, one question continues to intrigue us even today: To what extent did each of the early Christians have personal contact with the Spirit? As we have already seen, every baptized believer was promised the "gift of the Holy Spirit." But what did that gift entail, and did it mean that every disciple experienced one or more of the so-called "spiritual gifts"?

To begin with, a potentially-significant difference between receiving *the gift* of the Spirit and *gifts* of the Spirit seems to be highlighted specifically in the case of the disciples in Samaria. Peter and John had been sent to Samaria to pray for them, because, even though they had been baptized in the name of Jesus, "the Holy Spirit had not yet come upon any of them." Yet, how could that be if the Holy Spirit was promised to all who were baptized? It's one of those times when we must slow down the film, as it were, and examine it carefully, frame by frame. When we do that, we begin to see that in some instances "the Holy Spirit" was evidently shorthand for "gifts of the Holy Spirit."

For example, among the Samaritans who had been taught and baptized by the evangelist Philip was a former sorcerer named Simon. He had witnessed Philip healing and casting out evil spirits, and doing other great signs and miracles. As a former magician, he was obviously impressed that Philip was not using mere trickery, but exercising a powerful spiritual gift. Now, seeing Peter and John bestowing that same gift on others by prayer and the laying on of hands, Simon offers them money, saying, "Give me also this ability so that everyone on whom I lay my hands may receive the Holy Spirit" (Acts 8:18-19). Not surprising, his request garners nothing but a sharp rebuke! The miraculous manifestations of the Spirit were not for sale.

A somewhat similar incident occurred when Paul encountered twelve men in Ephesus who had been baptized of John but who knew nothing of the Holy Spirit. Paul took them and baptized them into the name of Jesus, and then "when Paul placed his hands on them, the Holy Spirit came on them, and they spoke in tongues and prophesied" (Acts 19:1-7).

Twice, then, we see that spiritual gifts were imparted by the laying on of hands, not simply by baptism. So what are to make of Peter's promise that all those who were baptized would receive the gift of the Holy Spirit? (The fact that *different kinds* of gifts were received in these two cases suggests that even the laying on of hands did not guarantee a uniform manifestation of the spirit in every disciple.)

Probably the best solution to this seeming enigma comes when Paul is discussing the various spiritual gifts given to the disciples (in 1 Corinthians 12). "There are different kinds of gifts," he explains, "but the same Spirit." Among the disciples, various manifestations of the Spirit were given for the common good—whether "the message of wisdom," "the message of knowledge," or faith, or gifts of healing, or miraculous powers, or prophecy, or distinguishing between spirits, or speaking in tongues, or the interpretation of tongues. "All these are the work of one and the same Spirit, and he gives them to each one, just as he determines."

Then comes the crucial line: "For we were all baptized by one Spirit into one body...and *we were all given the one Spirit to drink*" (12:13). Because everyone in the early church had been baptized, each of them had received the same "gift of the Holy Spirit" to which Peter referred on Pentecost. That is, a measure of the Holy Spirit mystically dwelling within one's self—and, by extension, within the entire church. ("Don't you know that you yourselves are God's temple and that God's Spirit lives in You?"— 3:16) Thereafter—separate and apart from that indwelling—the same Holy Spirit gifted various disciples with *special* gifts, or manifestations, for the building up of the body and the spread of the Kingdom. I say "various disciples," because no text suggests that every disciple received a special gift of one kind or another.

In extraordinary circumstances, of course, we know that spiritual gifts and special healings were bestowed even before immersion, as a sign of acceptable candidacy. Such was the case, for example, when Cornelius became the first Gentile convert (Acts 10:44-48). But for first-century disciples, the work and power of the Holy Spirit was not limited to exceptional cases. The early church was saturated through and through with the Holy Spirit. It enlivened, emboldened, and enriched the primitive church, meeting its every need. Unlike the mute idols which the Corinthians had worshiped as pagans, the Holy Spirit was active and alive and working through them in ways we today can barely comprehend.

But Aren't Those Days Gone?

If we cannot always be certain about the nature and use of spiritual gifts among first-century disciples, it might at least be helpful to explore whether there is anything which the various spiritual gifts had in common; and perhaps whether there were any distinct differences. For instance, when we look at the lists of the many gifts given to the early church, we see some which clearly involve supernatural manifestations of divine power. They include tongues, prophecy, interpretation, miracles, and healing (1 Corinthians 12:27-30).

Other, equally providential gifts appear not to involve the supernatural beyond the "gifting" itself. These include (from 1 Corinthians 12) the important role played by the apostles and other teachers, as well as "those able to help others" and those with gifts of administration. In Romans 12, they include serving, encouraging, contributing to the needs of others, giving leadership, and showing mercy.

Clearly, not all spiritual gifts in the model church were of the same type. In fact, those listed in the second category seem to be no different from gifts given to "holy men of old" in the centuries leading up to the birth of Christ. By contrast, the gifts involving *supernatural manifestations* were either virtually non-existent in previous centuries (as in the case of "tongues") or limited to a relatively few prophets of God. Joel's prophecy, therefore, could not have been more insightful: in the apostolic age, the Holy Spirit was going to work among God's people in a dramatic, revolutionary way!

With the spotlight focused sharply on this second category of gifts, it is instructive to consider how those gifts were actually bestowed upon those who exercised them. Apart from special cases (like Cornelius and Saul) and leading evangelists (like Stephen and Philip), the bestowing of the gifts seems to have been associated closely with the apostles. And that would not be without good reason.

When Jesus miraculously appeared to the apostles in the upper room following his resurrection, John tells us that "he breathed on them and said, 'Receive the Holy Spirit...'" (John 20:22-23). And, "if you forgive anyone his sins, they are forgiven...."

Knowing that only God can forgive sins, we begin to understand what a unique working relationship the Holy Spirit had with these specially-chosen ambassadors for Christ. Even when Jesus told them (following the so-called Great Commission) that "these signs will accompany those who believe," there seems to be more than a tenuous connection between the apostles and those who would drive out demons, speak in tongues, pick up snakes, drink poison, and heal the sick (Mark 16:17-18).

Indeed, in the early church we see a number of instances in which the apostles impart miraculous gifts by the laying on of their hands. That, of course, was the very issue over which Simon the sorcerer got into trouble with Peter and John—wanting to buy their ability to bestow gifts of the Holy Spirit (Acts 8).

In another familiar case, Paul exhorts young Timothy "to fan into flame the gift of God, which is in you through the laying on of my hands" (2 Timothy 1:6-7). Whether that gift was in any way different from the gift of teaching "which was given you through a prophetic message when the body of elders laid their hands on you" (1 Timothy 4:14), we simply aren't told. That Paul imparted some gift in addition to the one announced by the "prophetic message" makes one wonder if it might not have been something uniquely apostolic.

What all this suggests is at least the possibility that any supernatural gifts directly associated with the apostles might well have ceased along with their passing. Although that conclusion involves more conjecture than one might wish, it is somewhat bolstered by yet another line of reasoning. Considering that this category of supernatural gifts had in common the dramatic, visible working of Holy Spirit power, it seems reasonable to believe that tongues, prophecy, interpretation, miracles, and healing were "a package deal." That is to say, what's true about one is likely to be true about all.

Think, then, about the apostles' power to bring the dead back to life. We know that Peter raised Tabitha (Dorcas), and

Paul revived Eutychus when he fell from the third-story win-
dow. Apart from modern medical resuscitations of the so-called
"clinically dead" (which is to say *not* dead), is there any evidence
to suggest that this manifestation of Holy Spirit power has ever
been repeated since the time of the apostles? If not, then there is
no compelling reason why the Holy Spirit might not also have
ceased working through the other supernatural gifts in the same
miraculous "package."

Should anyone insist on a rationale for this cessation of
supernatural gifts, he might well find it by going back to where we
began, with Paul telling the Thessalonians: "our gospel came to you
not simply with words, but also with power, with the Holy Spirit
and with deep conviction." Now that we (unlike the Thessalonians)
have God's full revelation in hand, the miraculous working of the
Spirit would no longer be needed to confirm what, in the apostolic
age, was the piecemeal unfolding of that very revelation.

If that line of reasoning seems unsatisfactory to you, I
confess it is not altogether satisfying to me, either. I'm one of
those neurotic "tidy desk" folks. Everything has to be precisely
in its place, or I go slightly crazy. So, with this many loose ends
flying about, I, for one, could wish for greater certainty. On the
other hand, any scenario in which the charismatic gifts are said
to have continued past the apostolic age is equally fraught with
difficulty, if not more so.

Convince me that the dead are still being raised, and I
might have second thoughts. Show me a "word of knowledge"
from today's television evangelists that isn't patently a sham,
and I might reconsider. Let me know when tongue-speaking
"Pentecostals" no longer have to have translators at their inter-
national conventions, and I'll sit up and listen. Persuade me that
the Holy Spirit has ever given a modern prophecy which con-
tradicts what it taught in the first-century, and maybe we can
talk. Short of all that, I fear I will just have to settle for the untidy

conclusion that miraculous manifestations of the Holy Spirit did not survive in the centuries beyond the early church.

Watch Out For Swinging Pendulums!

But suppose for the moment that we've gotten this difficult "detail" right. Is this to say that the Holy Spirit no longer works among his people in direct and powerful ways? That he is forevermore confined between the covers of our printed Bibles? Or reduced to a kind of vague "providential working" for the good of those who love the Lord?

Unless we are prepared to take our scissors and cut out the last half of Acts 2:38, the only answer to those questions is: *Impossible!* If we've been immersed, we've been as filled on the inside as we've been washed on the outside. Hear again the words of Scripture speaking of "...the Holy Spirit, whom God has given to those who obey him" (Acts 5:32). As if for emphasis, Paul repeats almost verbatim what he said in 1 Corinthians 3, only three chapters later: "Do you not know that your body is a temple of the Holy Spirit, *who is in you*, whom you have received from God?" (6:19). No surprise, then, that Paul prayed on behalf of the Ephesians that the Father would "strengthen you with power through his Spirit *in your inner being...*" (Ephesians 3:16).

The gift of the Holy Spirit is not a meaningless euphemism. The Spirit is literally and truly as much a part of our inner being as is our own spirit! What good is it, then, for us to have the Holy Spirit dwelling within us if nothing actually happens as a result?[1]

I find it fascinating that Scripture suggests almost exact parallels between the miraculous spiritual gifts and those which are non-miraculous. Consider, for example, the gift of tongues compared with Paul's prayer for the disciples in Rome: "May the God of hope fill you with all joy and peace as you trust in

[1] Aware that this is an area which historically has engendered great debate, I merely share with you the results of my own study, and beg you not to let any differing perspectives shift the focus away from the obvious, compelling, central message of this book. For on one thing virtually all of us can agree: the Holy Spirit no longer works in the same directly miraculous way today as in the first-century apostolic church.

him, so that you may overflow with hope by the power of the Holy Spirit" (Romans 15:13). Overflowing joy, peace, and hope? What is that, if not ecstasy!

And speaking of tongues..."Be filled with the Spirit. Speak to one another with psalms, hymns, and spiritual songs. Sing and make music in your heart to the Lord...." (Ephesians 5:19). What is music of the heart, if not ecstasy!

And our prayers? There, too, "the Spirit helps us in our weakness. We do not know what we ought to pray for, but the Spirit himself intercedes for us with groans that words cannot express" (Romans 8:26). Inexpressible groans from our heart to his? Is it not an ecstacy of assurance that results from Spirit-assisted prayer?

Compare also the role of prophecy. Do we not see a natural parallel in Paul's prayer for the Ephesians? "I keep asking," says Paul, "that the God of our Lord Jesus Christ, the glorious Father, may give you the Spirit of wisdom and revelation, so that you may know him better. I pray also that the eyes of your heart may be enlightened in order that you may know the hope to which he has called you, the riches of his glorious inheritance in the saints, and his incomparably great power for us who believe" (Ephesians 1:17-19).

The same Holy Spirit who miraculously revealed the mind of God through prophecy, works even now to give us greater understanding of the hope that lies within us, and to lead us to a fuller appreciation of God's power in our lives. The continual, ongoing gift of the Holy Spirit is wisdom and discernment. In our study day by day, we are given understanding and insight into the "faith that was once for all entrusted to the saints." Paul's prayer ("that the eyes of your heart might be enlightened") is echoed in the words of the hymn by Clara H. Scott:

> Open my eyes, that I may see
> Glimpses of truth Thou hast for me;

> Place in my hands the wonderful key
> That shall unclasp, and set me free.
> Silently now I wait for Thee,
> Ready, my God, Thy will to see;
> Open my eyes, illumine me,
> Spirit divine![2]

Make no mistake. That divine discernment will never paint a different picture from the one painted in the first century. The brush of inspiration has been set aside, and the canvas has dried. But, even now, the Spirit's enlightenment can open our eyes to see that original masterpiece in a light we may never before have noticed.

The Spirit can also teach us to love as we have never loved before. "This is how we know that he lives in us," says John, "We know it by the Spirit he gave us" (1 John 3:24). Either that is nonsensical redundancy at its very worst, or profound proof of a radical kind of brotherly love that could only come as a gift from above. Has not "God...poured out his love into our hearts by the Holy Spirit, whom he has given us" (Romans 5:5)? When we love each other—"madly, truly, deeply"—we give proof to the world that the Holy Spirit is still a powerful force among his people.

As it was in the early church, so it is today: the fruits of the Spirit all begin with love (Galatians 5:22-23). Love that heals. Love that casts out evil. And love that revives, not just dead relationships, but most important of all, those who are dead in their trespasses and sins.

No, the Holy Spirit does not work the same kind of miracles today as in the apostolic church, but—make no mistake about it—the Holy Spirit *still works*!

---

[2] Our fear that the Holy Spirit might actually be active even today could hardly be more manifest than in our typical version of this hymn, in which the original word "Spirit" has been replaced by "Savior." Of course, if it is thought that nothing supernatural whatsoever takes place today, then we probably shouldn't sing that line at all, whether the agent is the "Spirit" or the "Savior."

Note also that the invocation in the hymn is not addressed directly to the Holy Spirit, but to God (which is to say, the Father), and only secondarily to his Spirit as the agency through whom God works.

Don't Quench the Fire!

Must we, therefore, continue to ask, "What does the Spirit do?" Is it not enough that we are "led by the Spirit" (Galatians 5:18); and that we are able to guard the pattern of sound teaching from the apostles "with the help of the Holy Spirit who lives in us" (2 Timothy 1:13-14)? That's not just you and I as individuals, but the whole church—as a temple in the Lord—in whom we "are being built together to become a dwelling in which God lives by his Spirit" (Ephesians 2:22).

In whatever way spiritual gifts actually worked in the apostolic age (and we may never know exactly how), it is abundantly clear that the primitive church was being guided, guarded, and directed by the Holy Spirit in every aspect of its existence. Today, when we hear that over-worn phrase—"Guide, guard, and direct us"—in congregational prayers, we should remind ourselves that it once had a profound reality attached to it. What's more, if we *really mean* that prayer, we must be open to the only avenue by which it can be answered: a powerful, active, genuine working of the Spirit!

Ever wonder why the Lord's body today seems so bereft of spiritual power? Could it be we *really don't* mean that prayer after all? That we would be frightened to death to think it might be answered in the only way it could be answered? That, should we ever experience it, our deistic view of an inactive Holy Spirit would be exposed?

No wonder we have Paul's warning (in 1 Thessalonians 5:22): "Do not put out the Spirit's fire; do not treat prophecies with contempt." Yes, absolutely—"Test everything," including the "details" of how the Holy Spirit apparently worked in a unique way among the early disciples. But once we have those details right (if we do), "Hold on to the good." Make sure the more important story-line doesn't get lost. Or distorted. Or confused.

Or, worse yet...quenched!

PART II

TOWARD AN IDEAL RESTORATION

*They will rebuild the ancient ruins and restore the places
long devastated; they will renew the ruined cities that have been
devastated for generations.*

ISAIAH 61:4

CHAPTER SEVEN

IN AN UNWORTHY MANNER

It is not the Lord's Supper you eat....

Visiting recently with a small congregation of God's people, I was asked at the last minute to preside at the Lord's table. In the few moments remaining before our time of worship began, I quickly chose some scriptures and gathered my thoughts for what I hoped would be a meaningful introduction to the Supper. At the appointed time, I approached the table and gave a brief exhortation about the new covenant in Christ's blood, and about how even the experience of the Israelites under the old covenant called us to bring our own "sacrifice" of holiness to the memorial we were about to share.

After offering a prayer of blessing for our taking of the bread, I made my way to the first occupied pew and handed the plate to a sister who was sitting near the end. That's when I realized I had broken the rules and not the bread! With one swift punch of her finger into the middle of the large flat wafer, the whole "loaf" instantly became two distinct pieces, and thereby was sanctified for use. Another quick pinch of the wafer, and our sister passed the bread along, apparently assured that, by her hand, the scriptural mode of partaking the Lord's Supper had narrowly escaped desecration.

What was I thinking when I came away from the table without splitting the wafer in two? Had I not just read from Luke 22:17-20 in which Jesus "took bread, gave thanks and *broke it*" before giving it to the apostles? Isn't that why many congregations strictly observe this tradition each week before the bread is passed to the congregation? Indeed, wouldn't such a practice be consistent with following New Testament pattern to a T?

Interestingly, neither this sister nor apparently anyone else in the congregation had similar qualms about using multiple cups, despite the fact that Luke also tells us Jesus "took *the cup*, saying, '*This cup* is the new covenant in my blood, which is poured out for you.'" As we all know, there are brothers and sisters who feel as strongly about using only one cup as many Christians do about literally breaking the loaf before it is passed.

Before we dismiss any of them as being theologically naive, we must remember that no less a theologian than Martin Luther made virtually the same argument to justify his belief that Jesus' presence is actually manifested in the bread. "*Hoc est corpus Meum*," he bluntly insisted, repeating (in Latin) Jesus' very words.

There appears to be no end to the controversies which easily spark today over whether we ought to take one detail or another literally. Yet, the only thing more amazing than how incredibly literal we can take certain obscure details is how incredibly blind we can be to patently obvious matters of far greater significance.

A Memorial Within A Meal

In this regard, perhaps the most universally-overlooked feature of the Lord's Supper as practiced in the primitive church is that—from all appearances—it was observed in conjunction with a fellowship meal. That is, a normal, ordinary meal with the usual variety of food. However, unlike normal, ordinary meals, this combined table fellowship and memorial was shared among the disciples for the special purpose of strengthening, not just their physical bodies, but their common bond in the spiritual body of Christ. Hence, Jude's reference to their "love feasts" (verse 12).

Without question, on the occasion of its inaugural intro-duction—there in the upper room on the night Jesus was betrayed—the memorial was part of an actual meal being shared, which included bread, wine, and whatever "dish" it was into which Jesus dipped the bread before handing it to Judas (John 13:26-27). That this memorial to Christ's sacrificial death should have been instituted in the context of a shared meal is consistent with the "breaking of bread" practiced by the early disciples.

In the New Testament record, we find three ways to "break bread." The first, of course, was the literal breaking apart of the bread, as Jesus did that night before he distributed it (Luke 22:19). It would have been something like our tearing off a piece of French bread as it's passed around the table, except that, by Jewish custom, Jesus did the breaking for all those who were eat-ing with him.

Undoubtedly because bread played such a large part in first-century meals ("Give us this day our daily bread...."), the eating of the meal itself was also referred to as "breaking bread." It was this second way of breaking bread which set the stage for the institution of Christ's memorial. As Luke tells us, Jesus and his disciples had gathered specifically to eat a meal together. "When the hour came, Jesus and his apostles reclined at the table..." (Luke 22:14-15). "In the same way, *after the supper* he took the cup..."(Luke 22:20).

From its very inception, therefore, the Lord's Supper was an integral part of a *real meal*. That *real meal* was not unlike the fellowship meals which the larger body of Pentecost disciples shared throughout the week when they "broke bread in their homes and ate together with glad and sincere hearts..." (Acts 2:46). On the Lord's day, of course, their common, ordinary fellowship meals took on an added significance as they came together specifically to celebrate Christ's memorial.

It appears that, in time, the Lord's Supper itself was referred to as "breaking bread." For example, Paul used this expression when comparing the feast of idols (in which they were not to participate) with their participation in the Lord's Supper. "Is not the bread that we break a participation in the body of Christ? Because there is one loaf, we, who are many, are one body, for we all partake of the one loaf" (1 Corinthians 10:16-17).

It is likely that this use of the phrase was also intended in Acts 2:42, where we are told that the disciples "devoted themselves to the apostles' teaching and to the fellowship, to *the breaking of bread* and to prayer." (Otherwise, having two separate references in a single paragraph to their frequent sharing of ordinary, everyday meals hardly makes sense.)

A much clearer example is found when the disciples in Troas "came together to break bread...on the first day of the week" (Acts 20:7). Because of its association with the "first day" (the day on which the disciples regularly met together), the breaking of bread on that occasion seems to have had the double connotation of both meal and memorial. Whatever actual form it took, it was a "memorial within a meal"—a time to remember the Bread of Life while "breaking bread" with one another.

When Abuse Shows Use

Oddly enough, what we know most about how the Lord's Supper was observed in the early church is revealed (in 1 Corinthians 11) when Paul rebukes the disciples at Corinth for profaning Christ's memorial. I am aware that most of us have traditionally understood this passage to condemn the eating of a common, ordinary meal at a time when Christ's memorial is being observed. (Virtually everyone can quote verse 22, "What, don't you have homes to eat and drink in?") So bear with me as I attempt to show the passage in an altogether different light. I'll put forward the most forceful case I can as to how I believe the text was intended, then leave it to you to decide for yourself.

The first thing we learn is that the disciples had "come together as a church" (11:18). It was not just the day-to-day, private fellowship which they shared. *"Your meetings,"* said Paul, "do more harm than good" (11:17). So what are we told about their "meetings"? Unfortunately, the news from Corinth is pretty embarrassing. "When you come together," Paul wrote sharply, "it is not the Lord's Supper you eat, for as you eat, each of you goes ahead without waiting for anybody else" (11:20-21).[3]

During what was meant to be a time of table fellowship for the whole church (in which the Lord's Supper was to be the centerpiece), some of the disciples were filling their stomachs and even getting drunk before others had arrived. (You don't have to consult a Bible commentary to guess which disciples arrived early and which couldn't get there on time. Public transportation for the poor hasn't changed much in twenty centuries!) Paul was livid. "Do you despise the church of God and humiliate those who have nothing?" (11:22).

Here is where one must be careful not to be thrown off track by Paul's ensuing question: "Don't you have homes to eat and drink in?" (11:22). Nor by his concluding line: "If anyone is hungry, he should eat at home, so that when you meet together it may not result in judgment" (11:34). Far from prohibiting a fellowship meal in conjunction with the Lord's Supper, it is clear that Paul is saying (in current vernacular): If the reason you are participating in the fellowship meal is to feed your stomach, then you'd do better to stay home and pig out! "So then, my brothers, *when you come together to eat*, wait for each other"

---

3 From A.T. Robertson's *Word Pictures In the New Testament*, "It is possible that here the term applies both to the Agape or Love-feast (a sort of church supper or club supper held in connection with, before or after, the Lord's Supper) and the Eucharist or Lord's Supper.

(11:33). Otherwise, when you start eating before everyone else has arrived, "One remains hungry, another gets drunk" (11:21).

That ordinary table wine was being consumed in large quantities (some were getting drunk!) underscores the significant point that, for the early Christians, gathering around the Lord's table was not the token ritual with which we are familiar, but an actual food-and-drink meal. Certainly, the bread and the wine consumed on those occasions were understood to be symbolic of Christ's body and blood, but they were not just "emblems"—not just our typical 21st-century crackers and grape juice!

For good or for ill, it is not a first-century Lord's Supper that we eat today. Our highly ritualized version comes nowhere near capturing the vibrant essence of the Lord's Supper in the model church.

One Loaf, One Body

What's crucial here is the obvious connection which Paul makes between the Lord's Supper and their eating together. In fact, that's the very problem. The abuse of what was meant to be a *fellowship* meal had undermined the whole idea of the Lord's Supper, which was intended to remind them, not only of their fellowship with Christ, but also of their fellowship with each other.

Indeed, that is Paul's point in reiterating the words of our Lord when Jesus spoke of the bread, saying, "This is my body." Playing on the word *body*, Paul moves the discussion from Jesus' physical body to Christ's spiritual body, the church. How, asks Paul, could they pretend to honor Jesus' body in the Lord's Supper while they were dishonoring Christ's spiritual body (their brethren!) during their fellowship meal? "For anyone who eats and drinks without recognizing the body of the Lord eats and drinks judgment on himself" (11:29).

What "eating and drinking" was Paul talking about: the Lord's Supper, or the fellowship meal? Both! That was the whole point of the exercise. The Lord's Supper gave meaning to their table fellowship, and their table fellowship gave meaning to the Lord's Supper. Each was a picture of the other.

You might want to read this slowly twice: Christ's spiritual body (the church) came together to "break bread"...in which the bread was symbolic of Jesus' body...which, in turn, was symbolic of Christ's spiritual body...which was *not* to be broken as it was *being* broken by the manner in which they were participating!

Subtle and nuanced though it was, that was Paul's message. At whatever time the bread and the cup of the Lord became the moment of focus—whether before, during, or after the meal—its acceptability had already been jeopardized by the social injustice surrounding the occasion. "Therefore," says Paul, "whoever eats the bread or drinks the cup of the Lord in an unworthy manner will be guilty of sinning against the body and blood of the Lord" (11:27). Whether then or now, division in the body desecrates the unity in Christ's body which the "one loaf" is supposed to symbolize.

In this regard, we probably have misunderstood even the symbolic relationship between the bread and Christ's crucified body. Never once (except in the King James Version's dubious rendering of 1 Corinthians 11:24) did Jesus speak of a "broken body," as we so often do around the Lord's table. (Check the footnotes of the KJV's Greek text.)[4] It is true that he broke the bread in anticipation of distributing it to his disciples, but when Jesus thereafter referred to the bread, what he said (according to virtually all translations) was: "This is my body, which is [offered] for you"—not "This represents my *broken* body."

That flesh would have been "broken" by the nails and the spear is not the same idea at all. Have you ever wondered why the gospel writers go to great lengths to tell us that—unlike the two thieves whose legs were broken—Jesus' body was pierced with a spear instead? John tells us clearly: "These things happened so that the Scripture would be fulfilled: 'Not one of his

---

4 As indicated in Robertson's *Word Pictures In the New Testament*, "klomenon (broken) of the Textus Receptus...is clearly not genuine.

bones will be broken,' and, as another Scripture says, 'They will look on the one they have pierced'" (John 19:36-37). The first of those two Old Testament references (from Exodus 12:46 and Numbers 9:12) came from the instructions which were given regarding the Passover lamb, whose bones were not to be broken. As *our* Passover Lamb, Jesus became the perfect antitype, whose body was never broken!

When we refer to Christ's "broken body," therefore, and even insist that the loaf literally be broken in two, we perpetuate a false notion about the unity of the body which the bread represents. Certainly, we may break the loaf in order to distribute it (as Jesus did), but we should never *think* of a broken loaf—or worse yet, a broken body, whether it be Jesus' physical body on the cross or his spiritual body, the church.

Contrary to our oft-repeated table talk, the bread of the Lord's Supper represents Christ's *unbroken* body! Which is to say, both on the cross and—now more important than ever—in the unity which we are to maintain as his Kingdom people.

Is Our Miniaturized Version Worthy?

Perhaps there are many ways to partake of the Lord's Supper in "an unworthy manner" which might prompt each of us to examine ourselves seriously when we participate in this sacred memorial. Yet, I hope that in some way this chapter will cause us to ask the question from a different angle: Is it really and truly the Lord's Supper that we eat from week to week? Or, having ritualized it beyond all comparison with the primitive church, is it possible that we ourselves might be observing Christ's memorial in an unworthy manner?

At the very least, could it be that there is something about the early observances of the Lord's Supper that we are missing out on because we've deviated from the pattern? Some blessing that we forego? Straying from the pattern doesn't always have to be something terribly *wrong*. Sometimes it's just *second-best*. Is it possible that we're settling for second-best?

Ironically, *not* wanting to settle for anything but the best might partially explain why the fellowship meal was eventually abandoned in favor of a more ritualized version of the Supper. Given the ever-present potential for hungry stomachs to crowd out hungry hearts, perhaps it was to prevent just such abuse that support grew for reducing it to merely a token meal.[5] If that's the case, of course, we ourselves can sympathize with such caution. All we have to do is look at our own balancing act between the auditorium and the fellowship hall, which all too easily gets out of balance.

Even so, it would be lamentable if nothing more than potential for abuse is the cause of our having dramatically altered the practice of the Lord's Supper from that of the model church. It's a long road from avoidance of scandal to virtual abandonment. The ritual we now euphemistically call "communion" (not wholly unlike the Catholic's sacramental Eucharist) doesn't hold a candle to the dynamic *koinonia* communion of the first-century disciples in their sharing together of the Lord's Supper within the context of a fellowship meal.

Fortunately, we haven't abandoned all the other practices of the early church which have equal potential for abuse. And who are we kidding when we presume that our scaled-down, substitute version of the Supper is itself free from abuse? Can any of us honestly say that we have not sat through innumerable observances of the Lord's Supper which seemed no more than "going through the motions?" And then there's the perfunctory (if sincere) prayers which all of us could finish from memory if the presider dropped dead in mid-sentence. And the intrusion of the collection plate into the body and blood of Christ. And the bare mention (if at all) of the purpose for our gathering. And the rush to get it over with.

---

5 Again, from Robertsons' *Word Pictures*, "It was conduct like this that led to the complete separation between the Love-feast and the Lord's Supper."

Ah, the rush....

When I think, particularly, of large congregations whose elders have actually put a stop watch to the Lord's Supper and brought in efficiency experts, as it were, to reduce to a minimum the time it takes to "pass the emblems," I'm mystified. When the question becomes, "How fast can we remember Christ's crucified body and shed blood?" have we not completely missed the point? (Some British brethren recently commented to me about how striking it was, when visiting American congregations, to observe how little time and attention was devoted to the Supper.)

It only confirms how little human nature has changed over the centuries. Dare spend too much time on the Lord's Supper so that the "worship service" extends into the lunch hour, and you'll have plenty of brothers and sisters rushing mentally (if not literally) out the door and to the dinner table. Paul's rebuke *then* is Paul's rebuke *now*: "What, don't you have homes to eat and drink in?" If the only reason we come together is to observe the Lord's Supper in check-list fashion (and the quicker the better), then—along with the Corinthians—we, too, might as well stay home and pig out!

And don't even get me started about the special opportunities being provided in order that folks can "take the Lord's Supper" earlier than usual on Sunday mornings during football season so they can get to the game, or to their televisions, by kickoff. In case anyone is still deluded about that, "It is not the Lord's Supper you eat, for as you eat, each of you goes ahead without waiting for anybody else." When football means more than Christian fellowship, the game is over and the home team has lost.

Having moved away from the New Testament pattern of remembering Christ, we've managed to avoid first-century abuse only to create a whole new set of abuses. But the potential for abuse must not deter us from attempting to re-capture the heart and soul of Christ's memorial, celebrating it with both the reverence and joy of the early church when they properly observed Christ's memorial at their love feasts.

Timing Is Everything

Is this to say that the disciples celebrated the Lord's Supper each and every first day of the week? Or that they never observed the Supper on any other day? As much as I would like to point in Scripture to a single definitive verse, the truth is that we have to put several pieces of a puzzle together in order to see the overall picture.

Of course, in the heady weeks immediately following Pentecost, "every day [the disciples] continued to meet together in the temple courts" (Acts 2:46). And we are told that "all the believers used to meet together in Solomon's Colonnade," evidently praising God and proclaiming Jesus as the Messiah. But there is nothing to indicate that they celebrated anything like an *agape* meal on those occasions, or even our more-familiar "communion." (Is there the remotest chance that the temple authorities would have permitted it?)

Even assuming that the "breaking of bread" in Acts 2:42 was, in fact, the Lord's Supper, we are not told specifically when, or how often, they shared that experience. Nor are we told when, or how often, "the whole church came together" for the purpose of tongues and prophecy (1 Corinthians 14:23); nor whether that time was specifically associated with the Supper.

What we do know, first of all, is that the disciples met together regularly. Well, at least most of them did. Like many even today, there were enough who absented themselves from times of shared worship and edification that the writer of Hebrews was moved to give the familiar exhortation: "Let us not give up meeting together, as some are in the habit of doing..." (Hebrews 10:25). If some of the disciples were truants, evidently most were faithful in meeting together regularly.

As we've already seen, the disciples in Troas apparently met together on the first day of every week. Of course, it's possible that the occasion being reported was nothing more than an isolated incidence. For that matter, even if the disciples in Troas met regularly each week, it wouldn't necessarily mean that Christians in other places followed suit. Yet, we are not left without fairly compelling reason to believe that such weekly assemblies were common for all first-century disciples.

For example, when Paul wrote to the Corinthians about the collection for the poor saints in Jerusalem (1 Corinthians 16:1-2), he instructed them: "Do what I told the Galatian churches to do. *On the first day of every week,* each of you should set aside a sum of money, [etc.]..." Surely, it begs belief that Paul was directing the Corinthian disciples individually to slip their money under a rug on the first day of every week. Arbitrarily naming a given day for personal savings would have made no sense.

The only reasonable interpretation is that Paul was *assuming* the disciples would already be meeting together on the first day of each and every week. So, as a practical matter, Paul told them to lay aside their money—as a congregation—during their weekly gatherings. It is these same normal weekly gatherings which seem to correspond naturally with what the disciples in Troas were doing: coming together on the first day of the week *to break bread.*

In this regard, it is noteworthy that the Corinthians apparently were not the only ones who met together for worship each week. From Paul's reference to the Galatian churches, it appears that they did as well. Although these brief fragments are circumstantial, the evidence is compelling that first-century Christians did, in fact, observe the Lord's Supper every first day of the week.

That they should do so is not in the least surprising. Certainly, Messianic Jews were already used to observing a weekly Sabbath, with all the ritual which that entailed. So, observing a weekly memorial of Christ would seem almost second nature to them. Nor is it a mystery that both Jewish and Gentile Christians would set aside the first day of the week as the Lord's Day, since that is the day on which our Lord rose from the grave. Had it not been for Jesus' resurrection, there would have been no Christian assemblies whatsoever. They met, not only to remember Jesus' death on the cross for their sins, but also to celebrate a risen Christ, the hope of their own resurrection at his Coming. "For whenever you eat this bread and drink this cup, you proclaim the Lord's death until he comes" (1 Corinthians 11:26).

Never is that Second Coming painted in more technicolor than in John's Revelation. How very appropriate, then, to hear him say: "On the Lord's Day I was in the Spirit, and I heard behind me a loud voice like a trumpet..." (Revelation 1:10). John was not alone in receiving a revelation on the Lord's Day. It was on the Lord's Day that the risen Jesus appeared reassuringly to a weeping Mary Magdalene, and also to Cleopas and the "other disciple" (possibly Luke?) in Emmaus. And, of course, it was in the evening of that same Lord's Day when Jesus showed his crucified body to the apostles, and removed every doubt about his resurrection.

I don't know about you, but this is the stuff of which goose bumps are made. Do we not see? Do we not understand? It is on this same Lord's Day, each and every week, when Christ reveals himself afresh *to us*! When he calls our name, like Mary's, and appears to us through our tears of guilt, and loneliness, and alienation. When—as with his apostles—he shows us again and again his crucified body to remove any and all doubt. And especially when he *breaks the bread* with us—as he did with the two disciples in Emmaus—and our eyes are opened to recognize him.

How then, by any means, can professing Christians still ask us whether they *have to take* the Lord's Supper every week, as opposed to monthly or quarterly? When Jesus said, "whenever you eat this bread and drink this cup...," he wasn't telling us to partake of the Supper just *whenever*, as if whenever we feel like it, or whenever it's convenient. In those inaugural words, Jesus was giving us the *meaning* of the memorial. It was the Spirit-led, first-century church which demonstrated the *mode*. By convincing evidence, that mode was weekly. Considering the wonders of its continuous "revelations," who would wish it otherwise?

Where To Focus the Spotlight?

If the case I've presented regarding the primitive practice of observing a memorial meal is anywhere near correct, the question naturally arises: What was the focus of Christian worship on the Lord's Day? Was it the Lord's Supper, or was it teaching and preaching? Indeed, was it the exercise of spiritual gifts?

The fact is, we aren't specifically told.[6] From Paul, we know that "When you come together, everyone has a hymn, or a word of instruction, a revelation, a tongue or an interpretation" (1 Corinthians 14:26). So their time together must have been filled with praise and edification. But there is no mention here of the Lord's Supper. Did these activities take place *earlier* or perhaps *later* than the Supper? Or even at times other than on the Lord's Day?

Certainly, if the example of the disciples at Troas is anything to go on, the primary reason for first-century Christians coming together on the first day of the week was *to break bread* (Acts 20:7). But from this same text we see that Paul also preached for hours on end. Was there always preaching? Did it invariably last so long?

Perhaps it is intentional that we are not given more details. Given the noticeable silence on the subject, surely we are put on red alert that there was *no* particular "order of worship."

6 Care should be taken regarding reports coming years after the close of divine revelation. Not only would there be a significant time lapse, but descriptions of how a particular congregation functioned might or might not have been typical of other congregations, or— more important—reflective of early apostolic practice.

It seems that there may or may not have been preaching at every meeting; and there may or may not have been the exercise of spiritual gifts on those occasions. All we know for certain is that their stated purpose for meeting together on the first day of the week was to break bread and, therefore, it appears that the memorial meal must have been a central feature of their gathered assemblies on the Lord's Day.

Today, of course, all that has changed. Having emasculated the vibrant fellowship meal of the early disciples and reduced it to little more than an emblematic ritual, we have already made a false start in our worship focus. In terms sheerly of time, perhaps the only part of our worship receiving less attention than the Lord's Supper is prayer. In some congregations, even announcements can come close to edging out the scant few minutes devoted to the Supper.

To radically restore New Testament worship, therefore, we must radically rethink the emphasis we put on the Supper. Certainly, it is good to sing and to pray and to edify one another in the Word. But the lesson of first-century worship is that, first and foremost, we meet together on the first day of the week *to break bread*. To remember *why* we sing, and pray, and edify. To remember the One who makes our life together possible. To remember the importance of our fellowship with one another in Christ. To remember that nothing else in all the world matters if Christ did not die for our sins.

But Could We Really Do It?

If only such a focus were possible! Recapturing that lofty vision of the Lord's Supper as the center of our time together on the Lord's Day is one thing. Actually implementing it according to the New Testament pattern is another thing altogether, particularly if we were to go all the way and observe the Supper as an integral part of a fellowship meal in the manner of the early church. Can you imagine it? Virtually every aspect of our Lord's Day assemblies would be thrown into mass confusion!

For starters, it would probably mean that we would have to spend double or triple the amount of time we normally devote to Sunday "services." And then there's all that food to prepare, not to mention the hours of thought which would have to be given to making sure that our fellowship meals do not overshadow Christ's memorial itself, as happened with the Corinthians. And, practically speaking, how would our singing and prayers and edification from the Word be integrated into such a setting?

The good news, I suppose, is that there could never again be a kind of "three songs and a prayer" mentality about our worship. You can be sure that having a first-century fellowship meal as the backdrop for our Sunday services would shatter our customary acts of worship.

What I wonder most is whether we could ever move comfortably from the almost funeral-like solemnity which surrounds our present Lord's table observances (which I often find personally meaningful and moving) to the kind of joyful celebration characteristic of a shared family meal (which, to be candid, sounds threateningly irreverent to me). In short, how do you mix a banquet with a funeral?

One thing is certain: those who object on principle to having kitchens in the church building would have to reconsider that position from scratch. Knowing what we know about first-century fellowship meals, the question isn't so much whether there ought to be a kitchen in the church, but whether the church ought to be in the kitchen. Or, put differently, whether we should be meeting from house to house for combined fellowship and worship as the early Christians did.

In the first century, the "kitchen" issue would never have arisen. Back then, there were no purpose-built houses of worship, complete with pulpits and pews, stained glass and steeples. In the absence of church buildings, there was simply no possibility that adding a fellowship hall would turn the church into a country club or social center as can so easily happen today. Unfamiliar with anything like our modern buildings, the primitive church met in homes... which had kitchens (of a sort)... which evidently played an important part in the memorial meal shared on the Lord's Day.

Maybe that's where it all went wrong in the first place. Maybe the church should never have left home. If Christians had been content to meet from house to house, there might never have been the temptation to dispense with the love feast and to settle, instead, for a miniaturized, stylized version of the Supper in buildings without kitchens.

So where does this leave us today, with our typically large congregations of up to five hundred, a thousand, or even three thousand members meeting together each Sunday? Could we ever hope to roll back the clock and duplicate anything like the house churches of the first-century, or—at a minimum—to adapt their weekly fellowship meal in some way so as to capture its essence in our modern context?

To ask these questions is to revisit the pivotal question posed in Chapter Two: "Is it not possible to work *within the system* to bring about any necessary changes?" Surely, the early church's weekly memorial meal is Exhibit A in the case for saying "no." To radically restore the centerpiece of New Testament Christian worship would be next to impossible within our current framework.

So the really tough question is, Are we willing to be that radical? Or are we, in truth, so locked into our traditional worship format that no amount of restoration zeal could possibly pull us away? Of course, we can always rationalize that times have changed, and that what's important is not precise replication but equally-meaningful edification. (After all, I'm reminded, the disciples in Corinth apparently had every detail right but still got it wrong.) But if we pretend to take restoration serious-ly, we are left with few options. From a first-century perspective, it seems not to be the Lord's Supper that we eat today, but only a pale imitation.

I confess that I, myself, am apprehensive about all the unknown implications which practicing the memorial meals of the first century might hold in store for us. But it's hard to ignore the obvious compelling question: Can we continue to treat the Lord's Supper as just a superficial Sunday ritual that receives lit-tle time or thought without being guilty of sinning against the body and blood of Christ?

CHAPTER EIGHT

AT HOME WITH WORSHIP

Greet also the church that meets at their house.

ROMANS 16:5

L ast Thanksgiving, our house in Nashville was bursting at
the seams with all of the Smith clan in town for the holiday.
By one o'clock, the turkey was roasted to perfection and
the side dishes were piled high with dressing, sweet potatoes,
butter beans, creamed corn, congealed salad, cranberry relish, and
piping hot home-made rolls. Yum! (Did I mention the scrump-
tious pumpkin and pecan pies, and Ruth's special coconut cake?)

When everyone was gathered around and the little ones
were quiet, I read a psalm of thanksgiving, spoke briefly about
how good it was to have the family together, and invoked God's
blessing on both our family and our food. Then we eagerly filled
our plates and scattered all over the house. With some twenty-
five folks sitting down for dinner all at one time, we ended up in
the dining room, at the breakfast table, and around folding
tables in the middle of our small living room, while some of the
teenagers made do with t.v. trays on the sun porch.

Needless to say, we all had a wonderful time, made even
cozier by being in such close quarters. All afternoon, the talking
and laughter never seemed to stop. And, of course, family being
family, there were also a few tears and hugs along the way. All
very much like your own family gatherings, I expect.

In fact, from what we can tell, it's also very much like the house churches of the first century and their memorial meals on the Lord's Day. Apparently, their love feasts were a mirror image of our own Thanksgiving celebrations, with home, family, food, love, prayer, and shared memories. Especially the memory of Christ.

Earlier, I questioned how it's possible to mix a funeral and a banquet. Admittedly, those two extremes are pretty much irreconcilable. But a joyous Thanksgiving meal is certainly not ruined by pausing in the middle of the festivities to reflect upon spiritual things, and to read the Scriptures and to pray. Indeed, this reflective time gives enhanced meaning to the whole occasion.

Meeting From House to House

For those of us who have ever "attended worship" with sizeable congregations in rather grand buildings, the most striking feature of the early disciples was their apparent practice of worshiping together in private homes, presumably in relatively small groups. I wonder, for example, if there is more than meets the eye when Luke tells us the manner in which Saul persecuted the church? "Going from house to house," says Luke, "he dragged off men and women and put them in prison" (Acts 8:3). Of course, this might have taken place during the week in the homes of various disciples. But it is also possible that Saul employed a strategy of surveillance, watching covertly as small groups of disciples gathered together for worship on the Lord's Day and then catching them in the act.

If that were the case, what an irony that Paul (by that time a disciple himself) would later reflect on how he had taught the gospel in Ephesus both "publicly and from house to house" (Acts 20:20). Paul might have been referring to times of private study with individual families in their own homes; or, equally possible, to his meetings with various house churches throughout Ephesus. We know that, in his first letter to the disciples in Corinth, Paul specifically refers to one such congregation in Ephesus, saying, "Aquila and Priscilla greet you warmly in the Lord, and so does the church that meets at their house" (1 Corinthians 16:19).

Paul had first met Aquila and Priscilla in Corinth not long after Claudius had expelled them from Rome in A.D. 49, along with all other Jews. When Paul moved on from Corinth to Ephesus, they accompanied him and helped to further the work there. The next thing we know, Aquila and Priscilla have moved back to Rome, and are once again hosting one of the local congregations in their home. In his general letter to the church in Rome, then, we read where Paul asks the disciples there to greet his former co-workers, Priscilla and Aquila, and also, "the church that meets in their house" (Romans 16:3-5).

It is worth noting from this special greeting that apparently not all the Christians in Rome worshiped together. It was evidently to a number of different house-church congregations in Rome that Paul conveyed expressions of love from their various sister congregations in Ephesus, saying, "All the churches of Christ send greetings" (Romans 16:16).

We get an even clearer picture of multiple house churches in the same locality from Paul's letters to the "faithful brothers in Christ at Colosse" and to Paul's friend, Philemon. In the first instance, Paul tells the Colossians to give his greetings "to the brothers at Laodicea, and to Nympha and the church in her house" [or Nymphas and the church in his house, KJV] (Colossians 4:15). Whether the congregation meeting in Nympha's house was directly in Colosse or in one of the towns nearby is not certain.[7]

Then we have Paul's second greeting: "To Philemon our dear friend and fellow worker, to Apphia our sister, to Archippus our fellow soldier and to the church that meets in your home..." (Philemon 1-2). The text isn't altogether clear whether the congregation was meeting in Archippus' house or Philemon's; yet, either way, it is definitely a different group from the one meeting with Nympha, despite their being in near proximity.

7 It is also possible that, in this particular text, Paul means nothing more than "the Christians in Nympha's household."

All of which may explain how, in Jerusalem, there could be three thousand disciples (and growing daily) without their necessarily meeting all together in one place on the Lord's Day (even assuming that all 3,000-plus remained in Jerusalem long beyond Pentecost).[8] For instance, when Herod had Peter thrown into prison, Luke tells us that "the church was earnestly praying to God for him" (Acts 12:5). This undoubtedly included the whole church in Jerusalem, but what we are shown, up close and personal, is a microscopic view of what may have been one of the newly-established house churches, gathering specially for prayer during this time of crisis. After Peter was miraculously released from prison, "he went to the house of Mary the mother of John, also called Mark, where many people had gathered and were praying" (Acts 12:12). It would not be surprising if the reason the disciples were meeting there that night was because that's where they normally met together for worship.

If, in fact, they were a house church, it seems likewise to be the case with those who met in Lydia's home when, this time, Paul and Silas were imprisoned. "After Paul and Silas came out of the prison, they went to Lydia's house, where they met with the brothers and encouraged them." (Acts 16:40). Whether specially for prayer, or regularly for worship, there seems to be little question but that first-century Christians met together in small groups as house churches.

Historically, of course, we know that it was not until the third century that Christians began to erect what we today would recognize as church buildings. Piecing together archeology and history, it appears that the primitive church typically met in a room (sufficiently large enough for probably 40-50 people) in the house of a wealthy member. Perhaps someone like Philemon, for example, who was rich enough to be a slave owner. Or perhaps Lydia, evidently a prosperous business-

8 Some commentators, including McGarvey and the Expositor's Bible Commentary, observe from Acts 2:46 that such a large number could only meet in the temple courts. However, they do not address the question of where the church met on the first day of the week to observe the Lord's Supper.

AT HOME WITH WORSHIP

woman. Although their spacious houses might have accommodated the entire congregation in a single city, this larger church,
for purposes of teaching and edification, might also have been
broken into smaller groups, meeting in various other homes for
the Lord's Supper. Or, indeed, it might have been just the other
way around, as Paul's discussion in 1 Corinthians 11 suggests.

That no evidence exists of large congregations meeting in
spacious "church buildings" for observing the memorial meal
together (whatever its actual nature) tells us much about what
we aren't always told by way of detail: that first-century
Christians obviously met together in a variety of homes, large
and small. Among the early disciples, faith and Christian practice began at home, in more ways than one.

From Temple, To Synagogue, And Home Again

The question for us, of course, is whether the house
church was a divinely-intended arrangement, or merely a historical happenstance owing to economic necessity, the pressures
of persecution, or perhaps the lack of available public meeting
places. Indeed, is it possible that what God intended was a revolutionary kind of worship which house churches facilitated in
a way that previous arrangements could not? Was there something about the intimacy of the home which was uniquely
appropriate to the intended function?

The temple, for example, had an enormous size appropriate to its divine purpose. The sacrifice of hundreds of animals needed
a place of great space and visible pomp. In such a sacerdotal system, the priests and Levites were scurrying around doing their
many priestly duties, all of which needed elbow-room.

Not so in the primitive church. For, both then and now,
we ourselves are the priests offering up sacrifices of the heart
through our High Priest, Christ, who gave himself as the blood
sacrifice for our sin (Hebrews 9:11-14). We are also the new temple of God in whom the Holy Spirit dwells (1 Corinthians 3:16).

So it was that—for our forbears in the faith—space and pomp and ritual were no longer necessary for worship.

Even the first-century synagogue was more focused on teaching and preaching than on the kind of table fellowship practiced by the early Christians. Although the disciples continued to meet in the synagogue in order to engage their Jewish brothers (and sometimes even curious Greeks) in dialogue about the crucified, risen Messiah, the table fellowship which they shared on the Lord's Day was quite a different experience. For that purpose, meeting in homes provided a perfect venue.

Yet it also appears that more than just the memorial meal took place in the house churches. Merely consider that, in Troas, where the disciples had come together to break bread, Paul preached to them throughout the night "in the upstairs room where [they] were meeting" (Acts 20:8). The house church, then, was also a natural setting for edification and exhortation.

As between the synagogue and private homes, there is more than a hint of contrast when, after preaching on the Sabbath in Corinth, "Paul left the synagogue and went next door to the house of Titius Justus, a worshiper of God" (Acts 18:7). Although we are not specifically told that Paul preached there, apparently he did, for the text tells us that "Crispus, the synagogue ruler, and his entire household believed in the Lord; and many of the Corinthians who heard him believed and were baptized" (Acts 18:8).

In this regard, we should not overlook that Jesus himself taught in private houses as well as in the synagogue and in the temple courts. There was the time, for example, when Jesus was invited to Matthew Levi's house for a great banquet and (quite possibly on that occasion) taught the parables of the lost sheep, the lost coin, and the lost son (Luke 5:29-32; 15:1-32). There was also the time when Jesus was in a house where he had gone to eat, when suddenly he was surrounded by a crowd so big that the meal was essentially brought to a halt and he began teaching (Mark 3:20-34). And the time, too, when Jesus healed the para-

lytic who was let down through the roof of a house by his
friends when they could not get to Jesus because of the crowds
that were surrounding him as he taught (Luke 5:17-19).

The synagogue may have been the normal place of Jewish
instruction and discussion, but we see instance after instance in
which private homes served as a place for proclamation and
teaching, both for Jesus and for the disciples in the first-century.
It should not be surprising, then, that people who were taught
and converted in homes throughout the week were found
assembled in homes as well on the Lord's Day. (Nor, incidentally, should we overlook that the houses mentioned in the forego-
ing texts were large enough for even "crowds" to meet in.)

One simply has to wonder: Was it only a matter of fortuity that homes were used for teaching, or is it possible that there
is something special about the setting of a home in which, not
only doors of hospitality, but also hearts are opened? House
church or no house church, in what setting is personal evangelism most effective? Have we robbed ourselves of special opportunities by shifting the venue of evangelism from the warmth of
hearth and home to the relative coldness of auditoriums in
church buildings? Have we thereby moved from the personal to
the impersonal? From individual Christians teaching their own
neighbors to having "gospel sermons" preached to mostly
unidentifiable visitors—or, worse yet, to non-existent visitors?

One thing is certain: the house church arrangement on
the Lord's Day stood in stark contrast to both the priestly system
of the temple and the rabbinic office in the synagogue. In the
house church, the role of official clergy virtually vanished in the
midst of a simple fellowship meal. As did structured ritual and
liturgy. And sacrosanct tradition.

Spontaneous Informality

What all of this suggests is that the primitive church had an
intimacy, informality, and degree of mutual participation largely

foreign to our own experience. The importance of this emerging contrast is not simply between our modern church buildings and houses, per se, but between what typically takes place in a church building as compared with what might take place more suitably in a home. Each has its own natural ambience. Each has its own constraints, dictated primarily by the sheer difference in size.

Just imagine for a moment a congregation of 200-300 members in one of our medium-sized church buildings. To think of this many people sharing a memorial meal together each first day of the week fairly boggles the mind. But not even that is the immediate concern. The more challenging question is, How can a congregation that size possibly have the kind of informal spontaneity which the early church apparently had during their gathered assemblies?

I realize that the nature of our Lord's Day gatherings has been altered significantly by the cessation of spiritual gifts such as tongues and prophecy. Still, one gets the sense that the primitive church would have known nothing of our spectator-oriented services where members of the congregation participate only minimally through singing and partaking of the emblems. Most of the time today we are a *listening audience*, sitting in an *auditorium*. We listen to announcements, prayers, sermons, and (if done at all) brief talks around the Lord's table. Hopefully, we are actively participating in thought, but mostly our role is passive. By contrast, we hear Paul saying to the church in Corinth, "When you come together, *everyone* has a hymn, or a word of instruction...," etc. (1 Corinthians 14:26).

The gathered assemblies of the primitive church appear to have been far more participatory than what we experience; and, almost of necessity, therefore, more spontaneous and informal. So much so, in fact, that Paul is careful to caution that "everything should be done in a fitting and orderly way" (1 Corinthians 14:40).

Have we taken Paul's caution to an extreme? How much more extreme can it get than having a printed "order of worship" from which any deviation on the part of someone in the audience would be viewed with horror, and any spontaneous contribution of thought or song considered shockingly out of order?

It's all the difference between night and day. When is there ever time set aside in our assemblies, not for "scheduled" prayers, but for *prayer*? (That is, for prayers to be lifted up by whatever brother feels moved to do so.) What sermon today is followed by a time for questions and open discussion? When is the last time you heard comments being invited from among the brethren as the Lord's Supper was being observed? Or someone spontaneously leading (or singing) a hymn?

I know. I know. There's much to think about, not the least of which is responsible participation; and the varying levels of spiritual maturity among those who take part; and the ever-present questions about gender roles. But before we get to the details, let's not forget the overall picture. The primary difference between the first century and the 21st century is that— apart from times when sermons were being preached—there seems not to have been "an audience" as we know it today. When does a home ever have an audience? Just as a family interacts with one another around the house, in the house churches of the first century the family of God actively participated with one another in their mutual worship.

Why, then, the difference? Among other reasons, it was because they *could*. Practically speaking today, we often *can't*. In our larger congregations, there's simply too many of us. It wouldn't work. We're too big.

Lest we miss the point, let me reiterate that the issue is not so much whether we meet in an actual *house* as opposed to a *church building*. Rather, it's the contrast between *small* versus *large*; *participant* versus *spectator*; *active* versus *passive*; *personal* versus *impersonal*. It's simply axiomatic: The larger the gathering, the less personal, interactive, and truly participatory it's likely to be.

Over the years, we have spent an inordinate amount of time and energy arguing with others about the so-called "five items of worship." And yet it seems as if we never once stopped to realize that those "acts of worship"—as practiced among us today—are mostly an orchestrated religious spectacle for which we have reserved seats each week.

When we compare our worship services with the prayer-book, high-church ritual of the Catholics or Anglicans, we look incredibly informal by contrast. But compared with the truly informal, spontaneous worship of first-century Christians, the seemingly-benign ritual of our own modern-day services is "high church" indeed.

As earlier alluded, this is as true of most "contemporary worship" today as it is of the more traditional worship services in mainline congregations. Oh, there may be more hand raising, less formal attire, and fewer songbooks, but the slickly-crafted, high-tech, worship-team services of current popularity may be even less spontaneous and mutually participatory than ever before. "Production" is the word which immediately comes to mind. An energized, exciting, even deeply moving service is no less a *service*. Which is not to say we can't be more thoughtful in coordinating hymns, scriptures, and lessons, in order to "produce" an enhanced period of worship and edification. The key, in my judgment, is to encourage mutual participation which is thoughtful, meaningful, and—above all—worthy.

Think, for a moment, about the words we use to describe what we do when we assemble together on the Lord's Day. Words like "worship services"; and "attending worship"; and "worship hour"; and "worship leaders"; and "worship teams." Not only are these specific terms themselves foreign to Scripture, but nowhere do we find them even in concept. Might we not come closer to the idea by focusing on the word *assembly*, which seems to capture the essence of *ekklesia*?

If anything, we have inherited the idea of a "worship service" from Catholic and Protestant tradition. By that tradition, there are always people up front leading whatever worship is taking place, and then there's everybody else, sitting in the pews following along in the set-piece ritual. In effect, it's the *clergy* and the *laity*, which we pretend not to have, but undoubtedly do have, at least in function.

Yet, in today's larger congregations, especially, how could it be otherwise? When you build a stadium (to borrow an analogy from our other religion: sports), only a limited number of folks on the field get to play. Everyone else may be cheering from the stands, but few of them are exercising their muscles in the same way. Little wonder that the church has become so weak and atrophied. Our participation is mostly vicarious: standing and raising our hands when the cheerleaders tell us to (or sitting on our hands when our cheerleaders tell us that it's wrong to do otherwise).[9]

If only the problem of large numbers were always available as an excuse. However, the most interesting thing about our ritualized worship is how rigid it is even in the smallest of congregations. Consider, for instance, that our congregations consist, on average, of about ninety members; and that, therefore, thousands of congregations have only 40-50 members. That being the case, most congregations could easily worship in the same mutually-participatory way as the early Christians did. But if there happens to be only twenty-five Christians in a church building on Sunday, what you will find is a group of people who go through the exact same motions as a congregation of 2500.

Even where opportunities naturally present themselves for more informality, spontaneity, and mutual participation, we seem to be locked into a system from which we cannot extricate ourselves. A system which (the "five items of worship" to the contrary notwithstanding) bears little resemblance to the dynamic, interactive worship we read about in Scripture. Whether megachurch or mini-church, we all seem to have missed the point.

---

9 One of the more interesting aspects of the house-church dynamic is the way in which, by comparison, the visibility aspect of larger assemblies tends to impact the crucial issue of gender roles. The more recognizable a leadership role, the more women are limited in their participation. With the reduction of "official ritual" led by recognizable worship leaders (song leaders, for example), there may be a wider framework in which women might participate without "teaching or having authority" over men. Particularly would this be true, I believe, during times of open discussion. As long as the principle of male spiritual leadership is duly maintained in both practice and spirit, dynamics might vary with each situation.

Worship and Evangelism In a Blender

Of all the differences between 21st-century worship and primitive Christian practice, surely the strangest innovation is the perfunctory call for a "response" at the end of every sermon, accompanied by the near-compulsory invitation song. Dare omit the "invitation," and you will quickly find yourself in the middle of protest and outrage by red-faced members who, themselves, may never once have invited a friend or neighbor to church in order to be taught the gospel. Nor does it seem to be important if, as a factual matter, not one non-believer happens to be present among the congregation. "There could always be a Christian who needs to confess his sins before the church," comes the steeled response.

The truth is, if you double-click on the "invitation-song" icon, what will appear on the screen is a church in which confusion reigns supreme about why we are gathered together on the Lord's Day. At one and the same time, we treat it as an occasion for Christians to remember Christ in edification and worship, but also—somehow, some way—for reaching out evangelistically to those who aren't yet saved. In the early church, there was no such confusion. Although teaching and preaching to the unconverted did take place from house to house, on the Lord's Day the already-converted church met together as brothers and sisters in the family of God for the purpose of sharing their common faith.

This is not to say that visitors were barred from their assemblies or were never convinced from the worship which they witnessed that these were truly people of God with whom they wished to be associated. For example, Paul specifically addressed how the Corinthians should conduct themselves in their worship so that, if "some unbeliever comes in," he would be convicted of his sinfulness (1 Corinthians 14:23-25). Even so, there is nothing to indicate that the memorial meal on the Lord's Day was ever intended as an evangelistic outreach.

In fact, going against the very grain of restoration thinking, we have turned the idea of evangelism on its head. In the early church, the disciples came together to "encourage one another." (That is, to edify and exhort one another through the breaking of bread and the teaching of the Word.) Whereupon they would go out, as on-fire individuals, and spread the gospel to the lost.

Our concept of evangelism, by contrast, is both vicarious and corporate. Instead of personally going out and taking the gospel to a dying world, the idea now is to bring lost souls into our Lord's Day meetings so that someone else can present them with the good news of Christ. In practice, of course, that is more theory than reality. In the end, we have evangelistic sermons aimed at people who aren't even there. Either that, or we have sermons of exhortation which inevitably, at the last minute, are robbed of their punch by awkward, contrived transitions into the obligatory "invitation"...again, for mythical people who still aren't there. Because we haven't invited them. Because we don't seem to really care about the lost. Because that's not our job.

This weekly confusion between edification and evangelism has been a disaster. In one fell swoop, we have both rid ourselves of personal responsibility for evangelism, and shifted the focus away from the principal reason Christians are to come together in the first place. The result is that we have fulfilled neither duty very well. We are like deer caught in the headlights, not quite sure which way to turn.

Intimacy In the Church

It's hard to see how any such confusion could have made its way into the house churches of the first century. Not only would the central focus of their gathering (to share in the memorial meal) be all too obvious, but there was an intimacy that would have made standing up and singing an invitation song a complete nonsense. Particularly would this be true in cases where a disciple needed to "respond," as we say euphemistically.

To begin with, in the early church there would have been such a degree of intimacy that confessing one's sins before the congregation rarely would have come as a surprise, as it often does today when someone walks down the aisle. If a sin had been committed against a first-century congregation, you can be sure that everyone in their small group would already have known about it.

Not only that, but the intimacy of the house church would also provide a loving context in which those who needed to repent in a special way could do so with the full expectation of familiar, open arms. Surely, in those circumstances, there was no bland statement about "needing to be restored" privately whispered into the preacher's ear. When the family of God has met together for a love feast, the prodigal son needs neither an invitation song to "go forward," nor a delegated intermediary to convey his urgent desire for forgiveness.

On the flip side of that intimacy comes an accountability rarely known in our large, modern congregations. It is inconceivable, for example, that first-century disciples could get "lost in the cracks" as happens today in huge congregations where folks can come and go with little notice either way. It's hard to be a "floating" member in a congregation where everybody knows your name. Or, as someone recently observed, "Nominal Christians don't clutter house churches!"

Moreover, if drastic church discipline should ever be necessary, only the house-church scenario makes much sense of Paul's instruction: "With such a man, do not even eat" (1 Corinthians 5:11). The ongoing table fellowship of the house church, both specially on the Lord's day and throughout the week, played such a significant part in the Christian's experience in the first century that the threat of its being withdrawn could actually be an incentive for the sinner to come home. Back to the table. Back to the fellowship. Back to the family again.

How could that possibly ever be the case in today's megachurches, or even in most of our medium-sized congregations? And this doesn't even begin to address the matter of shepherd responsibility (which we will soon discuss in more detail).

Suffice it to say for the moment that many flocks today are so big that there's simply no way the shepherds can know their sheep by name. Nor, worse yet, by need.

Let's Get Practical

Suppose it were all different. Imagine what it would be like if there were no sizeable congregations meeting in church buildings, but only small house churches like those in the first century. What would change? What would we notice first?

Maybe it would be the money. Wouldn't it be interesting to know how many millions of dollars have gone into bricks and mortar, not to mention their monthly maintenance? Are there not countless better ways in which money might be spent?

Or maybe it would be the absence of church signs and ads in the Yellow Pages. Is it possible that we could ever have a sense of identity in Christ other than one so dependent upon a printed church name, visible in black and white for all the world to see? Without sign-posted church buildings, would we ever again have reason to confuse our allegiance with a *place* rather than a *Person*?

Who knows? Perhaps it would be an instant open door to evangelism—explaining to curious folks what kind of a church doesn't have buildings...and why. First-century Jewish disciples must surely have had a lot of explaining to do as to why they were worshiping in private homes on the first day of the week instead of in the temple or synagogue on the Sabbath. Could that fact alone have contributed to the rapid spread of the gospel?

I would like to think that the absence of large congregations might perhaps bring about a greater sense of belonging. More than that, a greater sense of contributing. But would we really welcome that, or does the thought of playing a more active role in small group worship sound scary? If having to seriously participate is the cost of greater intimacy, I fear that many among us wouldn't be prepared to pay the price.

We've Created Our Own Problems

One of the serendipities of returning to something like house churches is the enviable prospect that we could avoid all sorts of controversial questions which we've been forced to debate because we've already departed from first-century practice. Consider, for example, the question about whether women should be permitted to "wait on the Lord's table." Given our current, ritualistic mode of observing the Supper, I, for one, happen to believe that the demand for more inclusiveness (supposedly as an expression of Christian equality) is a rejection of what I see to be a scriptural mandate for male spiritual leadership. In other words, I believe a *wrong statement* is being made. But how could this issue even arise in a house church setting, where everyone around the table "passes the trays" to each other? (In the early church, you can be sure that women "served the Supper," because it was the women who prepared and served the memorial meal. Of course, having to serve in that menial way would be offensive to some women today, which only highlights, at least for me, the symbolic importance of the kind of inclusion being sought.)

In a similar vein, consider also the traditional role of song leader in our congregations. Whether it's a question of gender or otherwise, the fact is that the early church probably didn't have "song leaders," as we know them—standing up in front, waving their hands to the beat. In a small group setting, no official song leader is needed, as my own extended family can attest. On the day after Thanksgiving last year, our home was invaded by a second wave of relatives (this time on my mother's side of the family), who brought yet another round of food and an even heartier appetite for singing. For a couple of glorious hours, our two-dozen voices were blended in vocal praise, with not one hand being waved to the beat. (Okay, cousin Tom's hand was being waved, but that's just Tom!) And it hardly mattered who sang the first note.

Then there's all the fighting we do over "worship teams," and (increasingly again) solos, and choirs. (Modern solos, incidentally, bear little resemblance to what Paul had in mind when he mentioned that "everyone [meaning *someone*] has a hymn...." It is one thing to recognize giftedness—just as we presently do with those who speak—but if solos were permitted to be sung by the worst singers in the congregation as well as the best, then we would be much closer to the point which Paul obviously intended, in which the message alone is important.)

Whatever other problems they may present, the first and most serious problem with all forms of "special music" is that, whenever and however used, they are part of a system of worship which is radically different from that of primitive Christian practice. In the first century, the "worship team" was the entire congregation! And of one thing we can be certain: In the intimacy of a first-century house church, there simply wasn't room for anyone confusing worship with a performance.

While we are on the subject of church music, it would be interesting to know whether the use of instruments is a greater or lesser temptation in smaller congregations. Certainly, someone might argue that instruments are needed more than ever when voices are few, but that matches neither personal experience nor the unquestioned practice of the early church. For at least the first five-hundred years (and continuing predominately for most of the next millennium), there was never any pretension that instruments were actually needed to accompany Christian worship, whether in the small house churches of the first century or in the church buildings of the ensuing centuries.

To this day, Orthodox Jews (following in the tradition of the synagogue), along with the millions of adherents in the Russian Orthodox and Eastern Orthodox communions, still do not use instruments (continuing the practice of the early church). The historical music of the church was so distinctly non-instrumental that it became referred to as *a cappella*—which is to say, "in the manner of the church." Anyone claiming to be a restorationist who calls for the introduction of musical instruments into Christian worship has just flunked the Shibboleth test of restoration thinking. But the instrument issue likely would not even have arisen if the rest of us hadn't already flunked the same Shibboleth test by departing from the small-group-worship model of primitive Christians.

One needn't resort to taking Ephesians 5:19 and Colossians 3:16 out of context in order to force an argument which those passages were never intended to address. (Nor jump through convoluted hoops debating the esoteric meaning of *psallo*.) The simple fact is that, in the first-century house church, instruments were neither needed nor used. No one disputes that instruments accompanied the Levite choir as sacrifices were being offered in the temple. But the clear, unmistakable message of Hebrews is that the entire ceremonial package of temple worship (of which the use of instruments was only one small part) was done away with in Christ.

It's the same line of progression as before:

Temple...synagogue...house church.

Priest...rabbi...disciple.

Pomp...tradition...simplicity.

No one more than I exults in the beauty of a large congregation singing majestic hymns in blended praise and edification. I believe that God has gifted us with a natural variety of voice and range which brings our unique style of four-part harmony within the parameters of his will. So it is that, along with many others, I am concerned that our current music emphasis is taking us to the brink of losing, in one generation, centuries of powerful, moving hymnody which has enabled believers to soar on wings of faith throughout the ages.

But in the battles over church music and the Restoration ideal, I'd settle, if need be, for the simple, antiphonal refrains which echoed off the walls of first-century house churches. Within the unadorned setting of their simple Lord's Day worship, the apostolic church was not focused on the beauty of its music. Rather, being filled with the Spirit, they taught and admonished one another purely and simply through the fruit of their lips—singing psalms, hymns, and spiritual songs. About that part of primitive Christian worship, no one takes issue.

Independent, But Networked

With the spotlight focused so sharply on the unique house churches of the early Christians, we are naturally curious about how those scattered, independent congregations interacted with one another. For openers, we know that they were in sufficient contact to allow Paul's letters to circulate. "After this letter has been read to you," says Paul to the disciples at Colosse, "see that it is also read in the church of the Laodiceans and that you in turn read the letter from Laodicea" (4:16). Yet, interestingly enough, our best insight comes from the way in which they shared with each other financially, both in times of special need and in the furtherance of the gospel.

Significantly, the first record we have of inter-congregational benevolence comes early in the ministry of the Apostle Paul, long before he ever penned his familiar instructions to the Corinthians about their "contribution." Luke first tells us about Agabus predicting famine throughout the Roman world (Acts 11:27-28), and then immediately informs us that "the disciples [in Antioch], each according to his ability, decided to provide help for the brothers living in Judea" (Acts 11:29).

Although they met from house to house in small groups, the early disciples were keenly conscious that they were part of a larger, universal body of believers. And when any part of the body suffered, the whole body felt its pain. Even miles away in distant cities or lands.

Note carefully that, in this instance, it was the disciples themselves who decided to make this generous love gift; and also that each one gave according to his own ability. Sound familiar? Later, we hear almost the same words from Paul as he tells the disciples in Corinth, "On the first day of every week, each of you should set aside a sum of money in keeping with his income..." (1 Corinthians 16:1-4).

Typically, of course, we hear those words badly para-phrased week after week in the mantra: "We have been command-ed to give of our means on the Lord's Day as we have prospered." From this textual miscue, we have concluded as a matter of doc-trine that *giving* is a required "item of worship" along with preach-ing, prayer, singing, and the Lord's Supper. Thus, our obligatory Sunday "contribution." Or, "offering." Or, worse yet, "giving back to God a portion of that with which he has richly blessed us."

The truth is, there is simply no evidence that the early church ever made weekly contributions as part of an apostoli-cally-mandated worship ritual. Their contributions, when made, were special collections intended to meet particular needs. From the text, it is obvious that Paul's familiar instructions were in response to questions which the Corinthians, themselves, had already put to Paul ("Now about the collection for God's peo-ple..."); and were simply a practical matter of implementation ("so that when I come no collections will have to be made").

If Paul's instructions about weekly contributions are to be regarded as a "command" for us today, consistency demands that we hold our funds until Paul himself comes and delivers them to Jerusalem. ("Then, when I arrive, I will give letters of introduction to the men you approve and send them with your gift to Jerusalem.")[10]

Nothing could be clearer from Chapters 8 and 9 of Paul's second letter to the Corinthians than that this was a unique con-tribution initiated by the disciples themselves. "Last year you were the first not only to give but also to have the desire to do so" (8:10). "I thought it necessary to urge the brothers to visit you in advance and finish the arrangements for the generous gift you had promised. Then it will be ready as a generous gift, not as one grudgingly given" (9:5). In fact, Paul says pointedly: "I

---

10 Unlike Acts 20:7 (an example carrying the force of precedent because of its connection with the Supper, and intended from its inception to be an ongoing memorial), this text is addressing what is obviously a special collection having no application beyond the time of its completion.

am *not commanding you...*" (8:8). Rather, "Here is my *advice* about what is best for you in this matter..." (8:10).

Although the contribution for the poor saints in Jerusalem was not Paul's idea but the Corinthians' themselves, Paul cleverly holds them to their commitment by citing the love gift which the disciples in Macedonia had earlier supplied for the support of the work right there among them in Corinth. "Entirely on their own," Paul recalls, "they urgently pleaded with us for the privilege of sharing in this service to the saints" (8:3-4). In fact, when Paul defends his apostleship later in this same letter, he talks about having "robbed other churches," meaning that "the brothers who came from Macedonia supplied what I needed" (11:8-9).

What's so interesting about these special love gifts being shared back and forth among the disciples is not just that it proves how very aware they were of each other, but that they were in a unique position to give generously. Some have suggested that today's larger congregations have the advantage of generating great sums of money for benevolence and mission work. Yet, it must also be said that this generosity usually comes with a hefty overhead which would have been unknown in the first century. When the Lord's body meets from house to house, and is therefore bereft of the buildings, staff, and budgets made necessary by sheer size of operation, every penny given goes directly to meet a specific need. Nothing is wasted on anything extraneous—particularly the creature comforts to which we have become accustomed.

Like cells in the body, ceaselessly multiplying and replicating, the house-church congregations in the first century collectively constituted a fast-growing organism which never lost touch with its outermost perimeters. And with every part of the body supplying *whatever* was needed *whenever* and *wherever* it was needed, this dynamic spiritual organism spread with remarkable speed and cohesiveness throughout the then-known world. Against all logic, being smaller meant being larger. More important yet, it's very diversity produced a unity among the disciples unparalleled from that time to this.

Yes, But...

So what do you think? Is there a chance in the world that we could ever give up our comfortable church buildings and meet, instead, in each other's homes? Is it even halfway conceivable that we might actually exchange our traditional, structured ritual for the spontaneous, mutually-participatory informality of first-century worship; or that we would ever feel comfortable sharing a memorial meal together each Lord's Day? Can we imagine what it would be like if, one Sunday, we didn't take up a "collection" because during the previous week we had given everything we had to meet a special need?

If pressed on the issue (which, so far, I've managed to sidestep), I don't know that I'm prepared to say unequivocally that the house church was a divinely-intended arrangement. Not in the sense, at least, that it plainly violates God's will if we meet, instead, in purpose-built houses of worship. However, I have no doubt but that moving away from the house-church concept has given rise to a system without scriptural support which has fundamentally changed the form and nature of worship as practiced in the apostolic church.

Here's a challenging exercise: When you meet together for worship next Sunday, give some special thought to the dynamics of what you observe. Knowing what you know about how the early disciples functioned when they assembled, what strikes you differently about your own assembly?

And one more radical thought: How might your personal faith-life be affected if your congregation were small enough to meet together in someone's house each Lord's Day...and that particular house just happened to be *your* home?

CHAPTER NINE

WHEN SHEPHERDS ARE SHEEPISH

*This is what the Sovereign LORD says: I am against the
shepherds and will hold them accountable for my flock.*

EZEKIEL 34:10

As I write these words, I'm looking out over the lush green hills of the English countryside above our cottage and the little village of Buckland which I've shared with you in previous books. But now all I can do is look. We can't go walking in the hills anymore, nor even down the public footpath that runs alongside our cottage to Laverton and on to Stanton. When it comes to our cherished daily walks, we are effectively quarantined.

Because of the current foot-and-mouth crisis, the whole countryside of England is closed. While the government is desperate to say otherwise (so that you will cross the Pond and keep the British tourism industry afloat), the fact is that our own village is as quiet as I can remember it in the fifteen years since I first made Buckland my part-time home. Considering the increased traffic on our single village lane in recent years, that's good news.

The bad news is that millions of sheep and cattle are being "culled." Make that, *slaughtered.* Sure, most of them would have been slaughtered eventually anyway, providing food for the table. But some are rare breeds on the brink of extinction, and others—especially cows—have been improved by generations of careful breeding, all of which is being wiped out in a single day. Even the killing of ordinary species under these circumstances is heartbreaking, especially since they are completely healthy specimens, guilty of nothing more than being in near proximity to an outbreak of infection.

Then there's the stench and smoke of the burning pyres, like some wretched ancient Gehenna where the flames never die. Of course, it's not only the rotting carcasses going up in smoke. Worst of all, it's the livelihood of the farmers. Those whose animals have already been culled are devastated. Those anxiously fearing a knock on their door by government vets are dying on the inside with every agonizing day that passes. Will they be the next to face bankruptcy? Will they be held prisoner on their farms for weeks while the incubation period passes?

The welcome peacefulness of the countryside belies the tragedy. There's a war going on out there. Actually two wars. One is against an unseen enemy that mercilessly attacks animals at random. The other is between the farmers and the government, whom the farmers accuse of pre-election political dithering. Even the morning headlines are filled with mixed-signals: "The countryside is closed!" "No, it's not." "We're opposed in principle to inoculations." "We are now considering minimal, strategic inoculations." "We're going to burn the slaughtered animals." "No, burial is best." "Sorry, we're going back to burning." Who's in charge? Who's taking responsibility for this sordid mess?

Actually, in a quite admirable sense, *everyone* is taking responsibility in this crisis, or at least doing their part to bring it to an end. I can tell you that Ruth and I wouldn't dream of stepping onto a farm and endangering our neighbors' sheep. In that same, one-for-all and all-for-one spirit, many farm and garden shows have been canceled; the multi-million-pound Cheltenham Gold Cup steeplechase has been put off; and even my old friend, George Foster, and his cronies have volunteered not to race their prized pigeons, lest the birds spread the virus through the air. Fighting foot-and-mouth is everybody's war.

What impresses me most about this crisis is the unrelenting determination of the farmers and shepherds to do whatever it takes to protect their herds and flocks. For all their resentment at the government's actions, it was the early indecision to which they objected most fiercely, not to the radical measures now being taken. Inoculation could stop the virus from spreading, but it would mean having the virus hanging around, just beneath the surface, forever. The only way to stamp it out altogether is to bite the bullet and use bullets. It's not a pretty picture, but it works. In a way that few others will ever appreciate, England's shepherds know that protecting their flocks means vigilance, quarantine, and—if necessary—drastic action.

A Parallel Spiritual Crisis

In the midst of all this, I can't help but think of the many obvious parallels with our own spiritual shepherds in the church. I'm more and more convinced that it's not merely cultural coincidence which explains why the Holy Spirit referred to elders, bishops, and overseers as "shepherds." I suppose it might be more relevant today to speak of management team leaders. But it wouldn't capture the same essence as *shepherds*. What business leader today would leave his plush office and (in a reprise of the parable of the lost sheep) seek out a single employee struggling with alcohol? What management team isn't inevitably going to consider "the bottom line" as their bottom line?

No, I tell you, the Good Shepherd himself is not to be compared to today's business professionals. For that reason alone, images of *shepherds* and *flocks* will never go out of date, even if the whole global community eventually exists in cyberspace with not a wooly creature in sight. If you want to talk about form following function, don't even think about updating to church committees and focus groups and team leaders as a pragmatic way of meeting contemporary needs. God himself knows the functions he intends, and he has given us the right forms for the job—right down to seemingly antiquated shepherds and sheep.

Unless I'm badly mistaken, this bucolic pastoral concept has more than a little to do with the difference between *organization* and *organism*. How we love *organization*, with its mission statements, flow-charts, budgets, position, power, and politics! But between a shepherd and his sheep, there is none of that— only provision and protection on the part of the shepherd, and reciprocal submission on the part of the sheep.

To more fully appreciate the difference, merely consider the clashing perspectives of the government and the shepherds in rural England when the crisis first began. Even after reports of the virus took on an alarming scale, the politicians seemed hesitant to attack foot-and-mouth, being more interested in avoiding "foot-*in*-mouth" as the election loomed. As it's turned out, ironically, they've "opened mouth and inserted foot" repeatedly in the long days since, realizing too late that their misplaced priorities only served to deepen both the agricultural and political crises simultaneously. Interestingly enough, had the politicians viewed themselves as servant shepherds watching benevolently over their constituencies, we quite likely would have had a quicker end to the nightmare.

This striking contrast ought to make us appreciate all the more Jesus referring to himself as the Good Shepherd, and help us understand why Jesus spoke so often about the relationship between a shepherd and his sheep. We see the same pastoral theme when Paul admonished the elders in Ephesus, saying, "Guard yourselves and all the flock of which the Holy Spirit has made you overseers. Be shepherds of the church of God.... [for] I know that after I leave, savage wolves will come in among you and will not spare the flock" (Acts 20:28-29).

Peter, too, makes use of the analogy. "To the elders among you," he writes, "I appeal as a fellow elder.... Be shepherds of God's flock that is under your care, serving as overseers—not because you must, but because you are willing, as God wants you to be...not lording it over those entrusted to you, but being examples to the flock. And when the Chief Shepherd appears, you will receive the crown of glory that will never fade away" (1 Peter 5:1-4).

How Big Was the Fold?

Whatever else the elders in the early church were called to be, first and foremost they were commissioned as shepherds of the flock of God among them. Which instantly raises a number of intriguing questions. Of what specific flocks, for example, were first-century shepherds overseers? How many sheep are we talking about? How big was each fold?

We know that when the disciples in Antioch sent financial support to their brethren in Judea, they did so, "sending their gift to the elders..." (Acts 11:30). Apparently, Luke had in mind the elders in Jerusalem. Which only begs the further question: How many elders were there in Jerusalem? Or, more to the point: Were there elders in each one of the house churches; or only one set of elders for the entire metropolitan area, as we might put it today? (And the same question could be asked regarding the "elders of the church" in Ephesus, since we've already seen that they, too, met in various house churches.)

A closer look at the Jerusalem elders may be somewhat surprising for many of us. When the historic conference was held to decide questions related to Gentile evangelism, we read that "Paul and Barnabas were appointed...to go up to Jerusalem to see the apostles and elders about this question" (Acts 15:2). At the end of the conference, "the apostles and elders, *with the whole church*, decided to choose some of their own men and send them to Antioch with Paul and Barnabas" (Acts 15:22). If this is all we had to go on, it would appear that there was only one group of elders for all the disciples in Jerusalem.

What's more, their wider influence even beyond Jerusalem can hardly be denied. For "as [Paul and Barnabas] traveled from town to town, they delivered the decisions reached by the apostles and elders in Jerusalem for the people to obey" (Acts 16:4). Have you ever stopped to think about the implications of that conspicuously-repeated pairing: the apostles and elders? Are we to take it that the Jerusalem elders had authority and influence on the same level as the apostles? Surely not, but there's simply no denying that the Jerusalem elders were unlike any group of elders we have ever experienced.

When Paul returned from Macedonia to Jerusalem to face inevitable arrest, the very next day he went to see Jesus' brother, James, who—from all accounts—was recognized as a leader in the Jerusalem church. At that meeting, we are told, "all the elders were present" (Acts 21:17-18). So once again comes the nagging question: Does this mean all the house-church elders in Jerusalem (collectively); or perhaps only one group of elders over all of the house churches in Jerusalem?

Our uncertainty is amplified all the more when we read Paul's instructions to Titus about appointing elders. "The reason I left you in Crete," said Paul, "was that you might straighten out what was left unfinished and appoint elders *in every town*" (Titus 1:5). Arguably, of course, this could mean a number of different groups of elders overseeing various, distinct congregations within the same town. (That's certainly the idea we get when we read that, at the end of their first missionary journey, Paul and Barnabas returned to Lystra, Iconium, and Antioch and "appointed elders for them in each church," Acts 14:21-23). Yet, Paul's actual words to Titus are *every town*, not every house church, or every congregation.

I don't mean to belabor the issue, but it has to be said that we've simply never given much thought, if any, to city-wide elders. We've always assumed that "the flock of God among you" must surely apply to each congregation. On the other hand, we've never really linked these intriguing passages to the existence of smaller house churches—a factor which might possibly alter the picture considerably. Did a number of different house churches ever collectively comprise a larger "congregation"?

Let me reassure you that, after taking my usual diversionary stroll, I'm not actually going to end up talking about elder "jurisdiction" as such, but rather the *nature* of New Testament elders. It's just that, oddly enough, asking these "jurisdiction" questions is one of the best ways to learn what elders were all about in the early church.

A Long History of Elders

To gain some measure of clarity about this and other issues related to God's spiritual shepherds, it may be helpful to trace back to their origins. We would be greatly mistaken to suppose that "elders" were unique to the early church. Long before the church was ever established, the Jews had a rich history of spiritual shepherds. In fact, Israel had elders even before it crossed the Red Sea and officially became a separate nation. When God spoke to Moses from within the burning bush, he instructed him, saying, "Go, assemble the elders of Israel and say to them, 'The LORD, the God of your fathers...appeared to me...'" (Exodus 3:16).

What elders? When and how were they appointed? What were their qualifications? Curiously enough, nowhere is there any hint about the circumstances under which the role of elder first came into being. It's as if Israel's elders suddenly appear from out of nowhere. Then we begin to see them everywhere.

For instance, we tend to forget that the elders of Israel accompanied Moses and Aaron when they approached Pharaoh (Exodus 3:18). In this instance, it appears that there was only one group of elders representing the entire nation. Presumably, they were the same elders who were with Moses when he brought forth water from the rock (Exodus 17:1-7); ate with Moses' father-in-law, Jethro (Exodus 18:12); were the first to be told what God had said to Moses on the mountain (Exodus 19:7); laid their hands on the bull offered for Israel's sins of omission (Leviticus 4:13-21); and were witnesses when the priests were consecrated for their ministry (Leviticus 9:1).

And yet, "seventy of the elders of Israel" (clearly not all of Israel's elders) were invited specially to come into God's presence for the confirmation of his covenant with Israel (Exodus 24:1-18). Mystery of mysteries, "Moses and Aaron, Nadab and Abihu, and the seventy elders of Israel went up *and saw the God of Israel*...But God did not raise his hand against these leaders of the Israelites; they saw God, and they ate and drank." (Can you imagine how transformed the Lord's body would be if elders today *saw God* as intimately as Israel's spiritual leaders—particularly as we join them to "eat and drink" in God's presence each week?)

These "seventy elders," incidentally, presaged yet two other groups of "seventy," the most familiar being the council of elders we know as the Sanhedrin, before whom Jesus was tried and condemned. We see a less-familiar "seventy" in the wilderness, when Moses despaired that he alone couldn't carry the burden of dealing with so many grumbling Israelites. "The LORD said to Moses: 'Bring me seventy of Israel's elders who are known to you as leaders and officials among the people. Have them come to the Tent of Meeting, that they may stand there with you. I will come down and speak with you there, and I will take of the Spirit that is on you and put the Spirit on them. They will help you carry the burden of the people so that you will not have to carry it alone'" (Numbers 11:16-17).

Here, seventy of Israel's elders were specially commissioned to assist Moses in his judicial leadership of the nation. Since these particular seventy were selected from among elders who were already set apart as "leaders and officials," it tells us that Israel's leaders typically were chosen from among one special group: her "olders." There was something special about Israel's older generation that made them uniquely qualified to serve as leaders, whether administratively or spiritually.

In fact, being an "elder" seems not to have been so much an "office" (except for those who were specially chosen to be "officials"), but rather a key *role* played by mature, hoary-headed, "wise old men." In the ancient world, that was as true of heathen nations as it was of Israel. For example, we see "the elders of Moab and Midian" who sought Balaam's advice about the Israelites (Numbers 22:7); and the deceptive Gibeonites, whose reference to "our elders" obviously denoted their leaders (Joshua 9:11).

Bearing in mind our initial question about the "jurisdiction" of elders in the first-century church, these examples of elders in ancient times might appear to be less than helpful. Yet, what we learn is that "Israel's elders" (and quite possibly elders in the early church as well) operated on a variety of different levels. For example, on a level just below Israel's "national elders," as it were, we see Moses calling together twelve separate groups of Israel's elders at one time. "Assemble before me all the elders of your tribes..." said Moses, as Israel prepared to cross into the Promised Land. So obviously there were elders of *tribes* as well as elders for the whole nation; and from among these same tribal elders, the "national elders" evidently were chosen.

On yet another level down, we see elders exercising leadership among a *special gathering* of the Israelites, when all the other tribes waged civil war against the tribe of Benjamin. (The Benjamites had refused to punish the men of Gibeah who had raped and killed a Levite's concubine.) It was the "elders of the assembly" who came up with that creative, if ethically-dubious, plan to repopulate the decimated tribe of Benjamin (Judges 21:15-23).

Despite appearances, it is not as if a group of men had been appointed specially as *ad hoc* elders for this extraordinary assembly. Rather, in any assembly—no matter how large or small—Israel's leadership was always on the shoulders of whatever "wise old men" were present. Young men may have fought the military battles, but it was the sage old grey-beards who sorted out all the other problems.

Appointing Elders From Town To Town

When we come to the next level down, we are brought back to the very beginning of our discussion, and to the question about city-wide elders. It's interesting that what we see most frequently mentioned in the history of Israel's elders is their leadership *town by town*. Among many examples which could be cited, these "town fathers" were responsible for apprehending murderers who might flee unlawfully to one of the cities of refuge (Deuteronomy 19:11-12); for admitting to those same specially-designated cities any manslayer who had a lawful right to their protection (Joshua 20:1-6); and for presiding over the bizarre ceremony where an unsolved murder happened to occur outside their town (Deuteronomy 21:1-9). As these and other examples illustrate, Israel's elders were respected as wise judges over criminal, civil, and religious affairs.

Interestingly, however, they didn't sit on elevated "benches" in wood-paneled courtrooms like our modern judges. Instead, throughout the Scriptures they are almost always seen sitting at the gates to the city. For instance, while the "worthy woman" of Proverbs 31 is busily buzzing about, doing more than any woman could possibly do in 24 hours, it seems that "her husband is respected at the city gate, where he takes his seat among the elders of the land." (Travel to almost any middle-eastern country today, and you'll see how little has changed.)

There at the city gate each day, these elders would act as a kind of informal court. The law said, for example, that if anyone had a rebellious son, "his father and mother shall take hold of him and bring him to the elders at the gate of his town"

(Deuteronomy 21:18-21). Thereupon the elders were to preside over an immediate death by stoning! The same went for any new husband falsely claiming that his bride was not a virgin. Where there was a dispute about the matter, the law directed that "the girl's father and mother shall bring proof that she was a virgin to the town elders at the gate" (Deuteronomy 22:13-21). And the same procedure was followed in cases where the brother of a deceased husband refused to carry on that husband's name. "If a man does not want to marry his brother's wife, she shall go to the elders at the town gate..." (Deuteronomy 25:7-10).

Perhaps the best-known matter ever decided at the city gates was the case of the "kinsman-redeemer," when the aging Boaz was given the right to marry the lovely Ruth. The "video" we are shown of the occasion (in Ruth 4:1-12) is priceless. Boaz goes up to the town gate and engages the city fathers in casual conversation until the kinsman-redeemer comes along. The text then tells us that "Boaz took ten of the elders of the town and said, 'Sit here,' and they did so." Whereupon Boaz negotiates with the kinsman-redeemer for the right to marry Ruth, and the deal is sealed with the handing over of a sandal. To which "the elders and all those at the gate said, 'We are witnesses.'"

If this traditional role of Jewish elders is anything to go by, it would not have been unthinkable for elders in the primitive church to have had a city-wide responsibility for all the disciples among them, despite a multiplicity of house churches. The only question remains as to whether that Jewish pattern was followed in actual fact. Certainly, since no town or city would have been completely populated by Christians, there is no compelling reason why that practice necessarily would have a precise parallel in the primitive church.

Moreover, there is at least a hint of yet another level of "elder involvement" arising out of the story of David's fasting for the stricken son born of his adulterous relationship with Bathsheba. The text tells us that "the elders of his household stood beside [David] to get him up from the ground, but he refused, and he would not eat any food with them" (2 Samuel 12:17). Having "elders" in a household is perhaps our best clue yet that "elders" even in the first-century church might have had a significantly different connotation than we have tended to assume.

What We Know, And What We Don't

The point of all this history is to say, first of all, that no single model of eldership responsibility (whether in the Old or New Testaments) is conclusive on the issue of "jurisdiction." There is nothing to rule out the possibility that the role of elders in the early church might well have encompassed more than one level of involvement—even simultaneously. Perhaps there were elders shepherding the disciples in each house church, depending upon their size and make-up. And perhaps elder oversight may have been exercised throughout a group of house churches which collectively comprised a larger, recognizable "congregation."

More thought-provoking for us, of course, is the third possibility—that elders in individual house churches might also have come together as a group of city-wide elders to discuss matters of importance to the entire community of believers. Indeed, that may well have been the case with the Jerusalem conference, when "the apostles and elders, with the whole church," were joined together in resolving the Gentile question. Nothing in the record of the early disciples suggests that the "whole church" in Jerusalem met together on the first day of the week for one enormous fellowship memorial; and, therefore, nothing necessarily precludes "Jerusalem's elders" from being gathered from among elders in a multiplicity of house churches.

When we think of "the church of God in Corinth," we immediately tend to think of a single congregation with a single set of elders. But we simply aren't told. As we've already seen, the Corinthians almost certainly met in house churches for the weekly love feast. And who's to know what might be implied about elders from the fact that the Corinthians were divided into antagonistic cliques favoring Paul, Apollos, Cephas, or Christ? Given all of those factions, it's hard to believe there would have been a single, united group of elders. And yet, Paul seems to regard "the church in Corinth" as a single entity for purposes of his many commands and admonitions, many of which obviously were written in response to correspondence he had received from the Corinthian disciples at large.

Perhaps the most striking thing about Paul's Corinthian letters (as well as several others) is the absence of any mention whatsoever of elders. It's at least possible that elders were not yet appointed at the time of these writings. We know that, even after the time of Paul's imprisonment in Rome, there were still evangelized cities where the appointment of elders was "left unfinished" (Titus 1:5). On the other hand, one of Paul's "prison epistles" was specifically addressed "To all the saints in Christ Jesus at Philippi, together with the overseers and deacons" (Philippians 1:1).

In that regard, incidentally, not even the church in Philippi was necessarily a single congregation with a single set of elders and deacons. Would anyone think it inappropriate to refer to "all the saints in Christ Jesus in Nashville"—speaking of all the congregations collectively, each with its own leaders?

Despite many more uncertainties than we could wish, at least in Paul's salutation to the Philippians we have a sharply-focused picture of the model congregation in the first-century church. In whatever arrangements they regularly met together for fellowship and worship, the dynamic organism of the local congregation was not without organization. It was plainly *saints*, *overseers*, and *deacons*—with the overseers filling a role which apparently had changed little from the "wise old men" of ancient Israel.

"Elders" Chosen From Among Elders

Throughout the years, much ink has been spilled (and not a little blood!) over who should be appointed as elders, given the texts of 1 Timothy 3:1-7 and Titus 1:5-9. If within those two texts are arguably found certain technical "qualifications" for elders (such as being married, and having believing children), more importantly, there are distinctive *qualities* which ought to be characteristic of any man serving as a shepherd. Among those qualities is the importance of being blameless, hospitable, self-controlled, upright, holy, and disciplined—together with a whole host of "nots," as in *not* overbearing, quick-tempered, violent, given to drunkenness, or a lover of money.

Of course, these are qualities which all Christians should aspire to have, not just elders. But from the word *elder* itself, there is an element of maturity implied, and a proven track record which has already earned the respect of all concerned. Nor would it seem that these specifically-listed qualities were ever intended to be exhaustive. More likely, they merely exemplify the kind of godly character which has always been expected of God's shepherds throughout the centuries—a character surely demonstrated by the Jerusalem elders at least two decades before Paul penned the two lists of elder "qualifications" which we tend to view so technically.

Job captured the essence of a mature, older man of God when he asked, "Is not wisdom found among the aged? Does not long life bring understanding?" (Job 12:12). God has set "olders" among his people to shepherd them with wisdom, understanding, and discernment. To counsel. To encourage. To rebuke. To render crucial judgments in difficult and trying circumstances.

Instead of our thinking that "the office of an elder" requires men of certain qualities, the idea, really, is just the opposite. Paul's insistence on the kind of qualities which are found so uniquely in older, wiser, godly men was meant to define their very function as "elders." It's a matter of taking what godly "olders" have already been doing informally for years and formally recognizing that leadership within the congregation.

Yet, if these special "elder qualities" commended by Paul to Timothy and Titus are of a type which *all* mature Christian men ought to possess, why is it that we constantly seem to be plagued with "an elder shortage?" In congregation after congregation the complaint is made: "We simply don't have men who are qualified to be elders." Could this be because we are so focused on what it takes to be an *officially-recognized elder* that we've failed to develop whole congregations of men who, with increasing age, ought to manifest spiritual wisdom, understanding, and judgment?

The early disciples didn't officially appoint as an "elder" any man who wasn't already respected as a spiritual leader in the congregation. To have an "elder shortage" is to have a congregation devoid of "wise old men" from among whom overseers can be specially recognized. Which is to say that the problem is far more serious than simply lacking enough men to make the short-list. It depicts a congregation in which the men, generally, are not maturing spiritually consistent with their age. Young boys aren't being brought up to be spiritual men; and those who are older seem content to remain spiritually stagnant. Little wonder such a congregation has an elder crisis.

Filling the Vacuum

The widespread lack of mature Christian men is one of the most devastating results of not having a strong mutual ministry. When what you have, in effect, is a rather exclusive clergy system, the "laity" simply don't develop as they ought. As long as men can remain mostly-passive spectators, they will never become the kind of elder statesmen who are naturally sought out as spiritual leaders.

Which only compounds the problem. In the absence of true elder statesmen, we are forced to settle for overseers who are chosen, not so much for their spiritual maturity, but for their demonstrated success in worldly matters. This is not to say that elders can't also be successful in their normal employment. But look closely, and you will see far too many elders whose *chief* qualification for the job is that they are good businessmen, respected professionals, or even (in more rural communities) the most successful farmers. Of course, this approach is a perfect fit for what has become the most common model among today's "elderships:" that of a corporate board of directors.

One of the tell-tale signs of this corporate model is the practice, in some congregations, of having set "terms" for those who serve as elders. And *voting* them into office, or out of office. Of course, that's simply not how shepherds and flocks work. Nor "wise old men." Worse yet, instead of the church taking the model of shepherd leadership into the world, we have brought the world's model of doing business into the church.

At that point, it becomes a matter of *chickens* and *eggs*. Do we have the "corporate board model" because of the kind of men we have appointed as elders; or are we appointing that kind of elders because they are most likely to be good "board members?" The answer, of course, is "yes." *Both!* No prizes for guessing why the *next* generation of the church then produces so few spiritual shepherds.

Elders As Gatekeepers

If elders are not to be "board members" for a "corporate church," what are they to be? From the historical association between Israel's elders and the city gates, one would not go far wrong to think of elders as *gatekeepers*. Ever wonder why Israel's spiritual leaders sat around at the city gates? A good guess is that they were keeping a close eye on who was coming into the community and who was leaving. In an era of great fluidity in "church membership," do elders today (especially in larger congregations) know who is coming in to be fed, and who is leaving, perhaps because they are *not* being fed?

Israel's gatekeepers were not only judges over matters in dispute, but as watchmen at the gate, they used their wisdom and understanding to judge with discernment between those who were bringing prosperity to the city, and those who were bent on destruction. With that in mind, Paul's warning to the Ephesian elders takes on added meaning. "I know that after I leave, savage wolves will come in among you and will not spare the flock" (Acts 20:29). Therefore, he tells them: Guard the flock over which you have been made watchmen.

One need only experience the present foot-and-mouth crisis in this green and pleasant land to appreciate how Britain's shepherds have become vigilant watchmen with eyes literally fixed on the gates to their fields. With today's "wolves" being a deadly killer virus, you can be sure that all the gates are locked shut, and warning signs clearly posted. Do our shepherds in the church understand the seriousness of today's spiritual crisis in which a virulent strain of cultural values is silently and inexorably destroying God's people? What's being done to shut the gates? What warning signs are being posted?

Using a similar pastoral metaphor, Jesus spoke of the way in which he—as the Good Shepherd—would come through the gate to save those within the fold. "The man who enters by the gate is the shepherd of his sheep," said Jesus. "The watchman opens the gate for him, and the sheep listen to his voice. He calls his own sheep by name and leads them out. When he has brought out all his own, he goes on ahead of them, and his sheep follow him because they know his voice" (John 10:2-4).

The three-fold application is obvious. Elders, first of all, are to be the watchmen taking responsibility for who comes and goes within their fellowship. Second, like Jesus, they are only able to lead their congregations effectively when they know each disciple by name. And finally, the congregation is willing to follow the lead of their elders because they recognize their *voices*.

Not the voice of a hired hand, mind you, but the voices of the shepherds themselves.

Elders As Teachers

There is much more to say about this later, but if we are ever to radically restore primitive Christian practice, we will have to seriously rethink the matter of whose voice is being heard by the congregation. Without in the least disparaging those who have committed themselves wholeheartedly to the preaching of the gospel, there is an ominous warning in Jesus' comparison between shepherds themselves and those who might be hired by shepherds. "I am the good shepherd," said Jesus. "The good shepherd lays down his life for the sheep. The hired hand is not the shepherd who owns the sheep. So when he sees the wolf coming, he abandons the sheep and runs away. Then the wolf attacks the flock and scatters it. The man runs away because he is a hired hand and cares nothing for the sheep" (John 10:11-13).

Not to put too fine an edge on it, the fact is that preachers come and preachers go (even dedicated, stalwart, and conscientious preachers, many of whom are hapless victims of a hire-and-fire mentality). But the shepherds always remain; and with them remains a responsibility which preachers will never have in quite the same way (if for no other reason than that preachers come and preachers go!). And so the congregation needs to hear a consistent, recognizable voice from those who are called to lay down their lives for the flock.

Of one thing we can be sure: in the first-century church, the shepherds didn't *hire* shepherds to feed their flocks for them. *They themselves fed the flock!* Much has been said about the incorrectness of addressing preachers as "pastors." But if we're truly honest, who today is feeding the flock? Whose voice, both figuratively and literally, is being heard week-in and week-out?

Perhaps the problem is not so much a matter of misapplied *titles* as misunderstood *roles*.

Sadly, there is an old joke about elders being "apt to teach" (as the King James Version puts it). Of a certain elder it is said: "He's apt to teach if he feels like it, but not if he doesn't!" Of course, the meaning of *apt* was never intended to be "inclined to," but rather "able to." From Paul we learn that a shepherd must be "able to teach" (1 Timothy 3:2), ostensibly because teaching is a principal part of the role which he is to play. In his letter to Titus, Paul highlights that responsibility, saying that the elder "must hold firmly to the trustworthy message [as taught by the apostles] *so that* he can encourage others by sound doctrine and refute those who oppose it" (Titus 1:9).

Indeed, it is clear that some of the elders in the apostolic church devoted themselves full-time to this calling. "The elders who direct the affairs of the church well are worthy of double honor," says Paul, "especially those whose work is preaching and teaching." Although it is possible to construe Paul's words as implying that only some of the elders engaged in preaching and teaching, the context has an altogether different emphasis. In the very next sentence we read: "For the Scripture says, 'Do not muzzle the ox while it is treading out the grain,' and 'The worker deserves his wages'" (1 Timothy 5:17-18).

Paul, here, is specifically referring to those elders who have given up other income-earning jobs to do, full-time, the teaching which all elders must be "apt" to do (even, presumably, if only privately, one-to-one). Indeed, we see the same association between elders and teaching when Paul tells us that Christ "gave some to be apostles, some to be prophets, some to be evangelists, and some to be...[as if said in one breath]...*pastors and teachers*" (Ephesians 4:12). Like Siamese twins joined at the hip, to be a *pastor* is inseparable from being a *teacher*.

Teaching, of course, is what the Good Shepherd himself did. And what the apostles did. When seven men were chosen to serve the Grecian widows (Acts 6:1-6), the apostles said to the disciples, "It would not be right for us to neglect the ministry of the word of God in order to wait on tables." There's not a thing wrong with waiting on tables, but the apostles had a special role to fill: proclaiming God's Word.

And, as also indicated, being given to prayer. Even in this, however, what we are shown about elders and prayer seems equally pastoral. In one of Scripture's most intriguing texts, James tells the person who is "sick" to "call the elders of the church to pray over him and anoint him with oil in the name of the Lord" (James 5:14-16). Maybe physical illness is all that James had in mind. But, if so, why does he add: "If he has sinned, he will be forgiven?" And, "Therefore confess your sins to each other and pray for each other so that you may be healed?" The most likely answer is that James considered the role of elders to encompass not only the pastoral feeding of the Word, but also the physical and spiritual healing of sin-sick souls which can come when godly men of the Word lift up prayers.

In the matter of the Grecian widows, the division of responsibility between the apostles and the men chosen to "wait tables," helps to make more sense of that curious pairing: *the apostles and elders*. In many respects, the apostles were prototype elders. As we saw earlier, the Apostle Peter made a special appeal to elders, speaking "as a fellow elder" (1 Peter 5:1). And the Apostle John began both his second and third letters by referring to himself as "the elder."

Does this mean that today's elders have "authority" like the apostles? No, not in the sense of having miraculous authority over demons, death, and disease; or exercising Spirit-directed, divine authority over the whole church. However, the Hebrew writer says in no uncertain terms: "*Obey* your leaders and submit to their *authority*. They keep watch over you as men who must give an account" (Hebrews 13:17).

Looking more closely, we see the precise source of that authority, when the writer says, "Remember your leaders, *who spoke the word of God to you*" (13:7). When shepherds are teaching God's Word, they are also conveying God's authority, and therefore are to be obeyed. (It's not unlike the call for children to obey their parents *in the Lord*.)

We see this point even clearer when Paul says, "Now we ask you, brothers, to respect those who work hard among you, who are over you in the Lord and who admonish you" (1 Thessalonians 5:12). Note the connection between "over you" and "admonish you." *Admonishing* (through the proclamation of the Word) is the very means by which elders have their oversight authority.

If there is any significant difference between Israel's "gatekeeping" elders and those in the primitive church, it might well be an added emphasis on *feeding*, not just judging and guiding. Without priests and rabbis, the burden of teaching would have fallen more than ever on the shepherds' shoulders. In that light, perhaps we would do well to call our overseers "pastors" instead of "elders." Maybe it would remind us of their primary role, not as a decision-makers, but as shepherds who feed their flocks.

In the fields beside our cottage, I've seen an amazing picture scores of times. It's of a shepherd with a bucket in his hand, and a whole flock of sheep following closely behind. For elders, bishops, overseers, and especially "pastors," that's what it's all about: leading by feeding. *Personally* feeding.

But just look who's carrying the bucket these days....

When Shepherds Go AWOL

One of the most interesting commentaries on Israel's spiritual leaders comes at the end of Joshua's life. With a glow of commendation, the text tells us that "Israel served the LORD throughout the lifetime of Joshua and of the elders who outlived him and who had experienced everything the LORD had done for Israel" (Joshua 24:31). What a refreshing contrast that is compared with the way the book of Judges ends, despairing that "In those days Israel had no king; and everyone did as he saw fit" (Judges 21:25). It just shows the influence for good that elders can have among God's people; and how quickly that influence can dissipate when elders shirk their leadership responsibility.

To me, the most intriguing part of that woeful epitaph at the end of Judges is the phrase: "In those days Israel had no king." Surely, this wasn't meant to suggest that Israel's moral and spiritual standards would somehow be superior under the rule of a king! History would soon prove that Israel's kings ushered in the nation's greatest period of idolatry, war, and destruction. Undoubtedly, then, the point was that, in the absence of a king, there was no authority whatsoever in Israel, whether good or bad. It was a time of political, moral, and spiritual anarchy.

So where were Israel's elders in the midst of all this chaos...?

Significantly, the only mention of Israel's elders during the entire period of the judges is of their questionable plan to repopulate the tribe of Benjamin (a scheme which involved both deception and coercion in aid of evading a solemn oath.)[11] Given such a serious lapse in judgment on the part of those who should have been the wisest, most understanding and discerning among all of Israel, it's no wonder that "everyone did as he saw fit." Where utilitarian pragmatism (whatever works!) is the order of the day among the shepherds, you can be sure that the flock will follow suit.

There is profound irony in what we are told about how kings came about in Israel in the first place. The fact is that "all the elders of Israel gathered together and came to Samuel at Ramah. They said to him, 'You are old, and your sons do not

---

11 That the Bible records this incident is not necessarily to say God approved of the elders' actions any more than God approved of Jacob's deceiving Isaac—despite how God later used Jacob in revealing himself to mankind.

walk in your ways; now appoint a king to lead us, such as all the other nations have'" (1 Samuel 8:4-5).

Who was it that wanted to do things the way the world did them? Israel's own spiritual shepherds—the very men on whose shoulders God had placed responsibility for leading his people! Never underestimate the willingness of those in charge to abdicate their responsibility and put it on someone else's shoulders. Nor the seductive lure of leading as the world leads, instead of leading in the manner God has called them to lead.

Of all the things in the church today which need to be radically restored, nothing is of greater urgency than bringing elders back to their role of prayer and proclamation (which, at least relative to prayer, has seen great strides over the past couple of decades). Wherever it still lingers, the board-of-directors approach to "eldering" is, by any measure, an abomination. Interminable "elders meetings" to decide matters having little to do with the spiritual health of the flock are a mockery. And abdicating responsibility for teaching and preaching of the Word by hiring professional "pulpit ministers" (as distinct from full-time elders) couldn't be more misguided.

What will it take for us to see how far removed most of our congregations are from the pattern of leadership in the early church? To honestly admit that there's been a paradigm shift of the greatest magnitude? To have the courage to fundamentally change how we are fed and led?

When the dereliction of Israel's elders finally resulted in Jerusalem's destruction and the exile of those self-same elders, the lament of Lamentations (5:14) said it all: "The elders are gone from the city gate...." Simultaneously, that statement spoke to both cause and effect. The reason Israel's elders were "gone from the city gate" is because they had long since abandoned what they were supposed to do at the city gate! They had let somebody else do their job. They had been content to be administrators and decision-makers, but they had forgotten what it meant to be *shepherds* among God's people.

If you are one of our many dedicated shepherds today, wondering why—despite hours of endless meetings—your flock seems so often to go astray, catch the next plane to England and come to Buckland. I'll show you some other shepherds in the midst of their own crisis.

In fact, that's one of them over there. The one with his eyes on the gate...and a bucket in his hand.

CHAPTER TEN

PULPIT MINISTERS: PATENT PENDING

One of the tragedies of our time is that the minister is both
overworked and unemployed; overworked in a multitude of tasks that
do not have the slightest connection with religion
and unemployed in the serious concerns and exacting labors of main-
taining a disciplined spiritual life among mature men and women.

SAMUEL H. MILLER

The letter which came across my desk was from a congregation where I had spoken several years ago. It's one of the many medium-sized, mainstream congregations which form the bedrock of the church. Fundamentally sound in doctrine, it is energetic in pursuit of Kingdom objectives, and traditional in its worship format, yet without fear of being innovative within the bounds of propriety. For many years, I have had a special friendship with several of its members, and count the whole congregation as faithful brothers and sisters in Christ.

As the letter explained, they were in the process of hiring a new pulpit minister, and the Search Committee was asking for recommendations of potential candidates. I suppose I shouldn't have been surprised by the "Pulpit Minister Job Description" which was attached. Over the years, I've received numerous similar missives. But this time something was different. As I began to read, my heart sank lower and lower with every line. I don't know. Maybe it's just that my antennae are fully extended these days. In case you've never seen one of these "search letters," you may find it as jolting as I did. (Or perhaps not. The fact that such letters are fairly standard speaks volumes in itself.) The two-page "Job Description," beginning with the following preface, unwittingly painted a picture which, I fear, is all too familiar:

The person filling this position shall be an experienced pulpit minister, firmly rooted in the Word, who lives a Christ-centered life. He will be supported by a Youth Minister, a part-time Associate Minister, a part-time Counselor, eight (8) elders, 23 deacons and secretarial staff members. The pulpit minister must be able to interface with a broad range of believers. He will serve under the direction of the elders, who have the responsibility for the entire staff.

Duties and Responsibilities
1.   Challenge the members and facilitate their spiritual growth and dedication.
2.   Preach on Sunday mornings and evenings and be responsible for the Wednesday evening devotionals; may develop and present scheduled radio or TV sermons.
3.   Plan sermons, with the advice and counsel of the elders, which are consonant with the needs of the congregation.
4.   Teach a Bible Class at least once each week (Sunday morning or Wednesday night).
5.   Write or edit a weekly Bulletin which is distributed to all members, other congregations, and individuals who request it.
6.   May provide material for the Sunday morning and Wednesday night Announcements.
7.   Present a balanced ministry that addresses service, faithfulness, morality, relationships, spiritual growth, leadership, temptations and other areas that affect families and individuals.
8.   Provide ministerial counseling to members in times of crises and/or refer them to professional counselors.

9. *Be acquainted with every ministry of the congregation in order to maintain harmony and unity.*

10. *Attend meetings of the elders and of the elders, deacons, and ministry leaders. Submit monthly activity reports to the elders prior to their meeting.*

11. *Work with other staff members in optimizing programs of the congregation.*

12. *Maintain regular, posted office hours—available for meeting with members.*

13. *Visit the sick and shut-ins as time allows.*

14. *Speak at special functions and conduct mission meetings at the direction of the elders.*

15. *Whenever possible, attend functions outside the church setting where our members are involved—e.g., civic clubs, school activities, ball games, plays, etc.*

Qualifications

Hold a baccalaureate degree in a pertinent field, or equivalent
Have a demonstrated record of progressive professional development
Be able to communicate effectively; computer literacy preferable
Have at least five years of pulpit ministry experience, or equivalent

Thereafter followed a listing of "Credentials Required," including a résumé; statement of ministry philosophy; salary and benefits history; recent sermon tape; and the usual three personal references. Under the heading "Salary and Benefits," we learn that the salary is to be "commensurate with education and experience," and are given further information regarding sick leave; medical insurance; annual leave; absences for gospel meetings; opportunities to attend lectureships and seminars; the retirement program; and holidays (which happily include the 4th of July and the employee's birthday).

Birthdays? Civic clubs? Monthly activity reports? What can I say? Where do I begin?

That any congregation in the first century would ever have drafted such a job description simply begs belief. Can there be any lingering doubts about typical "elderships" today being little more than boards of directors who, "having responsibility for the entire staff," hire pulpit ministers to do the work that God has assigned to elders themselves?

And maybe even the work of deacons as well...?

CEO and "One-Man Band"

If I went no further than to make the case that today's preachers are invariably overworked "one-man bands," I expect I would be elected unanimously as union president for the Brotherhood of Pulpit Preachers, and every minister around would hit the picket lines at midnight! What we see listed in this particular job description reflects the expectations in virtually every congregation I have ever known. It's all there: preaching, weekly bulletins, announcements, counseling, organizational meetings, office hours, hospital visitations, and, of course, showing up for those all-important ball games.

And we wonder why the preacher's sermons aren't more thoughtful! And why we rarely sense a genuine struggling with the text, or the depth of insight which comes only through long hours of solitude with the Word. As someone who knows the time and effort it takes to prepare meaningful lessons, my hat is off to preachers who must come to the plate and attempt to hit a spiritual home run, Sunday-in and Sunday-out. That alone would be hard work without also having to juggle half-a-dozen other ministerial balls in the air at the same time.

Yet, surely we shouldn't be surprised at the multi-tasking wizardry expected of our pulpit ministers. It fits perfectly with the corporate model which most congregations have adopted, all the way up the line to the Chief Executive Officer. The one who is the *real* leader in the congregation. The one who sets the course and is expected to deliver. The one who often manages the day-to-day operations.

Certainly, I'm also aware that, for every congregation where the governing board of elders weakly follows behind the CEO-minister, there are an equal number of "elderships" which are so possessive of their power and authority that the preacher is the last to learn what's going on, and has no say whatsoever in matters affecting the congregation. His job is to perform every piece in the repertoire of the "one-man band," and then go off into a corner. Far from his presence being required at elders meetings, the preacher is regularly excluded unless specifically summoned.

Whether the elders take an active or a passive role as overseers, one thing is painfully obvious: Each model is typically characterized by an absence of involvement on the part of the elders in directly feeding their flocks. That's the preacher's job. That's why we hire him. That's why we require him to be specially trained in religious studies and be an above-average communicator.

Incidentally, did you notice in the job description that there was no mention of any teaching role that the elders themselves might be taking? (I know for a fact that the capable associate minister in that particular congregation is also an elder, but even that is not usual.) Wouldn't it be interesting to see a "Job Description for Elders?" Is there any chance it would include teaching and preaching as a primary function?

Unfortunately, once the corporate model replaces the biblical model, the problem becomes cyclical. When the elders hire a professionally-trained minister to preach the Word, they become almost as dependent upon his expertise in the Scriptures as the rest of the congregation. (What's worse, the less they, themselves, study and teach the Word, the less likely they are to challenge his understanding, and thus the more likely to be swayed by his views.) Then it all comes full circle. To whatever extent the elders lack proficiency in the Scriptures, they are almost forced to hire a professional preacher to proclaim the Word for them.

And so they search for the best pulpit man they can find. The most bombastic, if that's what seems to count. Or the most energetic and entertaining. Or the most soothing. Or (rarely) the most spiritually challenging. Yet, whatever the preferred pulpit presence, everything else beneath the surface is basically the same. The choice is between a *bombastic* "one-man band," or an *entertaining* "one-man band." Or between a *soothing* one, or perhaps a *scholarly* one. But in the end, the popular man in the pulpit had better be certain to make his appointed rounds at the hospital...and did we mention getting out to all those ball games?

Despite their availability in a limitless range of colors and styles, "one-man bands" are all pretty much of a type: simultaneously overworked and under-utilized. *Overworked* in pastoral and ministerial roles which others have been called to fill; and *under-utilized* in the work of evangelism for which they should be specially gifted.

Before any more "search letters" circulate among us, I propose we need to make an altogether different kind of search for a pulpit minister—a search of the Scriptures to see if there was any such role in the apostolic church. I realize I'm treading where angels fear to tread, but it simply has to be said: Search the text high and low, and you'll never find any semblance of what we know of today as pulpit ministers.

To begin with, of course, there is not the slightest hint in Scripture of weekly bulletins, announcements, organizational meetings, office hours, nor certainly civic clubs or ball games. All of that comes straight out of the popular Handbook For Denominational Ministers. Call them what you will—"pulpit ministers," "preachers," or "evangelists"—the role and function which they traditionally discharge is no less a human invention than infant baptism, sprinkling, and confirmation.

I assure you that this blunt indictment does not come with any sense of joy on my part. After all, I'm only talking about a number of personal heroes in the faith who have given lifetimes to pulpit proclamation of the Word; and about my own father who was the quintessential pulpit minister for over forty years, preaching his last sermon on the morning of the day he died. And then, of course, there's myself. I have been the "pulpit minister" (albeit self-supported) for two congregations in the northwest, and have preached in countless other pulpits over the years. The stones I'm throwing are falling dangerously close to my own glass house. Yet, what else can we conclude in the face of a biblical record devoid of such an office? How can we have denounced so blithely the denominational "pastor system" without ever being honest enough to look into our own mirror?

Not To Be Confused With Evangelists

Surely at this point you must be asking: "But what about *evangelists*? Don't we have more than ample textual support for evangelists?" Indeed we do, beginning with Paul's assertion that God "gave some to be apostles, some to be prophets, some to be evangelists..." (Ephesians 4:11). But are today's pulpit ministers (or "preachers," if you prefer) really and truly *evangelists*?

Take a closer look at the job description we saw earlier. Apart from vague references to "scheduled radio or TV sermons" and conducting "mission meetings at the direction of the elders," the focus was clearly inward: "challenging the members" and meeting "the needs of the congregation." Not one direct word about evangelizing the lost. Nothing to suggest that converting people to Christ was the primary purpose for which the minister would be supported. When we think of a preacher today whose principal responsibility is to carry the good news of salvation out into the teeming masses of the unsaved, we tend to think of them only as missionaries in some foreign land.

If there is a time for evangelists to disciple those whom they have converted (and there is), those disciples must first be converted. Or as Paul put it: "How, then, can they call on the one they have not believed in? And how can they believe in the one of whom they have not heard? And how can they hear without someone preaching to them? And how can they preach unless they are sent? As it is written, 'How beautiful are the feet of those who bring good news!'" (Romans 10:14-15).

The metaphor of beautiful feet bringing good news doesn't exactly fit feet which are firmly fixed in pulpits. The role of an evangelist is to *be sent*. To convict and to convert. To establish and to train, and then to be sent out all over again—each time turning over the work of "pastoring" these new disciples to the shepherds whom God has set among his sheep for that very purpose.

In this regard, it is instructive to look *where* the first-century evangelists did most of their preaching. You can be certain it was not in the pulpits of comfortable church buildings before familiar audiences. It was out and about among people of misdirected faith, or no faith at all. If it was not in the synagogue on the Sabbath, "as was usual," (Acts 13:5; 13:14; 14:1; 18:19; 19:8), it was wherever else devout Jews were worshiping. When Lydia was converted, for example, Luke tells us that he and Paul's whole entourage "went outside the city gate to the river, where we expected to find a place of prayer." Paul took his opportunities when and where he could get them: whether on Mars Hill among the Athenian philosophers (Acts 17:16-34); or in the lecture hall at Ephesus (Acts 19:8-10); or publicly and from house to house (Acts 20:20). Philip, of course, proclaimed the good news in a chariot along a dusty road, and then "traveled about, preaching the gospel in all the towns..." (Acts 8:26-40).

Does this sound anything like our resident pulpit ministers today who mostly preach to the choir of the already-converted? True, Paul's teaching in the lecture hall of Tyrannus "went on for two years," but his "daily discussions" produced the result that "all the Jews and Greeks who lived in the province of Asia heard the word of the Lord." Not just those who were already Christians. And not just on Sundays and Wednesday nights. This was a protracted, two-year, *daily* gospel meeting aimed directly at reaching the lost.

The Rising Demand For a Professional Clergy

Are you old enough to remember when our preachers were hired on the basis of their intimate familiarity with the Scriptures, and not on whether they possessed a B.A. or an M.Div—or even a diploma from a "preachers training school?" In many congregations today, that would never do. Even accounting for the fact that educational standards have risen across the board in the last several decades, there is no doubt that we are demanding higher and higher levels of professionalism from those who fill staff positions in the church.

On one level, of course, the only requirement for evangelists in the first-century church was that they be persecuted. "Those who had been scattered [because of persecution] preached the word wherever they went" (Acts 8:4). At one point, that must have included most of the disciples in Jerusalem, since "all except the apostles were scattered throughout Judea and Samaria" (Acts 8:1). It goes without saying, of course, that no baccalaureate degrees were required. Or five years of pulpit ministry experience; or statements of ministry philosophy; or salary and benefits histories; or whatever the equivalent of "sermon tapes" would have been.

More important still, I wonder if our search letter's requirement that the minister "be able to communicate effectively" had the same connotation in the primitive church as it does today. Certainly, no one questions the effectiveness of first-century evangelists. Though rejected by multitudes, they nevertheless turned the world upside down for Christ! But not because they were skilled orators or smooth talkers. And certainly not because they were professionally trained seminarians. Lest we forget, there weren't any "schools of preaching" back then; nor Bible Departments in Christian universities; nor yet graduate schools of religion issuing advanced degrees in a wide variety of specialized fields.

That these successful evangelists were not "professionals" became a source of perplexed derision for the theologians in the Sanhedrin. "When they saw the courage of Peter and John and realized that they were unschooled, ordinary men, they were astonished..." (Acts 4:13).

Of course, Paul, the ultimate evangelist, was an educated theologian in his own right. "Under Gamaliel," said Paul in defense of his apostleship, "I was thoroughly trained in the law of our fathers..." (Acts 22:3). (As we learn in Acts 5:34, Gamaliel was one of the most renowned and respected teachers in the first century.) So obviously there is no penalty for formal biblical study or dedicated scholarship.

And yet, what I can never quite understand (because it seems so incongruous with Paul's eloquent writing), is his self-deprecation when it comes to the skills of oral communication. Paul says, for example, "When I came to you, brothers, I did not come with eloquence or superior wisdom as I proclaimed to you the testimony about God." And again, "I came to you in weakness and fear, and with much trembling. My message and my preaching were not with wise and persuasive words, but with a demonstration of the Spirit's power, so that your faith might not rest on men's wisdom, but on God's power" (1 Corinthians 2:1-5).

Just when we are ready to think that Paul purposely hid his eloquence under a bushel so that his communication skills would not upstage the power of the message itself, we hear his astounding admission: "I may not be a trained speaker, but I do have knowledge" (2 Corinthians 11:6). Can it really be? The Apostle Paul, truly not an eloquent speaker? It's hard to imagine.

But if, in fact, that's the case, what's even harder to imagine is that he would ever be hired today as a pulpit minister! In current parlance, he wouldn't qualify as "an effective communicator." What, not a silver-tongued orator? Not smooth and articulate? Who would ever want to sit and listen to someone like that speak until well past midnight? No wonder Eutychus fell asleep!

It's hard to say which is the greater problem: that we've elevated style over substance to such a degree that we can no longer tolerate thoughtful, but unexciting preaching; or that we've created a role and function in pulpit ministers which virtually begs for a professional style of communicating which was unknown in the apostolic church.

When the *qualifications* for preachers of the gospel change that dramatically, alarm bells ought to go off, warning us that our *definition* of a preacher has also changed dramatically. Pulpit ministers may have to be "effective communicators," but biblical evangelists only had to *communicate effectively*. And that they did.

The key wasn't "being a professional." The key was *professing*.

On the Road; On the Payroll

To say that first-century evangelists were nothing like today's professional preachers is not to say they weren't paid. It's all well and good to point to Paul's occupation as a tentmaker as he supported himself in Corinth while proclaiming the gospel (Acts 18:1-4). There are times and circumstances, even today, in which this practice would be good precedent. But Luke immediately tells us that, "When Silas and Timothy came from Macedonia, Paul devoted himself exclusively to preaching..." (Acts 18:5).

Piecing together the relevant texts, it appears that this shift from self-support to full-time evangelism was made possible by virtue of a generous gift from the Philippian brethren (apparently brought by Silas and Timothy). "As you Philippians know," he later would write, "in the early days of your acquaintance with the gospel, when I set out from Macedonia, not one church shared with me in the matter of giving and receiving, except you only..." (Philippians 4:15).

Not only do we have this example of an evangelist being financially supported, but through Paul we also learn specifically that "the Lord has commanded that those who preach the gospel should receive their living from the gospel" (1 Corinthians 9:14). Adding punch to that command, Paul cites the familiar Old Testament reference to "not muzzling the ox treading out the grain," then asks rhetorically: "Who serves as a soldier at his own expense? Who plants a vineyard and does not eat of its grapes? Who tends a flock and does not drink of the milk?" (1 Corinthians 9:7-9). "If others have this right of support..." Paul concludes, then why shouldn't he?

Indeed, why shouldn't every evangelist!

Evangelists In the Early Church

Of course, we have accepted the principle of supporting preachers for as long as they have been around. Therefore, the only real issue is whether these fully-supported preachers ought to serve principally in pulpits or somewhere outside the pulpit. For a brotherhood of pulpit preachers who regularly advocate restoring first-century Christian practice, actually doing "the work of an evangelist" (2 Timothy 4:5) must certainly be that part of the restoration plea which hits closest to home. Especially when the word "Evangelist" is printed on their business cards or on the sign outside the building. Is this the same kind of "Evangelist" we read about in the primitive church?

Appearing, as they do, in the early stages of the church, Stephen and Philip provide some of our first insight into the function of evangelists, although theirs was a more complex role than anything we might expect today. For one thing, they both exercised spiritual gifts. "Now Stephen, a man full of God's grace and power, did great wonders and miraculous signs among the people" (Acts 6:8). And "when the crowds heard Philip and saw the miraculous signs he did, they all paid close attention to what he said. With shrieks, evil spirits came out of many, and many paralytics and cripples were healed" (Acts 8:6-7).

Even more intriguing, these two evangelists were among "the Seven" earlier chosen to supervise the daily distribution to the Grecian widows (Acts 6:5; 21:8). It doesn't exactly take us back to the ministerial "one-man band" concept, but it does demonstrate that men "full of the Spirit and wisdom" can be used in more ways than one for the advancement of the Kingdom. Who knows what further evangelistic role Stephen might have played had he not been an early martyr to the cause? All we know is that he was killed for the very reason that he was proclaiming Jesus as the crucified and risen Messiah.

Hurriedly leaving Jerusalem in the wake of Stephen's death, Philip traveled to Samaria where he "preached the good news of the kingdom of God and the name of Jesus Christ," resulting in many Samaritans' being baptized (Acts 8:4-13). And, of course, we know that Philip preached to the Ethiopian eunuch, and "in all the towns until he reached Caesarea." Interestingly, it is in Caesarea that we next see Philip, when Paul is his house-guest on the way to Jerusalem to face arrest. "Leaving the next day," says Luke's record, "we reached Caesarea and stayed at the house of Philip the evangelist..." (Acts 21:8).

Suddenly, of course, questions begin to fly!

Is that Philip, the *former* evangelist; or Philip, the *current* evangelist? Over twenty years have passed since we last heard of Philip doing any evangelizing. Assuming Caesarea has been his home throughout this time, has he become a "located preacher"? Is he now a "pulpit minister," preaching weekly sermons to one of the congregations in Caesarea (and acting as CEO, hospital visitor, and bulletin editor); or is he still engaged full-time in reaching out to the lost? Or indeed both? The fact is, we just don't know. But since Luke calls him an "evangelist," the most likely scenario is that he is still doing what he was doing when we last saw him: preaching the gospel to the lost.

No law says an evangelist has to constantly be on the move; just continually moving others to Christ. The question is not whether the evangelist is "located," but whether the one who is "located" is an evangelist.

Paul's Special Envoys

Paul's charge to Timothy, which we mentioned earlier, comes laden with the obvious question: Just what is "the work of an evangelist?" I suggest it's not without reason that today's "pulpit ministers" have evolved from the early "evangelists." For, unless we are careful with the historical context in which the first-century church existed, it is easy for us to mistakenly assume that Timothy—the prototype evangelist—was also the prototype pulpit minister.

When, for example, Paul says to his young protégé, "Devote yourself to the public reading of Scripture, to preaching and to teaching" (1 Timothy 4:13), he seems to describe an outwardly-focused evangelist, preaching to the unsaved. Yet, when he says, "If you point these things out to the *brothers*, you will be a good *minister* of Christ Jesus..." (1 Timothy 4:6), our ears immediately hear a description sounding more like today's pulpit ministers.

To be sure, Timothy was both an evangelist to the lost, and in some sense a "minister" to the saved. But we must bear in mind what's going on behind that dual role. The text tells us that Timothy—along with Barnabas, Silas, John Mark, and Titus (and possibly Apollos)—served in a unique, almost "semi-apostolic" role in the fledgling church (especially when appointing elders). These men were Paul's deputies, if you will—his personal emissaries. They traveled about, acting on Paul's behalf.

Paul told the Thessalonians, for example, that he had sent Timothy to them out of necessity, since he himself was unable to leave Athens. "We sent Timothy," he said, "to strengthen and encourage you in your faith, so that no one would be unsettled by these trials." Timothy's special mission to Thessalonica was not exactly evangelistic, but neither did he become what we might call an "interim pulpit preacher." His mission of encouragement accomplished, Timothy returned to Paul, bringing "good news about [their] faith and love" (1 Thessalonians 3:6).

On another occasion, during Paul's third evangelistic mission, we see that Paul "sent two of his helpers, Timothy and Erastus, to Macedonia, while he stayed in the province of Asia a little longer" (Acts 19:22). And we also see Timothy's role as Paul's personal emissary in the letter to the disciples in Corinth. "If Timothy comes, see to it that he has nothing to fear while he is with you, for he is carrying on the work of the Lord, just as I am" (1 Corinthians 16:10-11).

Finally, from Paul's "prison epistle" to the Philippians, we learn that Timothy was by his side in Rome. "I hope in the Lord Jesus," says Paul proudly, "to send Timothy to you soon....I have no one else like him, who takes a genuine interest in your welfare.... You know that Timothy has proved himself, because as a son with his father he has served with me in the work of the gospel" (Philippians 2:19-22).

The point of all this background history on Timothy is to inject a note of caution for anyone who might wish to cite Timothy as precedent for an "evangelist" being a "pulpit man" in some local congregation. While it is true that Paul's two personal letters to Timothy seem to encourage his teaching among those who are already disciples, it should not be thought that Timothy was ever the kind of pulpit minister with which we are familiar.

After all the years of mission evangelism, the time had come for discipling the hundreds, if not thousands, of new converts in Asia, Macedonia, Achaia, and elsewhere. Without the benefit of having the New Testament in hand, as we have, these babes in Christ needed instruction about "how people ought to conduct themselves in God's household" (1 Timothy 3:14-15). They needed to know about godliness and the Christian lifestyle; about relationships between masters and servants, families and widows; and about elders and deacons, and the principle of male spiritual leadership. Above all, they needed to be warned to "keep the pattern of sound teaching"; to "correctly handle the word of truth"; and to watch out for false teachers who "will say what [people's] itching ears want to hear."

Standing in Paul's own shoes, as it were, Timothy was to "command certain men not to teach false doctrines"; to entrust Paul's teaching "to reliable men who will also be qualified to teach others"; and to "lay hands" (but not hastily) on those who were to be specially gifted or commissioned.

There is no doubt that, like Timothy, today's pulpit ministers can "preach the word" and—through the Scriptures— "correct, rebuke, and encourage" so that "the man of God may be thoroughly equipped for every good work." Then again, there is no reason why the elders couldn't do the same. And that, really, is what makes Timothy's ministry to the wider church in those initial years so unique.

We know, of course, that Timothy himself received a spiritual gift "when the body of elders laid their hands" on him (1 Timothy 4:14). But the fact that Paul goes to great pains to set out the qualities and responsibilities of elders and deacons tells us that, still at this time, many of the congregations were not fully established with spiritual leaders.

This situation explains why, in a letter remarkably similar to Timothy's two letters, Paul tells Titus that he had left him in Crete to "straighten out what was unfinished and appoint elders..." (Titus 1:5). Apparently, Titus' work of "finishing and appointing" did not end even there in Crete. The last we hear of him, he's gone off to Dalmatia (2 Timothy 4:10)—surely not to be a "pulpit minister," but once again to evangelize and set the church in order—then leave the work in the capable hands of godly pastors.

Go Into All the World

So what is the role of an evangelist? Call it "church planting," if you will. When the Corinthian disciples came down with a bad case of "preacheritis," Paul brought them up shortly, saying, "I planted the seed, Apollos watered it, but God made it grow....The man who plants and the man who waters have one purpose..." (1 Corinthians 3:5-9). Then changing the metaphor, he said to them: "I laid a foundation as an expert builder, and someone else is building on it" (3:10).

The role of an evangelist, then, is planting and watering; and laying foundations for others to build on. With either metaphor, it's *breaking new ground*. It's gathering up sheep to bring into the fold.

If there is any modern parallel with first-century evangelists it's our "missionaries," whose function is uniformly understood as reaching out to the unsaved. They both convert the lost and mentor those who have become disciples. Sadly, however, we find it almost impossible to conceive of having "missionaries" in our own backyard. "Aren't we already living in a 'Christian nation?'" many will think, if not actually ask. "Isn't the Great Commission for *pagan* cultures?" Surely, we know better than this. Breaking new ground isn't about geographical boundaries. Indeed, gathering up sheep is sometimes the most difficult with those who are nearest the fold.

If we need evangelists in Eastern Europe and Africa and China, we also need evangelists in Dallas, Atlanta, and Nashville. Evangelists who go out. Evangelists who take to the streets. Evangelists who have such a burning desire to reach lost souls that they might even forget it's the 4th of July or their own birthday!

Thankfully, we occasionally see refreshing ads in the classifieds like these which appeared recently:

Evangelist Sought *to plant new church. Want to grow a church in economically-diverse, unchurched area with help of a small group of dedicated Christians from a nearby congregation.*

Evangelist Needed *for an assembly of 120. Personal worker desired ahead of speaking ability.*

Outreach Minister Sought. Do you have a passion for the lost?

Would to God this is all we saw in the classifieds! Can you imagine what a dynamic difference it would make if, suddenly, all of our pulpit ministers hit the road as evangelists? And if elders shouldered the mantle of spiritual leadership and started taking over the work of leading hundreds and thousands of new disciples into spiritual maturity? And if young men aspired to be elders and evangelists instead of professionally-trained CEO's of large congregations?

The good news for cost-conscious "elderships" among us is that it wouldn't cost a penny more. And, for worried pulpit ministers, no one need be out of a job! All we'd be doing is redefining job descriptions. (Or, dare I say, restoring the New Testament church!)

Certainly, it would *look* different, and I'm sure it would *feel* different—probably even a bit underwhelming at first. But odds are we would soon sit up and take notice at the sight of dying embers of evangelism being fanned into an unstoppable conflagration. Talk about your "church growth" theories!

From Pulpit Ministry To Mutual Ministry

Last week, the Church of England's local parish magazine was popped through the mail slot at the cottage. Following the recent re-assignment of the local rector (or should I say, "rectoress"), the local village church has been without any regular vicar. As I skimmed through the newsletter, I could hardly believe what was being written...by one of no less importance than "The Venerable Hedley Ringrose, Archdeacon of Cheltenham." (I can never quite work out the various echelons in the Anglican hierarchy.) In the process of attempting to shore up drooping spirits during this discouraging interim, the Archdeacon made the following profound admission—all the more surprising coming from someone representing the Church of England's vaunted clergy:

> *Changes in English society have coincided with a declining number of stipendiary clergy to serve the parishes of the Church of England. This means that the pattern that we have come to think of as traditional, in which one Vicar takes all the ministry alone in one or even two parishes, has become unrealistic. But such a pattern isn't as old as we might think, and neither is it consistent with the New Testament principle of every-member ministry practised in the early church. I'm not suggesting that you won't have another parish priest, but only that the model will be different and our expectations need to change to fit the existing situation.*

"Pattern" theology in the Church of England? "New Testament principles?" "Every-member ministry?" I almost pinched myself to make sure I wasn't dreaming!

Yet, it was a reminder that, despite our historic commitment to "pattern" and New Testament principles, we ourselves may have given up on the idea of what the Archdeacon referred to as "every-member ministry." All it takes is a chapter in this book on the role of elders, and this very chapter on the role of evangelists, and—voilà—we quickly have our own clergy. Which is to say: the evangelists convert; the shepherds feed; and the rest of us...well...we just faithfully "attend."

Logically, it all stands to reason: If *they* are evangelists, *we* must not be. That's *their* job, not *ours*. (We're even paying for their support!) Actually, it's not logical in the least. Who ever said that having full-time, paid evangelists excludes others from sharing the gospel with the lost? We've already seen where at least two of "the Seven" (and probably all of them) were not only "deacons" in serving the Grecian widows, but also evangelists. And when one of them—Stephen—was brutally killed for proclaiming the gospel, "all those who had been scattered preached the word wherever they went." Not just Philip, "the evangelist," but *all* of them.

Nor is it to say that one has to be an appointed elder in order to teach and admonish. In the case of Apollos (ironically, an evangelist), we see Priscilla and Aquila "inviting him into their home and explaining to him the way of God more adequately" (Acts 18:24-26). And "older women" are instructed to train the "younger women" (Titus 2:4). Clearly, teaching the gospel and mentoring other disciples is not the exclusive, private reserve of our spiritual shepherds.

Not even in the assembly. How else do prospective elders become "able teachers" unless they have spent considerable time teaching alongside those who are already experienced pastors? To say that our shepherds should be feeding us through the Word doesn't rule out being fed by other men as well. Show me a congregation in which all of the men are actively involved in a mutual ministry of the Word, and I'll show you a congregation where there will never be an elder shortage, nor a lack of well-trained evangelists.

Do you not find it interesting, incidentally, that we are given a number of references to women teaching, when only men are permitted to instruct the assembled church? If that gender distinction served no other purpose, it should remind us— both men and women—that more formal callings do not preclude other avenues of similar service.

Just because I am not a *paid* evangelist, doesn't mean I have no responsibility to share the gospel with the lost. Just because I am not a *designated* pastor, doesn't mean I shouldn't also be teaching. And just because I am not an *appointed* deacon, doesn't mean I am not to be a servant. As a Kingdom servant, for example, Phoebe was a "deaconess" in the same way that you and I are to be "deacons," whether or not we are officially appointed to serve the church in the special administrative role contemplated for the men exercising that responsibility.

The Archdeacon of Cheltenham may wear a title unheard of in Scripture, but he was certainly right when he talked about "every-member ministry." Within the guidelines set down by the apostles, there should not be anyone among us who is not a proclaimer of the gospel. Or not in some way a pastor. Or not a deacon in the service of the Kingdom. God has called each of us into a mutual ministry for the building up of the body.

Of course, it's what happens when we are assembled for the memorial meal, and the edification and worship that accompany it, which most naturally defines our mutual ministry. Each a song, each a word, each a prayer. The very concept of worship focused around a pulpit flies in the face of the dynamic, mutually-participatory house churches in the apostolic age. Houses don't have pulpits!

Unlike Ezra's famous pulpit, which had people standing for hours listening to God's Word being read aloud (Nehemiah 8:4), today's pulpits have a curious way of appearing in matched pairs with pews. Comfortable pews. Spectator pews. Uninvolved pews. Given the vibrant mutual ministry of the primitive church, one wonders how pulpits and pews ever got invented—not to mention everything else that goes along with them.

Pulpit ministers may be an invention, but mutual ministry is not. Nor is the widely-neglected role of the evangelist. And in spreading *that radical word* we ought to be fervently evangelistic!

But could it really ever happen? No, not converting the world, but converting our own elders into "teaching pastors," and our pulpit ministers into "pulpit-less evangelists?" Is it totally unrealistic to think that an entire brotherhood might break with almost two centuries of tradition and empty its pulpits onto the streets?

Far be it from me, of all people, to be Pollyannaish, but I live in hope of one day seeing the following ad in the classifieds...and then hearing that there are thousands of eager responses:

Tired of being a "one-man band?" *Congregation of involved disciples seeking on-fire evangelist to bring lost souls to salvation. No experience necessary. Academic degrees optional. Must be willing to leave pulpit and go out into the world. Salary sufficient to keep your mind free from concern about your family's welfare. Prayer support from mature shepherds waiting to feed all the lost sheep you can find. Deacons on call to facilitate any special needs you may have. Disciples eager to point you to prospects and open their homes for teaching opportunities. Other disciples available to visit any sick or shut-ins you may encounter. And FYI, ball games are already covered by enthusiastic parents. Apply to* www.IWant-ToDoTheWorkOfAnEvangelist.com.

CHAPTER ELEVEN

A YOUTH-DRIVEN CHURCH

*I was born in the wrong generation. When I was a young man,
no one had any respect for youth. Now I am an old man and no one
has any respect for age.*

BERTRAND RUSSELL

Sacred cows, I'm told, are not to be touched. If there is anything more sacred these days than youth ministries, I'm not sure what it would be, unless it's the popular youth ministers themselves. So I know in advance that this chapter is going to be a tough sell. I also know that my task is made all the more difficult by the subtleties of the concerns underlying what seem to be the unassailable virtues connected with youth programs of all sorts in the church today. To dare raise questions in the face of all the good that is associated with youth ministries is not unlike attacking motherhood and apple pie. Yet, in the pursuit of radical restoration, no aspect of our faith and practice can be exempt from reexamination.

It would be easy enough, of course, to begin by asking where we find any divine precedent in Scripture for either youth ministries or youth ministers. Certainly, there is no mention that "God gave some to be apostles, some to be prophets, and some to be youth ministers..." However, I am in no doubt that the appeal to scriptural precedent will not alone make the case these days. We are already comfortable with too many other things for which scriptural precedent is lacking. And so we must take the long way home.

As we begin the journey, I beg your indulgence as I lay out "the big picture." Without it, I fear there is no way to explain the serious concerns involved. And for that purpose, if I may, I want to take us back one last time to Shakespeare—in particular, *King Lear*.

The Tragedy of King Lear is a story about authority, legitimacy, hierarchy, and the natural order of things—particularly the natural order of generations. It's a tale in which the older generation (in the person of Lear himself) foolishly relinquishes the right of leadership, while the younger generation (represented by two of Lear's three daughters) wilfully seizes on that capitulation, to the ruin of virtually everyone involved.

With a vanity unbefitting the wisdom of his more than eighty years, Lear decides to distribute his kingdom among his three daughters, proportioned on the degree to which they avow their love for him. Absolutely gushing with professions of adoration, the manipulative two older daughters, Goneril and Regan, are rewarded for their pretensions by each receiving a third of the kingdom. But the favored youngest daughter, Cordelia, refuses to mock with such calculating flattery the father she truly loves, and ends up offending him instead. So much so, that what would have been her third of the kingdom is divided between the two sinister sisters; and the virtuous Cordelia is shuffled off penniless to marry the king of France (who lovingly takes her to wed, sans dowry).

It is not long, of course, before Goneril and Regan begin to show their true colors, and virtually strip their father of any remaining influence and dignity he had retained for himself. Faced with this unexpected turn of events, Lear leaves the unwelcoming shelter of his daughters' homes and launches out into the elements, braving a fierce gale while railing against the unnatural act of parental abuse. The storm raging around him is nothing to compare with the swirling winds of confusion and anger he feels within:

> *...This tempest in my mind*
> *Doth from my senses take all feeling else*
> *Save what beats there: filial ingratitude.*
> *Is it not as this mouth should tear this hand*
> *For lifting food to't?*

Even an increasingly-demented Lear understands that filial ingratitude is as nonsensical as "biting the hand that feeds it" (as the phrase is more popularly repeated). For the child to be cruel to the parent is perverse. It is Nature gone amuck, as wild as the storm which mercilessly lashes the defeated old man. Shaking his fist at that very lightning-filled terror, Lear shouts above the din:

> *Singe my white head; and thou all-shaking thunder*
> *Strike flat the thick rotundity o'th' world,*
> *Crack nature's moulds, all germens spill at once*
> *That makes ingrateful man.*

"Crack nature's molds!" he begs, so that such ingrates never again be born. But, already, it's the rupture of Nature's course that is the very source of Lear's lament. By Nature's mold, children ought to treat their elders with respect. When that is not the case, confusion reigns—as Lear's fool (who is no fool) reminds him:

> *When priests are more in word than matter;*
> *When brewers mar their malt with water;*
> *When nobles are their tailors' tutors;*
> *No heretics burned, but wenches' suitors;*
> *Then shall the realm of Albion*
> *Come to great confusion.*

Something's gone terribly wrong in England—indeed, in human nature—when priests don't practice what they preach; and, especially, when noble lords are expected to be mere tutors to their own servants. To upset the natural hierarchy of relation- ships is to spit into the wind. To invite anarchy. To play havoc with the created order.

Ever wonder where we got the expression, "putting the cart before the horse?" It comes from the mouth of Lear's fool. As he stands to one side listening to a conversation between Lear and Goneril, the fool amuses himself with a running social commentary drawn from the events unfolding in his presence. He first sets up the more-familiar line by singing a brief little ditty which explains the subject of his musing:

> *The hedge-sparrow fed the cuckoo so long*
> *That it's had it head bit off by it young.*

Any "fool" can see what's happened, says Lear's own fool. The king has shown kindness to his daughters only to have it rewarded with insolence. Whereupon his next interjection brings us to the now-familiar (if slightly altered) expression: "May not an ass know when the cart draws the horse?"

As with the hapless sparrow: when the offspring devours the parent, the cart is before the horse. As with Lear and his daughters: when the young show disrespect to their elders, the cart is before the horse. And as with God's own people: when the older generation follows the lead of the younger generation, the cart is before the horse.

Who ever heard of a cart pulling a horse? It's crazy! It's mad! It's something so obviously wrong that even a fool knows better.

Then again, even Lear should have known better than to let it happen. It is he himself who was the fool. For as his wise fool reminds him, "Thou hadst little wit in thy bald crown when thou gavest the golden one away." Too late, alas, Lear finally recognizes his mistake and upbraids himself for his folly:

> O Lear, Lear, Lear!
> Beat at this gate that let thy folly in
> And thy dear judgement out.

Which brings us to the ironic fact with which the impudent Goneril taunts her aged father: "I do beseech you to understand my purposes aright, as you are old and reverend, should be wise." The operative words being *"should be"*! Had Lear exercised the wisdom of his age, he would not have invited the troubles thrust upon him by a younger generation. It was a lesson learned the hard way: that responsibility lightly relinquished is respect likely to be extinguished.

Abandoning Natural Relations

They are not in the same book, of course, but Shakespeare and the Apostle Paul are on the same page. In his Roman letter, Paul also addresses the issues of authority, hierarchy, legitimacy, and the natural order. At first appearance, Paul seems to be coming out of left field. He begins his argument by censuring pagan idolaters, of whom he says: "Although they claimed to be wise, they became fools [here we go again] and exchanged the glory of the immortal God for images made to look like mortal man and birds and animals and reptiles" (Romans 1:22-23). In short, "they exchanged the truth of God for a lie, and worshiped and served created things rather than the Creator..." (Romans 1:25).

What they had done—these idolaters—was to turn the *natural* order of things on its head, ironically by worshiping things in *Nature*! They had inverted the legitimate hierarchy of Creator over creature by illegitimately (even nonsensically) elevating the creature over the Creator. Might not Lear's fool have had some choice words about such folly? "Cart before horse," perhaps...?

Paul then suddenly turns his attention to an unlikely target: homosexuals. In fact, he rushes so fast from idolaters to homosexuals that he actually mixes the two together, as if to say that all idolaters are homosexuals. In truth, his point is just the opposite: that all homosexuals are "idolaters," at least in the sense that they, too, have brought confusion to the natural order. In turning to one's own gender for sexual gratification, the homosexual has "exchanged natural relations for unnatural ones" (Romans 1:26-27).

However, to dismiss homosexuals as "perverts" is to miss Paul's point: that homosexuals are "inverts." Like idolaters, they have inverted the natural order of things. They have toppled the sexual hierarchy. They, too, have "put the cart before the horse."

Paul's argument is ever so clever. He knows that in the case of idolaters and homosexuals the natural order of things is so obviously perverted that even a "fool" can recognize such folly in others. It's then that Paul springs the trap on our own folly. All of a sudden, Paul begins listing sins of which you and I are guilty.

With startling effect, we come face to face with the fact that we are no less guilty of being "inverts" than idolaters and homosexuals! For we were created to love, and yet we hate. We were created for peace, and yet we fight and slander one another. We were created to be honest, and yet we lie. The power of Paul's message becomes painfully apparent: Whatever the particular sins we commit, we are inverting the natural order of things—invariably, to our own destruction.

Given the rebellion of Goneril and Regan against their generous father, surely it is no mere coincidence that we see in their actions the inversion of hierarchy inherent in one of the very sins which Paul specifically includes in his list: "Disobedience to parents." Respect within the parent-child hierarchy is a graphic reminder of the submission shown by the wife, the obedience of slaves to their masters, and the deference to be paid to our spiritual shepherds.

Hierarchies of respect and submission not only foster healthy relationships between ourselves and others, but—most of all—teach us about our relationship with God himself. He is our Father and King; we are his children and subjects. He is "older," the Ancient of Days; we are "younger," the rebellious ones he "thought would call him 'Father'..." (Jeremiah 3:19).

The Hierarchy of Age

This brings us, at last, to the hierarchy of age which is at the heart of our present discussion. As his final days of leading Israel were rapidly coming to an end, Moses gave Israel a song of admonition in which he predicted their future rebellion against God, even before they entered into the land of promise (Deuteronomy 32:5-7). With striking similarity to King Lear and his disdainful daughters, Moses says of Israel:

> *They have acted corruptly toward him;*
> *To their shame they are no longer his children,*
> *but a warped and crooked generation.*
> *Is this the way you repay the Lord,*
> *O foolish and unwise people?*
> *Is he not your Father, your Creator,*
> *who made you and formed you?*

Moses then appeals to a sense of history and experience as the antidote to rebellion, and in the process introduces us to a generational hierarchy often overlooked in the midst of our youth-driven culture:

> *Remember the days of old;*
> *consider the generations long past.*
> *Ask your father and he will tell you,*
> *your elders, and they will explain to you.*

No matter how bright and sharp, or how dedicated and earnest they may be, the fact is that young people simply don't have the benefit of older age which engenders broader under-standing and—hopefully—the wisdom which comes with years of experience. Elders and fathers—*fathers, especially*—have a cru-cial role to play as storytellers to the young.

I suppose that few of us—certainly myself included—have taken Moses' advice as seriously as we should have. Over and over, I regret not having spent more time with my own father, asking harder questions and benefitting from his biblical knowledge and spiritual insight. So there's nothing new about generation gaps and the failure to take advantage of those who have blazed the trail ahead of us.

In our earlier chapter on elders in the apostolic church, we talked about the significance of "olders" being the ones to lead and feed. That's because they are in the best position to explain the spiritual verities which those who are younger (whether in age or in Christ) need to know. It's the "olders" who have the benefit of hindsight, and the years of accumulated study of the Scriptures under their belts. It's the "olders" who, like Israel's elders, have the kind of seasoned judgment that qualifies them to "sit at the city gates" and decide difficult cases.

It is no surprise, then, that immediately after the Apostle Peter exhorts elders to be shepherds of God's flock among them, he completes the generation hierarchy, saying, "Young men, in the same way be submissive to those who are older" (1 Peter 5:5). The hierarchy of age is not just an arbitrary pecking order, or some time-honored system of hazing. Much more than power politics is going on here. What Peter is telling us is that the process of spiritual regeneration is, among other things, *genera-tional*. It's inherited. It's handed down. What we know of God and his world is transferred from one generation to the next, from the oldest to the youngest.

So it was that both ancient Israel and the first-century people of God were always "elder" led, not "younger" led. That was the natural order of things. The created order. The way God intended spiritual leadership to be.

The Trouble When Carts Pull Horses

If all this seems a bit elementary, nevertheless it must not be taken for granted. Not these days, certainly; and, in fact, not at any time throughout history. In Isaiah chapter 3, we are told of the many ways in which Jerusalem and Judah brought disaster on themselves. Among the causes prompting God's judgment, we see that the elders had reneged on their responsibilities as spiritual leaders. "The Lord enters into judgment against the elders and leaders of his people," God said through Isaiah. "It is you who have ruined my vineyard" (Isaiah 3:14).

The most fascinating thing about the punishment which God promised as a result of the elders' languid leadership is that the "penalty" was specially tailored to the offense. Since the elders failed to lead from the top of the generational hierarchy, as it were, God said he would reverse that hierarchy and have Judah led from the bottom up. "I will make boys their officials; mere children will rule over them" (Isaiah 3:4).

However, this was not so much a *penalty* as it was a *prediction*. God was simply signaling the natural consequences whenever any older generation refuses to shoulder the responsibility for leadership. In the same way that every vacuum begs to be filled, you can be sure that, in the absence of strong leadership from the more mature, "the young will rise up against the old" (Isaiah 3:5).

It is not wholly unlike Esau's selling his birthright for a mess of pottage and thereby fulfilling the prophecy that "the older will serve the younger" (Genesis 25:23). Whoever could have predicted that the seemingly inconsequential fact of the older serving the younger would perpetuate animosity and war among their descendants even to this day? When those who are older sell out to the young, it doesn't take a crystal ball to know that there's sure to be trouble ahead.

Indeed, in Judah's case, the generational *coup d'état* had already happened! "Youths oppress my people," says God; what's more, "women rule over them" (Isaiah 3:12). When Judah's elders refused to lead, the natural order of things collapsed in every direction. Like a row of dominoes, not only the generational hierarchy toppled, but the gender hierarchy as well. One, two, three—we all fall down!

As the foolish King Lear proves so well, of course, there is no guarantee that older age invariably results in wise decisions or even clearer understanding. Merely consider that Solomon, the wisest man who ever lived, seemed to grow less wise with every passing year. But overall, the odds clearly favor advancing years bringing increased maturity. In that regard, I can't help but wonder if we aren't given the story of Solomon's son, Rehoboam, to press home this very point.

You'll recall (from 1 Kings 12:6-13) that when Rehoboam succeeded Solomon to the throne, the people petitioned him to lighten their burdens. So Rehoboam sought advice from two different groups as to how he should govern and tax the people of Israel. The text tells us that "Rehoboam rejected the advice the elders gave him and consulted the young men who had grown up with him and were serving him." The advice of the younger set— to govern with a heavy hand—eventually led to a division between Israel and Judah, and to countless years of bitter civil war.

I suppose it's not inevitable for problems to arise when the younger generation's way of doing things rules the day, but one can hardly ignore the "division" and "civil war" which currently plagues the church as a result of our own generational conflicts.

The Undeclared Generation Wars

In case you didn't notice, that last sentence contained two fairly significant assumptions. The first is that there is division and conflict in the Lord's body today. Surely, that must be obvious to all but the most isolated among us. It's not just the historic divisions between the "conservatives" and the "liberals," whoever either of those might be, on whatever issue we might be talking about. In fact, there are so many fissures lately that it's more a question of "splintering" than "splitting."

Among the more serious doctrinal concerns are the issues of *fellowship* (Can one be a Christian without being scripturally baptized?); *gender roles* (To what extent, if any, may women participate in leadership?); *instrumental music* (Is it really forbidden?); and *marriage, divorce, and remarriage* (fill in the blank for an infinite number of variations on theme).

Yet dominating them all, strangely enough, is one particular conflict which (though clearly an oxymoron) could be called "the worship wars." Basically, it's a battle over worship *style*: to clap or not to clap; song books or screens; traditional hymns or contemporary choruses; praise teams or not. Sadly, a large number of congregations have already divided over these relatively less significant issues, and more splits seem inevitable. In time, I suspect the weightier issues cited above will take an even larger toll. But for the past decade, most of our division has been over modes and methods of worship.

Which brings us to the second assumption: that these conflicts are largely generational. To be sure, the demand for more contemporary forms of worship is not limited to teenagers or even the "thirty-somethings." I can think, for instance, of one particular congregation where a staid, traditional worship format was recently replaced by an exciting, upbeat contemporary format, much to the delight of the entire congregation—most of whom are retirees!

That said, it appears that—across the board—the worship wars typically pit the younger against the older. The reason should be obvious, simply by looking at what the disputes are mostly about: *music*. Nothing defines a generation quite like music. Every generation has its own songs, and thus its own styles.

For at least a century, generational style differences had little impact on the church, no matter what was going on in the popular world of music. Parents and children may have fallen out over Elvis, or the Beatles, or Guns and Roses; but on the Lord's day, it was still "Night With Ebon Pinion," whether or not we knew what an ebon pinion was!

Then something occurred which had never happened before: popular music style invaded the church. (Certainly, major shifts in music style have happened in the distant past, but not in our lifetime.) From Christian radio and the denominations, we began hearing all sorts of new "contemporary songs" that didn't need four-part harmony, or even books. Screens and "overheads" would do nicely, thank you.

In fact, these new choruses were songs that you could sing even without a screen—say, around a campfire at a youth camp. Of course, there had always been "youth songs," with spirited actions to go along with the words (like clapping and raising hands), but now there were many more to choose from. They were even overtly biblical, frequently being nothing more than psalms set to melody. Not unexpectedly, young people were instantly drawn to the easy tunes and simple lyrics with their distinctive emphasis on feelings of the heart.

No one seemed to mind (or notice) all this until the young people's contemporary music began to encroach on traditional hymns during the "worship hour." And screens replaced books. And praise teams were introduced, ostensibly to teach the older folks the new songs. At that point, there was "trouble in River City" with a capital "T."

And as if these style innovations were not enough to set the cat among the pigeons, one began to hear (perhaps totally unrelated) the first whispered calls for introducing instruments. Soon, there were louder voices. Not surprisingly, it wasn't long before the center aisle in the auditorium became a no-man's land between young and old when it came to all things musical.

Divided We Fall!

I say "center aisle" figuratively. But in many instances, there has been a literal divide between the youth group and the adults in the auditorium. Certainly, that is the case in congregations where young people have regularly met separately from everybody else-whether on Sunday nights, or Wednesday nights, or, of course, at their youth rallies and retreats. Without begrudging them their own space and opportunities for fellowship, the fact remains that there are consequences to dividing up the congregation for *any* purpose.

For all their advantages, there are also inevitable down sides to carving up the family into "singles ministries," "seniors ministries," and "the college group." Once such categories are created, at some point the wholeness of the Lord's body begins to get lost in much the same way that focusing on minorities in society can actually produce more strife than unity. Generational apartheid is not to be desired any more than any other kind of apartheid. Nor has there been any diminution of the divine maxim that "a kingdom divided against itself cannot stand."

In the case of youth groups, in particular, their literal separation from the adults has tended to make them an entity unto themselves. A congregation within a congregation, having their own minister, their own music, their own modes of worship, and their own hermeneutics of heart and story. All of which works well enough until "the whole church comes together." At that point, "each one having a song" takes on new meaning. The fact is that we have *different songs*...and, for that matter, different ideas altogether about how enthusiastic worship ought to be.

"What's happened to all the excitement?" the youth group asks. By contrast with their high-energy youth rallies, worshiping with the older folks can be a real drag. To begin with, there's all those "pre-Columbian" hymns, as a friend of mine put it. And, of course, too, all those preachers who are simply out of touch. (One of the most capable preachers I know was just "eased into retirement" to make way for a more youthful face and a peppier pulpit presence.) That's why we've hired all the youth ministers. They can relate!

Never mind that the apostolic pattern was older men teaching younger men, and older women teaching those who are younger. We've happily settled for slightly-older men teaching the slightly-younger. It's not their fault, of course. Youthful youth ministers are doing the best job they can, despite often being alternatively either pressured or abandoned by both elders and parents. When Paul told Timothy, "Don't let anyone look down on you because you are young" (1 Timothy 4:12), he could well have been speaking to today's youthful under-shepherds.

And yet, the pressure for youth ministers to maintain a high level of energy and excitement has often come at the cost of widespread biblical illiteracy. All too often, our young people "have been destroyed for lack of knowledge." The report card reads: "A" for enthusiasm, heart-felt spirituality, and service to others (far exceeding my own generation); but anywhere from "C-" to "F" for knowledge of the text. (As with estimated fuel consumption figures, "Individual cases and youth groups may vary.")

As for "relating," the more young people become accustomed to energetic youth ministers, the more difficult it is for even the most sensitive and articulate older preachers and teachers to bridge the generation gap. And the less that gap is bridged, the more tempted we are to hire youth ministers who *can* relate! It's a Catch 22. But talk about getting the cart before the horse....None of this would have happened had we not already created an environment in which the congregation is purposely and intentionally segregated by age.

In that regard, the shoe needs to be put on the right foot. The problem is not so much that the older generation can't relate to the younger generation. (After all, they once were the younger generation!) Rather, the problem today is that young people can no longer relate to those who are older—or, worse yet, seem unwilling even to try, because they're somewhere off in another dimension, in their own youth-ministry world.

Yet, surely this is not a rebellion of their own making. From "Cradle Roll," to "Junior Church" during the worship hour, to separate teen sessions during weekend seminars and lectureships, our young people have been cut off from observing what the adults do when they worship. They no longer absorb by osmosis the deeper doctrinal principles which adults talk about. Nor do they often experience the "wave length" of thinking and emotions on which their older brothers and sisters in Christ operate.

At the very least, if children are thought to be mature enough to make the most important commitment they will ever make—being immersed into Christ—then they ought to be mature enough to think about the great spiritual issues of life along with adults. Unfortunately, many youth ministries (sometimes pressured by the expectations of parents to make sure their kids are baptized) have encouraged youth baptisms at earlier and earlier ages, only to compound that felony by maintaining the wall of separation between young and old.

Surely it is not without significance that when Israel gathered to hear Ezra read the law (from daybreak until noon!), the text tells us, not once but twice, that all this was done "in the presence of the men, women, and *all who were able to understand*" (Nehemiah 8:2). And when the congregation of Israel recommitted their covenant vows before God, once again the text tells us that all the men, "together with their wives and *all their sons and daughters who are able to understand*" bound themselves with an oath to follow the Law of God (Nehemiah 10:28). If young people are "mature enough to understand" and to join in a covenant relationship with God, then they need to be standing as one before the Lord with the whole congregation.

Youth In A Cultural Cocoon

Putting all of the blame on youth ministries, of course, would be both foolish and unfair. After all, we are part of a wider culture in which the older generation and its values count for little. Young people in America are increasingly a separate nation, having cut themselves off from the adult world. On a deeper level, of course, it is *they* who have been cut off from the adult world by parents who have parked their children in front of the t.v., and in day-care centers, and in latch-key homes, away from desperately-needed parental influence.

In his book *The Second Family: How Adolescent Power is Challenging the American Family*, Ron Taffel argues that, despite their growing up faster than at any time in history, today's young people are remaining completely cocooned in their peer group. "Let loose in their own world," says Taffel, "young people have no reason to stage an uprising or to rebel against family values. They are, in many ways, already gone, immersed in what I call the second family—the aggregate force of the pop culture and the peer group."

Is it just a coincidence that what Taffel terms the "second family" comes at a time when the "first family" has been decimated by divorce? (Even among God's people!) No wonder the youngsters are turning to the pop culture and their peer group for answers. If you're thinking this is the best reason yet to have youth ministries—to provide a godly alternative—the most that can be said is that it's a *better* peer group. But it's still a *peer group*, with all its collective inexperience and lack of spiritual depth. Where is the point of contact with the "olders"—those who can lead with wisdom and mature insight?

Nor can we overlook society's obsession with marketing almost exclusively to the young, seen especially in the entertainment industry (in movies and music) and sales of just about everything from burgers to cars to clothing. The first not-so-subtle message is that adults are irrelevant. (Like, who needs them, actually?)

But parents, too, must share the blame. From their earliest ages, children have been given unlimited choice in what they will eat, wear, and do. "Choice" is America's new god. Should we be surprised, then, when our young people believe that matters of doctrine are little more than menu choices at McDonalds?

Which leads to a second serious repercussion, which is a cultural consensus kowtowing to the young. What young people want is what young people get. How many parents these days can refuse to pull into the Golden Arches when the screaming demand is made for a Happy Meal? The cynical success of youth-targeted marketing gives new meaning to the phrase: "a little child shall lead them!" Parents may be at the wheel of the minivan, but far too often it's advertising-driven children who are at the controls in our youth-driven culture.

And in our youth-driven church.

Thanks to both media and culture, we now also speak different languages. The lines of communication have broken down. It's not just that no older person can get through to the young while they are talking and text-messaging on their mobile phones, or glued to the internet. It's that, even when we are talking face to face, what ought to be mutual points of reference have mostly gone by the board. It's as if we have two different operating systems. The young folks are using Windows, while the older folks are still using DOS. It's like mixing Apples and IBM's. Try as we might, we just can't get through to each other.

Even when today's younger Christians have legitimate reason to spurn some of the lifeless, traditional worship forms of their elders, they have been robbed of mature avenues of communication by which to convey those concerns to an older generation who need to hear their message. Worse yet, the older generation typically perpetuates the problem by "moving the mountain to Mohammed, rather than moving Mohammed to the mountain." However ineptly we might do it, we try our best to "speak where the young people speak, and be silent where the young people are silent." Instead of teaching them our own language—the language of adults—we abandon "maturespeak" for "youthspeak." Like, totally.

I should know. I keep catching myself doing it all the time. No one wants to build bridges to young people more than I do. No one is more torn about how to do it, given the current climate. If we *don't* use their language, we are seen as out of touch. If we *do* use their language, they never learn ours. Nor, more importantly, the language of the inspired ancients.

I Don't Mean To Be Un-American...

Speaking of different languages, this summer Ruth and I had a most wonderful experience with our brothers and sisters in Christ in Slovakia and the Czech Republic. Nearly fifty of them (almost half the disciples in Slovakia alone) gathered for a spiritual retreat just outside Bratislava, and throughout the weekend we came to know and love each other despite obvious language barriers. It helped tremendously that we had the world's best translator, Branyo Kuvik; and also that many of those from Eastern Europe had at least passing familiarity with English. But what amazed me most was the level of spiritual inquisitiveness on the part of the group, at least eighty percent of whom (among the Slovakians) were under 25. In very real terms, the whole church in Slovakia is a "youth ministry."

With great enthusiasm, they sang many of the contemporary choruses brought to them from the States, supplemented with a number of incredibly beautiful songs (in both lyrics and melody) written by one of the young men in the group, who, until a couple of years ago, couldn't even sing on key! And they dressed just as casually as American young people, and laughed together and had great fun.

Yet, there was one huge difference: they were diligent seekers of truth and doctrine. Almost nothing else mattered except coming to know God's will. According to the schedule, I was to speak for two hours each morning and two hours at night. The rest of the afternoon was "free" time, for walking in the woods, or playing games, or simply visiting with each other. But, except for fellowship late into the night, very little "free" time ever happened. Instead, they insisted on asking questions for literally hours on end. Couldn't get enough. Absolutely hungry for the Word.

If one were to look for an explanation, it might lie in the fact that they are first-generation disciples, emerging within a single decade after the fall of communism. Unlike most of us who have "grown up in the church," the Slovaks have come out of deep Catholic roots, and the Czechs, for the most part, out of atheism. They take nothing for granted. They don't have centuries of tradition to overcome. They're just eager to know all they can about God and his power in their lives.

What I learned from these zealous young disciples in a culture far different from our own is that it is not impossible (or even difficult) to communicate with young people despite *real* language differences. And, also, that we don't have to dumb down everything we say and do in order to "relate" to them. And, most gratifying of all, that they had a warm respect for my grey beard that is not often duplicated back home. For these young people, a spiritual father figure wasn't a barrier, but a blessing.

Yet, just look at the cultural differences. These are not young people who grew up with silver spoons in their mouths. They know little of western materialism. In fact, attending that very retreat (in the most modest of facilities and with only basic meals) cost them one-fifth of their monthly wages. They haven't had the unlimited choices of kids in the States. Fast-food is a rare luxury, and the latest name-brand clothing simply isn't an option for most of them. So, I suggest to you that the problem is not *young people.* Never has been, never will be. The real villain is a pampered youth culture in America that only has to say "Jump," and the rest of us quickly respond, "How high?"

A Parental Responsibility

If we are ever to be serious about radically restoring first-century faith and practice, we must face the cold fact that the apostolic church was never directly or centrally responsible for the spiritual growth and development of the young. Nor, certainly, for their social entertainment and fellowship.

The role assumed by the church in the past several decades is one that is *in loco parentis*—i.e, taking the place of parents. (Which is not unlike the role which government has assumed in secular education, juvenile justice, and family law.) It is yet another instance of a toppled hierarchy and the relinquishment of God-ordained responsibility. Everywhere you look, someone is passing the buck. Parents pass it to the church; the church passes it to the elders; the elders pass it to youth ministers. Yet this is only the latest incarnation of a long-standing practice of responsibility avoidance.

Long before the advent of youth ministries, the Sunday School had already become more than merely a supplement to parental instruction in the home. The idea of the church acting *in loco parentis* has been with us for generations...with telling effect. One shudders to think what percentage of young people have learned more of what they know about the Scriptures from Sunday School teachers than from their own parents. Considering how rarely we hear parents and children talk about studying the Bible together at home, the percentage must be astronomically high.

With the arrival of youth ministries, the problem of vicarious spiritual instruction has only been exacerbated. I can't recall knowing any parents who ever drove all the way across town so that their children could be in a more serious, demanding Sunday School class, but I can point you to multitudes today who regularly travel over hill and dale in search of the most dynamic youth group in the area. Driving children great distances for teen fellowship seems not to be a problem. By contrast, taking the time to teach them at home remains a low priority.

When Paul wrote, "Fathers, do not exasperate your children; instead, bring them up in the training and instruction of the Lord" (Ephesians 6:4), he was merely ratifying centuries of teaching about parental responsibility for children's moral and spiritual development. The Israelites had been warned, for example: "Do not forget the things your eyes have seen or let them slip from your heart as long as you live. Teach them to your children and to their children after them" (Deuteronomy 4:9).

Lest anyone think that this responsibility was fulfilled in some collective educational scheme akin to the later synagogue schools, listen again to where this training was to take place. "These commandments that I give you today are to be upon your hearts," said Moses to the people. "Impress them on your children. Talk about them when you sit at home and when you walk along the road, when you lie down and when you get up" (Deuteronomy 6:6-7).

How much of this is going on in homes of Christians today—whether around the dinner table (or, more likely, at Pizza Hut); or in the car on the way to and from Little League; or at bedtime (whenever that is for teens!); or at breakfast (not to be confused with Pop Tarts as the kids run out the door)? Has our frenetic lifestyle all but crowded God out of family life? Do we expect the church to pick up the pieces on Sunday morning?

Can you imagine what a difference it would make if parents (especially fathers) spent as much time in spiritual discussion with their children as youth ministers spend with them? For that matter, think what effect it would have on the Lord's body if parents (especially fathers) spent as much time in spiritual discussion with their children as they spend together at soccer practice. And why is it that moms and dads have plenty of volunteer time to help coach the soccer team, but insist on hiring others to "coach" the youth group at church? Do we think that children aren't going to sense that difference in priorities? The irony is that, whether parents recognize it or not, they are *constantly* teaching their children values. The only question is, What values are they teaching?

Numbers-Driven, Youth-Driven

When you step back and think about it, the very existence of youth ministries is tied to the size of congregations. Most larger congregations have them; few smaller congregations do. In the house churches of the first century, of course, a youth ministry would have been totally unnecessary, if not completely out of place. Quite probably, children too young to understand what was going on would have been treated like children in any other home gathering today: neither ignored, nor central to the purpose of the adults' meeting. Teens and adolescents old enough to appreciate the seriousness of the occasion were most likely considered part of the larger group. In a home setting, there was literally no room to have one group here and another group there.

When we run out of room today, of course, we simply have an added excuse to offer a "contemporary" second service more appealing to the younger folks (even if, in order to avoid a contentious "split," it effectively divides the congregation in half). And have you noticed that the "traditional" services in these two-service congregations have a way of gradually becoming more and more "contemporary," while the "contemporary" services virtually never become more "traditional?" The creeping incrementalism of the youth agenda has an insatiable appetite for appeasement.

The very fact that we have two services in many congregations today only serves to highlight the difference between churches in the first century and today's typically-larger churches. The larger the congregation, the larger the youth group. The larger the youth group, the stronger their voting power, which they exercise with their feet (along with their parents' feet). In an era of church-hopping and church-shopping, youth rules. With young people and their parents demanding bigger and better youth programs, elders fall over backwards to provide the most youth-friendly worship possible. (Just look at the competition each fall when the congregations nearest to our universities try to outdo each other in "capturing" the incoming students.)

No question about it: the last thing we'd ever want to do is to lose our young people to some other congregation! So what will it take...the most dynamic youth minister available? (Indeed, the most dynamic pulpit minister?) The most innovative, high-tech programs? An exciting, contemporary worship format? A greater degree of involvement for young women? Christian concerts, complete with instruments? Perhaps simply *more fun*? (Apparently, no promotion of spiritual life retreats and foreign missions tours is complete without a lot of hype about how much fun there will be.)

The worst part, sadly, is that all this is done, if necessary, at the expense of alienating those who are more spiritually mature. Those who have been the pillars of the Kingdom for a lifetime. Those who have borne the burden of keeping faith alive during the hard times. And those godly older folks who cringe silently with each new intimidating mandate for accommodating the young. (The high-handed insensitivity often associated with bringing about a shift in generational focus can at times be breathtaking.)

When any or all of this happens, the Lord's body has well and truly become a youth-driven church, and it's back to the cart pulling the horse. Back to the generational hierarchy being turned unceremoniously on its head, with "children ruling over their elders." And back to a magnanimous King whose children, despite his many gifts, treat him with unseemly disrespect.

No, not King Lear...the other One.

Hope For the Future

There is great irony that from this less-than-flattering picture I've painted of youth ministries I see great hope for the future. Why are young people so excited when they return home from a weekend retreat? I suggest it's because they have experienced something very similar to "radical restoration." While I continue to be concerned about what I believe is too often a lack of biblical depth in study and song, and lament that parents are not playing the primary roles they ought to play—nevertheless, look what is happening dynamically at those retreats. There is spontaneity, informality, intimacy, and mutual participation of a type which our young people rarely witness in our more structured assemblies. Typically, there are no "buildings" to speak of, and certainly there are no clocks around a campfire. Or pulpits and pews. Or printed orders of worship. Or set-piece prayers. And, of course, there's all that table fellowship which breaks down so many barriers.

For that matter, any of you who have ever been on a spiritual retreat for adults will probably recognize many of the same features. Have we ever made a connection between those uniquely uplifting worship experiences and what I'm talking about under the label of "radical restoration"? If you've come back from one of those weekends on a spiritual "high," then you yourself have tasted something of what must have been the exhilaration of first-century worship and fellowship.

Imagine, then, the healing that could come to a generationally-divided church if we were to radically restore the New Testament pattern of intimate, spontaneous, mutually-participatory worship and edification, focused around table fellowship in the memory of Christ!

After all, what is it to "retreat" if not to "go back"? To regroup, to renew, to reinvigorate—indeed, to radically restore?

CHAPTER TWELVE

LET'S GET PRACTICAL

If the order of your worship service is so rigid that it can't be changed, it had better be changed.

THEODORE A. RAEDEKE

A mong the questions I am most often asked when I speak about radical restoration is the burning issue, "How could we ever find other Christians—especially when we're traveling—if there were no church buildings with "Church of Christ" signs outside, and no ads in the Yellow Pages?" I have to admit that questions like these make me want to throw up my hands in despair! Surely, these kinds of concerns can't have high priority when confronted with the need to rid ourselves of denominationalism, root and branch, and start over afresh.

Yet, I realize that radical restoration threatens to rob us of all sorts of security blankets; and that, practically speaking, even the most mundane of details eventually would have to be considered. If I may hold for a moment the question about how we would find each other, I'd like to begin with one of the questions which surely poses the best possible problem we could face.

What happens when we outgrow our small group fellowship?

First off, we praise God! Next, we clone. We grow and clone. Grow and clone. Grow and clone. That's the process. That's the first-century way. We don't bulge; we clone! Organizations grow bigger and bigger (and more top-heavy

with bureaucracy). Organisms, by contrast, reproduce themselves. Again and again. Over and over. Each new cell maintaining the original vibrancy and structural integrity of the first.

"Yes, but how do we know *when* to clone?" invariably
becomes the next question. And the answer is: When there are
too many of us to have intimate, mutually-participatory, spontaneous worship together. When we can no longer seat everyone
at the fellowship meal, and when there are too many sheep for
the shepherds to personally know and feed.

"Well, sure," someone always asks, "but how many people would that be? Fifty? Seventy-five? A hundred? Where do
you draw the line?"

When I was a law professor teaching the law of negligence, I used to draw a continuum on the board—from simple,
ordinary negligence, through gross, criminal negligence, and on
to wilful and wanton conduct. Invariably, students would
squirm disconcertedly in their seats until one of them just could-
n't stand it any longer and ask, "But, professor, where do you
draw the line between the various types of negligence?" To
make the point that "the line" is always a matter of judgment in
individual cases, I would turn again to the board and arbitrarily
draw a line somewhere off the continuum. "You want a line?" I
would ask with more than a dose of irony, "There's your line!"

In the same way, I am reluctant to draw any arbitrary
"line" regarding magic numbers for size. However, I will share
with you someone else's "line" which, if not compelling, is altogether fascinating. In his book *The Tipping Point* Malcolm
Gladwell (staff writer for *The New Yorker*) talks about how ideas
spread in something like "social epidemics." In fact, he hits
amazingly close to the question at hand when he asks: "Have
you ever wondered, for example, how religious movements get
started?" Whereupon he describes how John Wesley's
Methodist Movement became a "social epidemic" in the space of
five or six years in the 1780's. But most fascinating of all is

Gladwell's discussion of what a number of observers have called "the Rule of 150."

Testing a tentative premise that our social channels of communication and interaction have a natural numerical limit, sociologists have gone back in history and discovered that primitive societies lived in villages which on average had 148.4 people in them. (Don't ask me how they reached such a precise figure. I'm just reporting!) Consistent with the basic premise, apparently the rule of thumb for military fighting units is also no larger than 200 men. "At a bigger size," says Gladwell, "you have to impose complicated hierarchies and rules and regulations and formal measures to try to command loyalty and cohesion. But below 150...it is possible to achieve these same goals informally." Sound vaguely familiar, given our distinction between organization and organism?

Gladwell then brings us even closer to home by introducing us to the practice of the religious group known as the Hutterites (who come from the same tradition as the Amish and the Mennonites). For centuries, they have had a strict policy that when any colony approaches 150, they split in two and start a new one. When Gladwell asked one the Hutterite leaders about "the rule of 150," he was told, "If you get too large, you don't have enough things in common, and then you start to become strangers and that close-knit fellowship starts to get lost."

Based upon all of this, Gladwell opines that "congregants of a rapidly expanding church...or anyone in a group activity banking on the epidemic spread of shared ideals need to be particularly cognizant of the perils of bigness. Crossing the 150 line is a small change that can make a big difference."

Referring to Gore Associates (the company that makes the water-resistant Gore-Tex fabric), which also follows "the rule of 150" as a matter of company policy, Gladwell concludes that, "In order to be unified—in order to spread a specific, company ideology to all of its employees—Gore had to break itself up into semi-autonomous small pieces. That is the paradox of the epidemic: that in order to create one contagious movement, you often have to create many small movements first."

None of that is strictly biblical, of course, other than the intriguing fact that when Jesus fed the 5,000 he had them seated in groups of hundreds and fifties! But it does seem to be consistent with what we know about how early congregations functioned, and probably tells us much about why they were so successful. All I'm suggesting is that we ought to give serious consideration to the idea that significant growth ought to automatically signal the need to divide up the congregation and begin a new work. If we ever seriously took that idea on board, then the grow-and-clone process would become as second nature to us as our present habit of building bigger buildings or having second services.

My own guess is that the prospect of either of those things—*bigger buildings or second services*—ought to be our best clue that we've done enough adding and now it's time to divide and multiply. If the reason for not planting a new congregation under those circumstances is mostly a matter of economics, remember again how little dependent first-century congregations were on financial outlay. In the absence of expensively-maintained buildings and staff, it apparently hardly mattered that one group began meeting as two. As is often said of marriage (with far less credibility!), two can live as cheaply as one.

But aren't small congregations fraught with their own problems?

Sometimes, it seems, small congregations are small for a reason. Certainly, it would be rare that remaining small is the intentional result of an ideological commitment to a process of growing and cloning. Often, it means nothing more than that folks haven't been able to get along, whether because of personality clashes, or such narrow-mindedness that the Lord himself wouldn't be welcomed in their midst!

And so there is no guarantee that small group fellowships similar to first-century house churches would be problem-free.

Right off the bat, there is always potential for developing the kind of cliques we see in the Corinthian church, centering around charismatic personalities. It seems that dominant leaders can always find at least a few folks to sit at their feet, and are content to settle for their unquestioning loyalty over greater growth.

Of even more concern is the possibility of having small groups that are socially or racially exclusive. If the Lord's body were ever to meet literally from house to house, those houses would likely be in neighborhoods, which themselves tend to be socially divided by color and class. If fellowship were consciously limited to those same divisions, then "small" would be *too small*. Was it not this kind of social ostracism during the fellowship meal that landed the Corinthians in trouble with Paul?

As for personality clashes, I suggest that God has set us in small church families for a reason: so that, as in natural families, we can learn to love each other, warts and all. I say this with some fear and trepidation, aware from personal experience how hard it can be to overcome personality differences in congregations too small to avoid rubbing elbows. The theory is right, of course. It's just that putting it into practice isn't always easy.

If we began to assemble in new, smaller groups, might we become exclusivist?

Yes, of course. We might. Others have. The risk is always there. Merely consider the Corinthians. If pride goeth before the construction of many a building, pride could just as easily follow after deciding *not* to build one. As in, "We are radically restored, and—by the way—you're not!" But it doesn't have to happen that way. And if we are truly "radically restored" in both heart and spirit, it won't happen that way.

I've said much about the value of remaining networked, but there is also a sense in which small group fellowships, having few, if any, tangible identity markers, will result in far fewer congregational comparisons. It's hard to shoot at invisible targets. And equally hard to be judgmental. In a small-group environment, each congregation can more easily go about doing what it needs to do, and answer to God for any shortcomings. Typically, it's big congregations (especially those with "big-name preachers") which can foster so much pride from within and judgment from without. Given that we're already more exclusivist than is good for us, the small group model might just help diffuse our arrogance.

How would we locate each other?

Now for that earlier question. As we have already seen, God's people in the first century appear to have been incredibly networked. Ironically, it may have helped that there were relatively few disciples in the early years. We hear so much talk today of "Christianity" and "Christians" that we take those words for granted. Indeed, our world is actually complicated by the fact that there are so many believers who call themselves Christians. That, of course, is what lies behind the maddening question about the Yellow Pages and signs outside our buildings. How, out of all those who identify themselves as Christians, can we find those who believe and practice the kind of biblical Christianity we collectively espouse?

Far from the name "Christian" being a problem in the first century, it was one of the very means by which disciples could connect with each other. After all, Christians were of only one kind in the first century. If you met someone who was a "Christian," you didn't have to ask what group he was a member of. It was just Christ's church, plain as that. The called-out ones. "Are you a Christian?" "Me, too." Nuff said!

Yet, we also know that the disciples were not initially known as Christians. "The disciples were called Christians *first* at Antioch" (Acts 11:26). This was during the inaugural time when the gospel was first being preached to Greeks, not just to the Jews. Interestingly, the Jewish disciples were never called "Messiah-ites" (which might have been a rough equivalent of the Greek word "Christian") or even "Jesus-ites." Instead, they were viewed (if perhaps as heretics) as part of the wider Jewish family, and referred to as "the Way." (We're not told why. Could it be because of their teaching that Jesus, as the Messiah, was *the* way...as well as *the* truth, and *the* life?)

Twice, Paul associated himself with "the Way," as we discover, first, when he addressed the crowd of angry Jews following his arrest in Jerusalem. "I persecuted the followers of this Way to their death..." (Acts 22:40), said Paul, explaining the incredible turnaround that led to his becoming a member of the very sect he had once zealously persecuted. Then, in his defense before the Roman Governor, Felix, Paul admitted that he worshiped the God of the Jews, "as a follower of the Way, which they call a sect" (Acts 24:14). Paul knew that Felix himself "was well acquainted with the Way" (Acts 24:22).

In fact, that is the very point. By this time, *everyone* who knew anything about Jewish religious practice was familiar with "the Way" and its disciples. So, anyone inquiring in, say, Corinth or Rome or Ephesus as to where the disciples of Christ might be meeting together wouldn't have difficulty finding their way to the right group. The only group there was. All they had to ask was: "Do you know the Way?"

Would that we, too, were so well known by our distinctive style of life and godly worship that *everyone* would know how to find us! Would that we were known far and wide, not just because of our exclusivist claim to be "the *only* way," but as a people who so honor God that our lives unmistakably point to the One who is *The Way*, for all the world to see.

I realize that village life in Buckland is hardly indicative of finding each other in heavily populated metropolitan areas, but I can't help but think about the visitors we had earlier today at the cottage. A couple we'd not met before from Cookeville, Tennessee were traveling in the Cotswolds and thought they'd drop by. Driving up the village lane, they spotted a gardener working in the cemetery, and asked if she knew where I lived. The young woman (who is not a villager, but lives in the area) surprised them by asking, "Is he the one that has something to do with the Bible?" Within minutes, they were outside our cottage, guided by nothing more than a reputation singularly fixed on "something to do with the Bible."

If we could foster those kinds of reputations in all our neighborhoods and communities, not only could we locate each other, but we might also locate folks with an interest in knowing more about what it means to have "something to do with the Bible."

As for out-of-town visitors looking for worship opportunities with God's people, we easily could take a page from congregations on "the mission field." Despite typically meeting from house to house, or in non-descript buildings lacking signs outside, fledgling churches in foreign countries have an uncanny way of being found simply by word of mouth. (I, myself, have done this many, many times over the years.) If we could ever begin to think of our own backyard as a "mission field," we might quickly discover that visitors could find us just as easily. Besides that, we've already got a massive directory of God's people throughout the United States. In today's world, "word of mouth" comes conveniently bound in a single volume.

Who do you make the checks out to?

Running a close second in the race for most-frequently-asked questions, is this one about writing checks. Of course, the question behind the question is: If we didn't have some kind of official *name*, how could we do business as a church? The good news is that we *couldn't* "do business." We could only get on with being busy about the work of the Kingdom, which doesn't require the kind of organizational trappings we're so addicted to.

Remember, first of all, that a truly radical return to something like first-century house churches would mean doing away with virtually all of our current budget items, such as buildings, and utilities, and staff. All of which lessens the chance that we would need the same kind of budgets and expenditures that our checks typically support. Given that paradigm shift, for instance, the benevolence of the church might actually be achieved on the basis of (...drum roll...) a cash economy! I know it's virtually unthinkable these days, but I'm reliably informed that cash is still legal tender, if perhaps woefully unable to produce air miles.

No, I'm not suggesting that we be completely silly about the matter of church finances; only that there is plenty of scope for re-thinking the whole system from top to bottom. If we could ever move away from the unwarranted idea of "giving" as a mandated "item of worship," and begin thinking of "giving" as a way of meeting special needs whenever they arise, we would not need the same kind of "treasury" to which we are accustomed. (The kind of treasury which, not unlike the U.S. Treasury, is collected as a matter of course, and then begs to be spent in ways both prudent and foolish.)

When *every* collection is special—to meet a *specific need* which has come to the attention of the congregation—it can be as simple as everyone's digging into their pockets and purses and coming up with the necessary money, which is immediately dispatched to those in need. Maybe that happens even during the week. Or perhaps on two or more successive Lord's days. Maybe a week goes by where there is no pressing need, and therefore no "contribution" is collected. The serendipity is that, however we take up the collection, we might well be surprised at how much more money would be raised by our knowing *precisely* the need being met.

Of course, mere mention of the U.S. Treasury raises an issue of importance for many folks: How can we take a tax deduction for charitable giving, if we don't document our contributions by writing checks? I suppose I've been running a certain risk over the years, but I have always reported my cash contributions to the

Lord's work, aware that, if challenged, I might not be able to prove my case to the IRS. Most often, the checks that I write in aid of benevolence are specifically directed to those in need, without using some church treasury as a conduit. If that means being unable to document my charity, then so be it. Perhaps I'm just over-ly sensitive in this regard, but I shrink from the thought that my benevolence is in any way conditioned on its tax implications.

However, I am reminded of a conversation I once had with the late Howard White, former president of Pepperdine University, whom I valued as a wise mentor. When I shared with him some of these heretical ideas, Howard suggested that it just wouldn't be good stewardship not to take full advantage of charitable deduc-tions, since the government, by effectively subsidizing our contri-butions, makes it possible for us to give even more. Perhaps he was right, or perhaps he was thinking too much like a fund-raising uni-versity president, as I reminded him with a smile.

The issue of checks versus cash apart, there remains the question of how to handle whatever ongoing commitments the congregation might have. What about the support of full-time shepherds, for example, or full-time (out-of-pulpit) evangelists? Or the minimal maintenance of any building which might be used in lieu of private homes? (Even meeting the expense of modest facilities for small group worship might require regular rental fees or utilities.)

To say that a congregation should not have the kind of treasury we typically have (supplied arbitrarily from the miscue of "being commanded to give on the Lord's day as we have been prospered") is not to say that having funds on hand and dispens-ing them as necessary is contrary to Scripture. Else what did Paul mean when he instructed the Corinthians to "lay by in store?" Practically speaking, some of our "special collections" might need to be made on a fairly regular basis. But hopefully, even these will take on new meaning because of the different way we speak about, and practice, our giving together as a congregation.

Which brings us back to those pesky checks and the payee blank which is still staring us in the face when we write out amounts that might be foolhardy to carry around in cash on our person. (Or, at the very least, the name on the bank account from which checks need to be written.) My personal preference would be almost any account name and payee *other than* "Church of Christ," simply to move us all beyond the current denominational usage of that term.

At the risk of promoting absurd results greater than the problem to be avoided, it might not be a bad idea if ten different congregations in a given city each had different names on their bank accounts, and thus checks. Among account names that immediately come to mind are: "Christ's church," "The Lord's church," "The Church," "The church of God," "The family of God," and—who knows—perhaps even "The Way."

At the end of the day, of course, it's not really a question about checks and bank accounts, is it? When all is said and done, what we find so unsettling is the thought that we would be essentially nameless. After all, our identity—who we really are—is inextricably tied to a name. Who am I, for example? Well...I'm *LaGard!* It seems not enough for me to be the *son of Frank and Mary Faye*, or (to extend the analogy) to be *a child of God*, or *a disciple*, or *a follower of Christ*.

Yet, if we take rightful pride in being "Christians only," then why can't we be just that—simply *Christians*? What does it matter that others have hijacked the name inappropriately? If anyone should ask about our "church affiliation," we can just tell them that we are citizens of the Kingdom of God who meet together regularly to remember Christ and encourage each other in our faith. And, would they like to know more...?

(As it happens, I took advantage of such an opportunity this very morning when our plumber—to whom I had given one of my books yesterday—asked what church I was a member of in the States. Thirty minutes later, we were still seriously discussing differences in churches, the nature of God, and the deity of Jesus—all because I adamantly refused to give the kind of easy answer he first expected.)

For fellow Christians who might wish to know with which congregation we worship, we could do worse than to begin using biblical language itself. Why not the simple response: "With the disciples who meet in the McCaskills' house;" or "With the brothers and sisters who worship together at the municipal hall?" Short of that, it would be a healthy start if we would simply quit adding the mandatory label, "Church of Christ" (which should already be implicit), to individual congregations. Instead of routinely saying, "The Greymont Church of Christ," why not simply "The Greymont congregation?" Or we could simply respond: "We worship at Bellwood;" or "We meet with the family of God at Brentview."

What's in a name? Sometimes everything; sometimes nothing at all. There is, for example, the matchless name of Jesus, at whose name one day every knee will bow. And then there are the names which just happen to be on checking accounts and checks. Unlike the name of Jesus, those names don't matter in the least.

One day last fall, I just knew I'd found the perfect answer to the check question. On a trip to South Carolina, Ruth and I stopped for lunch outside Knoxville, Tennessee. Next to the cozy log-cabin tea room where we had eaten was an antique store which we popped into for a quick browse. Along one of the aisles, I noticed a box on the floor with all sorts of rubber stamps, which obviously had come from some defunct business. Among the stamps, I found one so interesting that I immediately picked it up and rushed to show it to Ruth. "Here's the answer to the question about our checks," I said to her, turning the stamp so she could see the words. The words? "Payable to Maker!"

And why not? Everything we give is ultimately to our Maker.

How could small congregations afford to support missionaries?

For congregations which currently are larger than average, it could be done by minimizing the overhead. In most large congregations, the bigger the budgets for mission work, the bigger also the overhead. So, to whatever extent returning to the small-congregation model could reduce the expense of maintaining huge buildings and a sizable support staff, to that extent there will be more money freed up for mission work (even if the "mission" is the local neighborhood).

For congregations which are already small-to-average, little would change in terms of actual availability of funds. (I could be dead wrong, but my guess is that smaller congregations already have a higher ratio of giving-per-person than larger congregations.) Particularly if there were a shift from pulpit ministers to teaching pastors, then the minister-turned-evangelist could easily be supported by a single, small congregation, or perhaps in conjunction with another congregation which also contributes directly to his work.

At the risk of veering slightly off-issue, it simply has to be said that our present system of financing mission work is woefully inefficient. While I can't point to any specific Scripture that would confirm the observation, from what we are told—and *not* told—it appears highly unlikely that first-century evangelists had to spend an inordinate amount of time and expense seeking and maintaining support, as is the case today. It is an absolute scandal when our evangelists abroad are forced to spend weeks on the road back home drumming up monthly checks from a dozen different congregations, each of which seemingly takes pride in how many different mission efforts they are supporting. Not only is it financially wasteful and emotionally draining, but it doesn't speak well for any genuine, long-term involvement in the evangelism being done. Nor, for that matter, with the families who are often sacrificing more than we appreciate to do that difficult work.

The call to "mutual ministry" takes on a whole new (and altogether wonderful) meaning when individual congregations commit themselves fully over the long haul to a single evangelist and his family, whether in a local or a foreign work. That would be true congregational participation, giving all involved a greater sense of mutual responsibility, accountability, and joyful celebration.

And finally, there is this thought (suggested by a brother experienced in mission work): that our attachment to buildings and pulpit preachers has fostered, in turn, a culture of dependence among many foreign congregations whereby an assumed need for their own buildings and pulpit preachers has prevented their independence from long-term financial support. To what extent, then, might evangelism be advanced, especially in poorer countries, by returning to a less formalized model of church structures, both physical and organizational? Which leads us to the next question....

Must we really sell off all our buildings?

That depends. First, how emotionally attached are we to the buildings? My guess is that, the finer the building (and the more money we've personally invested in it), the more difficult it would be for us to give it up. Yet, ironically, the more attached we are, the more we *need* to give it up! When keeping the building becomes more important than our achieving greater spiritual growth in another setting, our notion of "the church" couldn't be more misguided.

Yet, even if we could easily walk away from whatever building we're presently meeting in, the question remains: Is it scripturally *imperative* that we meet in private homes? At the risk of supplying ammunition for the "form follows function" argument, I suggest that the pattern is not so much a matter of private homes as opposed to church buildings, but rather a matter of gathered assemblies being small enough to be intimate, spontaneous, and mutually-participatory.

Lawyer that I am, however, I would also argue against myself to say that function has an interesting way of following form. Show me a "church building" that has the usual pulpit and pews, and I'll show you a body of believers who probably don't function much like the first-century church. Form may not always be primary, but it's not irrelevant.

In that respect, it is equally possible that a congregation could begin meeting next Sunday in private homes rather than in their former "church building," and yet function pretty much the same way they've always functioned. At the very least, however, it would be more difficult for them to maintain the kind of rigidity of worship ritual to which they were accustomed. What's more, there is something about the hospitality of a home that simply can't be duplicated elsewhere, especially if a memorial meal is to be the centerpiece of the gathering.

When, as a practical matter, no one in the congregation has a home large enough to host the Lord's Day gathering, there should be plenty of places available for small group meetings, including schools, club rooms in housing developments, and rental space in retail buildings and industrial parks. If these venues seem dreary substitutes for our more conventional buildings, they would at least leave us with no illusions about what constitutes "the church." (For what it's worth, some of the fastest-growing community churches today are meeting in just such facilities instead of the traditional "church building." Rather than experiencing impeded growth, these fellowships have found renewed purpose and vitality—not to mention less wasted money—in shifting the focus away from bricks and mortar.)

At a minimum, what we need for the moment is a moratorium on all future building projects. Such a pause would give us time to step back and reconsider what we are doing and why. If we insist on going ahead with the "building phase," perhaps we might at least significantly alter the designs to better promote first-century form and function. Better yet, before we pour the foundation, we would do well to consider the profound implications of another building project—the one we read about in the Gospels, in which our Lord said, "Upon this rock, I will build my church." That he didn't have bricks and mortar in mind goes without saying.

Would down-sizing mean that we could no longer gather in large numbers?

I certainly hope not. I treasure the times when hundreds, even thousands, of us join together in fellowship to hear the Word proclaimed and to blend our voices in praise and edification. With even the most radical scenario possible (no visible presence what-soever apart from the Kingdom work in which we are all fervently engaged), I see no reason, either scriptural or practical, why the vis-ible church could not assemble together *en masse* as God's people. Somebody—*anybody*—spread the word! The informal networking of a radically restored body of Christians will soon get the message: We're having a giant family reunion! Everyone's invited.

In cities and metropolitan areas, let's stay in touch and get together even more often than we presently do. In states and regions and countries around the globe, keep alive the precious ties that bind our hearts in Christian love. Elders far and near, stay connected to your fellow elders in other congregations and share each other's burdens. Come together town by town and city by city to pray for the Kingdom. Congregational autonomy was intended to promote intimacy, not isolation.

Meet together as the wider family? Save me a seat. I'll be there!

What about the memorial meal itself? How would that actual-ly work?

Having already given more than my fair share of advice, it may now appear to be a cop out if I don't suggest specific ways and means of doing things. Nevertheless, I am hesitant to fill in the blanks left empty by Scripture. It's too easy for a suggestion to become a practice; a practice a ritual; a ritual a rule. My only advice is that the *real meal* eaten in fellowship as part of the *memorial meal* ought to be made as simple as possible so that there can be no confusion about which is more important. The last thing we would want to do is repeat the mistake of the Corinthians and turn the memorial meal into an unworthy picnic.

Other than that, I can easily visualize Christ's memorial being thoughtfully incorporated into the middle of the meal; or certainly prior to the meal; or, indeed, following it. (Ruth suggests that those who prepare the meal might appreciate having it first so they can concentrate more fully on the memorial.) What matters most is that we strive to recapture the intimacy of table fellowship while recognizing the broad implications of Christ's spiritual body "breaking bread" together on the first day of the week.

Would children be permitted to join in the memorial meal?

A family I know who meets in a house church with a few other families has relayed to me one of the surprising details they encountered the first time they celebrated the memorial meal together around the table. It suddenly dawned on them that the children would be eating the "love feast" alongside the adults. How, then, to handle the matter of children participating? In the end, the "problem" virtually resolved itself when they decided to have a time of prayer separating the fellowship meal from the time devoted to the memorial, even though they remained "at table" with one another.

What happens to the children and teens?

While on the subject of young people...I'm certainly not unaware that my call for eliminating youth ministries would be a shock to the system, and that the vacuum would have to be filled in appropriate ways. As one brother wrote to me recently, "Young people are in a unique position to influence other young people when maturity is progressing toward adulthood, and life-changing decisions are being made at that stage in life. What more opportune time to reach those impressionable young minds with the gospel of Christ than when they are searching for meaning to life's questions?" Indeed.

Perhaps even more crucial was his observation that "I see all around me a world of teenagers and pre-teens who are practically raising themselves as a result of divorce and neglect on the part of their parents' poor choices. Therefore kids with this background have no spiritual guidance from the very two adults responsible for that training. The youth of the church, Christian parents, senior members and youth workers are able to fill that void. Thus, the whole congregation is involved in the 'youth ministry' in one respect."

As I expressed earlier, I'm not at all sure that "the whole congregation is involved" under the current youth-ministry system, but there are ways in which it certainly could be. And *must* be! With parents taking the lead in teaching their own children and (where possible) including children from homes where parents are not a contributing spiritual factor, responsibility would be much closer to home. And particularly in house-churches, it would remain close to home. In small groups, children automatically become part of the fellowship, not a separate entity. At the earliest possible moment, they are right in there with the adults, thinking like adults and acting like adults.

Nothing of what I have said excludes times for separate youth fellowship. In the same way that today's youth ministers organize and promote camps and retreats, parents and other older disciples can provide similar times of interaction which nurture spiritual and social relationships between teens and pre-teens. Especially among a wide network of small group fellowships, there is no reason why young people should ever feel isolated or left out. To abandon "youth ministries" is not to abandon ministry to our youth. Hopefully, it is to do a more effective job of helping them in their search for meaning and in making mature, life-changing decisions.

Would there be a place for Bible classes for the young in small group fellowships?

I see no reason why not, as long as everyone is clear that the classes are not to be a substitute for parent-led teaching within each family, and as long as young people—especially teens—are incorporated into more mature adult studies as quickly as their maturity allows.

As thousands of us who grew up without youth ministries and cradle roll and "Junior Church" can attest, children from the earliest ages may be quietly coloring Bible scenes, or even squirming uncomfortably in their seats, but they are listening and observing without even being aware of it. On several occasions I have taught a lesson in which I use a mythical "Jumbo, the elephant" to make a serious point. Without fail, the face of every youngster immediately lights up, and, with that, I have their full attention...at least until I ungraciously dampen their fascination by 'fessing up that "Jumbo" isn't real! "Jumbo" or not, we should never underestimate what learning is taking place as the young ones sit among us.

An incidental concern for some is that "uncomfortable squirming" I just mentioned. "What's to be done with crying children in a house church or other small group settings?" I'm often asked. "After all, there wouldn't be special 'cry rooms' as we have in most buildings these days."

I suppose it would seem less than sympathetic for me to observe that God's people managed to survive for two centuries without having church buildings, much less "cry rooms." Beyond that, I can only say that I have vivid memories of switches from a peach tree just outside the building where my mother used to retreat to get my attention. To this day, I find even whispering "in church" difficult to do!

Being completely practical, if congregations were literally meeting in private homes, I suspect that distressed infants probably could be accommodated even more readily than in austere church buildings, "cry rooms" and all. Homes are tailor-made for children.

As something of an aside, I'm personally less concerned about the actual facilities than the attitude of some parents who, even in today's typical church buildings, seem oblivious to the way in which their disruptive children become a hindrance to everyone else's attempts at worship and edification. But I have no suggestions in that regard, being of the conviction that, if you have to tell folks what ought to be really obvious, you can never tell them! Still, on balance, I'd side every time with having the little ones right there with the rest of us. The church, together with the future church...singing, scribbling, squirming, and, yes, even screaming!

Where would we find enough elders for all the small group fellowships?

First off, many if not most of our present congregations are already "small group fellowships." At the very least, we would have no greater problem than we already have. Beyond that, however, I would suggest that a radical shift in our understanding of congregational leadership ought to go a long way toward resolving this question. The smaller our groups, the more participatory they should be (assuming we're not just going through the usual motions). The more participatory they are, the more likely it is that a greater number of men will develop into being strong spiritual leaders. If we could ever develop a church culture in which mutual ministry takes place on a wide scale, there ought to be an unlimited supply of mature older men from whom shepherds can be appointed in even the smallest of flocks.

But someone has asked, "What would we do in the meantime, when we haven't had twenty years of grooming elders?" I'm just optimistic enough to think that, if we ever got really serious about radical restoration, we could close the elder gap rather rapidly, not unlike the American space program playing some serious catch-up after the shocking news that the Soviets had launched Sputnik. After all, we wouldn't exactly be starting from scratch. We already have many dedicated elders in place (if perhaps in need of reassignment as teaching shepherds), and other men who are well on their way to spiritual maturity. In light of this new challenge, some high-intensity studies for the men certainly wouldn't go amiss.

What if my elders don't agree that I should leave the pulpit to be an evangelist?

This was the poignant question from one pulpit minister for whom accepting the idea of radical restoration conceivably could have crucial personal consequences. I have said repeatedly that there is no *need* for any pulpit preacher to lose his job. (And I might add youth ministers or any other kind of "ministers" we presently support.) In theory, we are only talking about a reassignment of responsibilities and functions. But as this preacher for a fairly large congregation said to me, "If I told my elders, 'Here's what I need to be paid to do; take care of the pulpit yourselves,' I would be cut off." Which is to say, fired. With a wife and children to support.

Sometimes I forget that I exist in an ivory tower. For almost thirty years, I have had the luxury of thinking aloud in the protective freedom of academia, where the search for truth is permitted for its own sake. That's what universities are all about, even (especially?) Christian universities. Among all the institutions of higher education, Christian universities need have no fear of the search for truth, since the Truth for which we search is divine. And so I consider myself extremely blessed not to face the pressure reflected in the question put to me by someone whose paycheck is so dependent on maintaining (if I may put it this way) the party line.

Yet, I recognize that the present function of the pulpit preacher is far more precarious, and in a sense *must* be. I can hardly urge stronger leadership on the part of elders and then turn right around and emasculate that same leadership by undercutting their responsibility to do what they think is right for their flock. But where does that leave a pulpit minister who feels led in a different direction?

The hard answer (easy for me to say) is taking a leap of faith. The same leap of faith that reformers and restorationists have always had to take—many with far more drastic consequences than any preacher today surely would ever face. Loss of livelihood and loss of life are not to be compared. Still, serious decisions of conscience such as these are not the kind of choices that anyone can make for someone else. We must each count the cost and search our own souls. Is that not what we preach from our pulpits? Is that not what we ask of everyone else?

But perhaps there are alternatives which we have yet to explore. Baby steps that can be taken before adult-like strides. Patiently working through some of the more difficult concepts; educating; preparing the soil and planting the seeds; allowing folks time to understand the need for some of the major concerns we've been talking about. No one is calling for a mass conversion overnight. Even the scholarly Nicodemus needed time to make sense of concepts that at first seemed downright ludicrous.

As I think about it, this preacher's question is not altogether different from the question that each of us must ask about radical restoration, even if our livelihoods are not threatened in the same way. For each of us, *something* will be threatened. None of us will be exempt from having to count the cost. Given the seriousness of what hangs in the balance, it's a time for all of us to do some serious soul-searching.

By definition, radical restoration is a radical idea. And radical ideas need time. And study. And prayer.

After all that, it may finally require a leap of faith. Then again, after all that it may not be such a great leap.

Chapter Thirteen

Radical to the Core

Faithfulness in little things is a big thing.

St. John Chrysostom

After all this talk about radically restoring primitive faith and practice, we come at last to the heart and soul of our discussion: Does it truly matter? Is it not how we live our lives before Christ that really counts? Will radically changing the way we meet together for worship and edification make a dramatic difference in the kind of people we are?

Certainly, those are all the right questions. For the answers, let me invite you to look back on our discussion of radical restoration and think carefully about some of the major paradigm shifts we've encountered:

- From a body of radically-thinking and radically-living people, to a people who fit rather comfortably in culture.
- From a dynamic first-century organism, to a 21st-century religious organization more defined by its doctrinal correctness than its fervor.
- From intimate, mutually-participatory congregations, to typically larger, mostly passive audiences in church buildings.

- From weekly fellowship meals centering on the memorial bread and wine, to a miniaturized, ceremonial version of the Lord's Supper.
- From an elder-led-and-fed flock, to an undeclared clergy system of pulpit ministers unknown to the early disciples.
- From parental responsibility for spiritual development of the young, to youth ministries which have divided the Lord's body into separate congregations and perspectives.
- From personally-professing evangelism to (in theory) evangelism by professionally-trained communicators.
- From evangelism in public places and from house to house among the lost, to preaching in pulpits before audiences mostly devoid of unbelievers.
- From spontaneous giving to meet special needs, to a formalized "contribution" regarded as an indispensable item of worship.
- From a non-denominational body of Christ having no official name, to an institutionalized denomination in both name and practice.

———————

Is it even remotely possible that this many significant paradigm shifts have had no impact on the kind of people we are?

The renowned Charles Haddon Spurgeon is credited with saying that "sermonettes make Christianettes." In a similar vein, I suggest that *institutional churches* make *institutional Christians*. And more particularly...

That multi-programed churches can make merely busy Christians.

That superficial churches can make shallow Christians.

That large, impersonal churches can make disengaged Christians.

That passive churches can make lifeless Christians.

That materialistic, culturally-compromised churches can make fleshly, worldly Christians.

By stark contrast, intimate, involved, mutually-participatory churches are more likely to produce spiritually-driven Christians who are intensely focused on God, crucified with Christ, infused with the Holy Spirit, in love with fellow disciples, committed to holy lives, separated from the world, filled with genuine piety, and passionate about evangelism.

With exceptions abounding, the more ritualized the church, the less spiritualized the soul. The more hierarchical the church, the less involved the individual. The larger the congregation, the smaller the role of the ordinary member.

More seems almost always to be *less*, while *less* has a far better chance of being *more*. Merely consider Christ's own picture of the Kingdom—that tiny mustard seed which, when it grows, takes over the whole world!

All of which is to say that the way we meet together for worship and edification does indeed make a difference as to the kind of people we are. Not only do ideas have consequences, but the institutions spawned by those ideas also have consequences we sometimes fail to fully appreciate.

As the Church Goes, So We Go

If, as it is said, "we are what we eat," then undoubtedly it is also true that we are what we imbibe together from week to week as an assembled body of believers. As Jesus put it, "a tree is recognized by its fruit." Or, turning to the flip-side, look at the fruit we are bearing—or, more importantly, *not* bearing—and you can tell much about the institutional "tree" from which our fruitlessness has come.

Yet, just think how different it could be! Suppose we really and truly radically restored the form and practice of the early church...and then began to mimic that pattern in our own, individual lives. Just look at the wonderful fruit which that could produce....

Reflecting the move from elaborate buildings to simpler arrangements, we ourselves would be encouraged to have simpler lifestyles all the way around. Less materialistic. Less concerned about our *houses* and more concerned about our *homes.* Less time worrying about furnishings and fittings, and more time concentrated on our family's faith and the physical and spiritual needs of others.

Mirroring the move from being mostly passive spectators to being actively involved in a vibrant mutual ministry, we'd be more passionate about life itself! More outgoing, more people-oriented, more willing to participate and to contribute and to serve. Less self-absorbed, and more sacrificial. Less complacent in a world fraught with evil. Sensing a greater responsibility for making a difference wherever God has called us.

Consistent with the move from highly-structured organization and ritual to a more dynamic, spontaneous organism, we could never again regard regular church attendance and one-day-a-week contributions as substitutes for radical acts of personal piety. Nor perfunctory prayers at the dinner table as the limit of our conversations with God, but rather nurture within ourselves an ongoing, minute-by-minute attitude of prayer. Nor consider singing together congregationally as our exclusive avenue of praise, but rather be so filled with the Spirit that, moment to moment, our hearts well up with melodies of praise.

And then there's the move from vicarious evangelism to personal evangelism. Would we not find ourselves more joyful in sharing our faith with others and more convicted about our own calling to take the good news of salvation to a lost world? And the minute that happened, would we not find ourselves studying the Word more diligently than ever; and living more exemplary lives in the presence of those we hope to reach for Christ; and praying for the lost—not just generically—but face by face and name by name?

I realize those connections may sound a bit contrived and the supposed results way too easy, but there simply has to be *some* correlation between how we worship together and the kind of people we "just happen" to be. Individuals will certainly vary within any kind of congregational model, and in every kind of congregational model there can be people who are genuinely and passionately sold-out believers. Yet, across the board, the people in congregations of all types have their own distinct characteristics.

Show me a congregation that is legalistic and judgmental, for instance, and I'll show you a bunch of folks who are likely as not to be rather sour and critical about virtually everything in life. Show me a congregation that reeks of money, and I'll show you a group of people who are likely more materialistic than average. While it's probably true that congregations *attract* certain personalities, or perhaps *reflect* the composition of their members, I posit that—individual personalities aside—they also *produce* different kinds of people.

Just in case you think I've got the process back-to-front, incidentally, I couldn't agree more with those who insist that it's regenerated people who bring new life to a congregation. After all, the people *are* the church! But show me a congregation that is radically transformed as a functioning spiritual body, and I'll show you people who, one by one, are radically regenerated. God paved the church to be a two-way street. Change the people as they ought to be, and you've changed the church as it should be. Change the church as it ought to be, and you've gone a long way toward changing the people as they should be.

Or more to the point, as *you and I* should be!

Jesus—A Radical Life

More and more, we are being called to be, not just a doctrinally-correct church, but a cruciform church. That is, a more cross-formed, cross-centered, cross-motivated people. A people whose eyes are fixed on Jesus. A people who ask WWJD (what would Jesus do?) It may be a faddish question, but it's a good one. What *would* Jesus do in the context of our own 21st-century culture when it comes to times of gathered worship and edification in the Kingdom? Would he do things differently from the Spirit-led, apostle-taught primitive church? Would he feel comfortable in one of our typical "worship services"? Would he serve as a pulpit minister, or involvement minister, or youth minister? What would he think about our current elder system?

The only problem with asking "WWJD?" is that we have an interesting way of coming up with answers which suit our own preconceived notions. At the risk of our doing just that, have you ever considered the striking parallels between Jesus' life and this present discussion?

Consider, for example, his "nameless" origins. By the world's standards, there was nothing about his birth and early childhood that stood out as a signpost of identity. The only signs Jesus knew anything about was the power of God working wonders in people's lives and the sign which Pilate derisively attached to the cross, mocking his kingship over the Jews. Jesus, the Name above all names, did not rely on having the "right name." It was enough that he knew who he was...and that all men would be called to him through the sign of "the snake lifted up in the desert" and the sign of "Jonah in the belly of the great fish."

Is it possible that signs outside the building have robbed us of a closer identity with Christ which might be richer and deeper by simply knowing whose we are?

As the son of man, fully divine yet fully human, the young boy Jesus left Jerusalem at the age of twelve and went down to Nazareth with his parents, "and was obedient to them." As simply as that, we learn that the Lord of the Universe himself paid deference to generational wisdom. And at the feet of his earthly parents, Jesus learned whatever it took for him to grow "in wisdom and stature, and in favor with God and men."

Do children lose something precious when parents opt out of the process of spiritual training?

Jesus said of himself, "Foxes have holes and birds of the air have nests, but the Son of Man has no place to lay his head." Maybe I'm overreaching here, but it does seem that, from his birth in a borrowed manger to his burial in a borrowed tomb, Jesus pointedly avoided all permanence of place, as if to remind us how easy it is to become attached to externals and miss what should be going on inside.

If "church" were thought of as a relationship instead of a place, might we not have an enhanced appreciation for why we come together each week?

Escaping the clamoring crowds, Jesus most often communed with only twelve men and perhaps a handful of other disciples. There were times for the multitudes, of course, but the most productive discipling seems to have taken place in small group settings. In the midst of intimacy and informality, hearts could be opened and minds could be stretched. Jesus didn't have to have crowds. His small handful of dedicated disciples turned the world upside down!

Would we not be more on-fire if we abandoned the lure of bigness and settled, instead, for the intimacy and informality which only smaller groups can provide?

Over and over, Jesus sat at table with those whom he was discipling. Whether with the Twelve in the upper room, or at the banquets thrown in his honor by Simon and Levi, or while celebrating the wedding at Cana—Jesus repeatedly placed a high value on table fellowship.

Might we not discover added meaning in The Supper were we to eat the memorial meal together—even if only from time to time— around a real table instead of the ceremonial one we're used to?

We've mentioned the obvious before—that Jesus didn't choose professionally-trained rabbis or priests to be his apostles. Yet it is also instructive that Jesus himself did not incarnate among the priestly or rabbinic ranks. Everyone marveled that "he taught as one who had authority, and not as their teachers of the law."

Would our own appreciation for the simple authority of God's Word be enhanced if we weaned ourselves away from the idea that we can only learn at the feet of professionally trained ministers?

And then there's the cross itself—a model of stripped-bare simplicity, abject humility, and personal involvement. It was hardly what the world would have recognized as successful or exciting...much less fun. And you can be sure that only the soldiers gambling for his clothes thought it was entertaining. How far we have traveled from the foot of the cross!

Nor was it a time for the thrill of a crowd. As the pall of Jesus' death gripped the disciples, everything about the moment tells us they must have found comfort and strength in the common bond they had forged with the few. Those they could trust. Those with whom they could openly weep. Those to whom they could reveal their deepest doubts and fiercest fears at such a time. Or at any such time....

Even before tears of sadness would become tears of joy at the breaking dawn of resurrection day, a revolutionary idea was already in the pangs of birth. Even while Jesus' body lay cold and lifeless in the tomb on that dreadful night, we see cruciform congregations already beginning to take shape: Small. Intimate. Interactive. Sharing. Caring. And, like Jesus' own body, soon to be wondrously and joyfully transformed beyond anyone's wildest imagination.

My own guess is that if we could ever find our way back to the foot of the cross, it wouldn't be just "the church" belonging to Christ that is truly restored in faith and practice, but a dynamic body of believers individually becoming more and more radical for Christ.

Heart-and-soul radical...to our very core.

Radical Discipleship

It was Jesus himself, of course, who was first "radical to the core." Just listen to what he said. *No calling was ever more radical.* "Come, follow me." "I have food to eat that you know nothing about." "Unless you eat the flesh of the Son of Man and drink his blood, you have no life in you." "Anyone who loves his father or mother more than me is not worthy of me; anyone who loves his son or daughter more than me is not worthy of me; and anyone who does not take his cross and follow me is not worthy of me." "Whoever wants to save his life will lose it, but whoever loses his life for me and for the gospel will save it." "Any of you who does not give up everything he has cannot be my disciple."

No lifestyle was ever more radical: "No one can serve two masters. Either he will hate the one and love the other, or he will be devoted to the one and despise the other. You cannot serve both God and Money." "Woe to you who are well fed now, for you will go hungry." "Blessed are those who hunger and thirst for righteousness, for they will be filled." "Do not store up for yourselves treasures on earth, where moth and rust destroy, and where thieves break in and steal. But store up for yourselves treasure in heaven...."

No spiritual purity was ever more radical: "Repent for the kingdom of heaven is near." "Not everyone who says to me, 'Lord, Lord,' will enter the kingdom of heaven, but only he who does the will of my Father who is in heaven." "Unless your righteousness surpasses that of the Pharisees and the teachers of the law, you will certainly not enter the kingdom of heaven." "It is better for you to lose one part of your body than for your whole body to be thrown into hell."

The relationship between that kind of radical discipleship and radical restoration is captured wonderfully by Brendan Manning in his book *The Signature of Jesus.* "The early church," he writes, "was built on small groups of people who came together to support one another in a whole new way of life. These primitive communities were visible evidence of an alternative to the status quo of their culture. Today we need small bands of people who take the gospel at face value, who realize what God is doing in our time, and who are living proof of being in the world but not of the world. These base communities or neighborhood churches should be small enough for intimacy, kindred enough for acceptance, and gentle enough for criticism. Gathered in the name of Jesus, the community empowers us to incarnate in our lives what we believe in our hearts and proclaim with our lips."

Powerful stuff! A radical people banded together in a radical church to show witness to a sinful world in need of radical transformation.

Still Not Convinced?

As much as I wish I could leave our conversation on this lofty, idealistic note, I am under no illusion that, either as a result of this book or any other similar prompting, the vast majority of our present congregations are going to make the kind of radical changes we've been discussing. Not that there is anyone among us who disagrees with the proposition that we ought to be "heart-and-soul radical" for Christ. It's just that we won't all agree as to whether such a radical Christian commitment necessarily demands radical changes in the way we have functioned for so long as God's people.

Some, I'm sure, will have been greatly offended at the mere suggestion that the "Churches of Christ" as we know them are denominational in name and practice, and thereby fundamentally flawed. Others, I suspect, will simply be mystified that anyone might think we have not already fully restored the New Testament church. Still others might find that at least some of our discussion has resonated with their own private musings over the years, but remain unconvinced about other parts of the package. I suppose there may be a few who might buy every word of it in theory, but see too many practical obstacles to our actually implementing radical change. And fewer still, perhaps, who can't wait for the revolution to begin!

I'll share with you one of my own reservations: the distinct likelihood that in the initial stages of radical restoration we'd be so focused on form and format that we'd lose sight of what it's all *for*! Just another round of changes for the sake of change. More gimmicks. The latest fad. Or, for those already so inclined, legalism *nouveau*—yet one more opportunity to get bogged down in doctrinal debate and details. Father, spare us!

Is there, then, any reason to hope? I frankly don't know. I, for one, would be shocked if any of our mega-congregations suddenly sold their massive building, split into ten separate congregations and began worshiping according to something like the house church model. And seriously astonished if any congregation of any size suddenly tore out their pulpit and pews in order to gather more informally in some other way. And even mildly surprised if there were many of us who took to regularly observing the Lord's Supper as part of a common fellowship meal.

Somehow I just can't visualize thousands of "Church of Christ" signs being torn down overnight, and "Church of Christ" ads suddenly missing from the Yellow Pages, and "Church of Christ" letterheads being tossed out—right, left, or center. Much less do I see hundreds of pulpit ministers fleeing their pulpits for the streets, exhausted though they may be from being one-man-bands. Or youth ministers in their scores handing their young charges back to their parents. Or anything like a high percentage of elders assuming primary responsibility for spiritually feeding the flock over which they are overseers.

So where do we go from here? Is there any way forward? I think so. Or at least I think there may be *many* ways forward. For those who are already running through the streets shouting for the revolution to begin, down-size your congregations, flee your pulpits, become real teaching shepherds, and spread the love feast table in memory and in fellowship! The rest of us wish you Godspeed. Show those of us who are less courageous, or simply not yet fully convinced, that it really can be done. All the way. To the extreme. Your unique role is to push the outer margins so that the rest of us have more room to manoeuver in the center. We *want* to believe; help our unbelief.

Suggestions For the Not-So-Radical

For the rest of us who are intrigued by the possibilities, yet still hesitant, maybe there are some things we could do—short of radical change—which could make a surprising difference. Perhaps even the smallest of things. At the risk of trivializing the whole process, think, for example, what it would be like if we took down the attendance and contribution boards at the front of the auditorium; and removed attendance and visitor cards from the pew racks; and quit assigning folks to be "official greeters." And dispensed with the printed "order of worship." Each of those seemingly insignificant things has its own important story to tell about who we are and what we're about.

And more important than those—throw away the clock...perhaps literally! We sing the song "Take Time To Be Holy," but rarely do we take it seriously at any level. Don't rush our special time with God and with each other. Take time for prayer. Lots of time. Not just two or three perfunctory prayers, but have a special time set aside for prayer. And take more time, especially, for the Lord's Supper. If we're not going to have a true memorial meal, the least we could do is to make the "Supper" the centerpiece of our time together, with songs, and prayers, and shared thoughts about why we observe that hallowed memorial each Lord's Day.

And is there any chance we might sing without a song leader drowning everyone else out? Do we really need someone waving his arms from the pulpit? It might take some getting used to, but surely we'd get the hang of it eventually. The idea is to take the spotlight away from the front and blend us all together. To listen to each other as we teach and edify one another through song, not just to sing for its own sake.

Remember, it's mutual participation we are after at every possible level. Whether song leading, or bringing thoughts around the table, or teaching and preaching—open it up for all the men to take responsibility. And train them to do it well, beginning not with methods but with prayer and study of the Word. Center a man on God, and the methods will take care of themselves.

But as the men grow, don't teach them to preach. That's right. Don't teach them to preach. Teach them to share their study...their struggles in the Word...their experience in living it out...and their hearts as they reflect on what they've studied. Let's not perpetuate an expectation for the same kind of sermons from those who continue to preach full-time. Let's allow them to *talk* to us about our spiritual needs. To feed and nurture is not necessarily to prepare a sermon with three memorable points. (Can you even remember any of the three-point sermons you've heard lately?)

If we simply insist on having a pulpit minister preach to us Sunday after Sunday, then for heaven's sake (literally) clear his desk of all the extraneous responsibilities we've burdened him with and let him mine the deepest fathoms of revelation in the solitude it takes to see God face to face. If the "Supper" could ever become the centerpiece of our time together, we wouldn't have to expect an exciting "home run" from the preacher each week. It would be enough that he shared one simple thought about God that we've never before considered. Something we can really take away with us. Something that might not soothe us, but would definitely stretch us and challenge us, whether it takes ten minutes or an hour and a half.

And when the elder or preacher is finally finished, forget the invitation song. That tradition belongs to another mind-set altogether. Why not finish instead with a time for discussion and feedback? We do something like that wherever I speak—during "Late Night With LaGard"—and folks are clearly hungry for the opportunity. But instead of just one man (namely me!) answering the questions, why not the elders? Pass the microphone around, if need be, so that everyone can ask the questions which have come to mind, or can share their own insights. Toss the teacher's ideas back and forth. Follow in Jesus' footsteps when invariably he asked: "What do you think?" "What do you think?" "What do you think?"

A Time For Reflection

So what *do* you think? Does any of this make sense? Is it even remotely possible to keep in mind the bigger picture without getting bogged down in details? Are there other things I haven't mentioned? Can you think of anything else that might be standing in the way of our individually being "radical to the core" as God's people?

What I've tried to do in the pages of this book is to call us back to the restoration ideal which we share in common. To be as objective as possible about the faith and practice of the apostolic church. To be brutally honest about how we stack up with the early disciples by way of comparison. To challenge our thinking about how we might close the obvious gap between ideal and reality. And to suggest practical ways we might recapture the spirit of our forebears in the faith.

But it's up to you at this point. If the picture I've painted seems altogether too radical, too extreme, then you must find your own center. If you're not at all convinced that I've made my case, then the time has come for you to make your own.

In fact, the time may well come when all of our minds will be made up for us. If our post-Christian culture continues unimpeded in the godless direction it's headed, the day could appear (and soon) when we will have no choice but to follow the lead of the early church. For of one thing we can be sure: the onslaught of official, hard-core persecution would quickly produce radically different congregations. We wouldn't have to worry about whether to sell our buildings. They'd be taken from us! We wouldn't have to think about meeting in small groups. It would be the only way we could meet! Nor would we likely maintain reservations about observing the Lord's Supper as part of a fellowship meal. Intimate, Christ-sharing table fellowship with brothers and sisters under a common threat would become a precious time indeed.

In all honesty, I can't say I look forward wistfully to such a time as that. I'm sure none of us does. Yet, I confess I crave that kind of fellowship here and now. An intimacy in worship that I have never before known. A vibrancy in mutual edification that I can only dream about. A life more pure and sacrificial than I have ever lived. A mind more alert to the Spirit's leading. A soul more in tune with my Savior. And a heart turned inside out for God—radical to the core!

Do you know what I mean? Have you ever longed to experience something better? Something *radically* better? Maybe now's the time. Maybe this is a way....

A way that you and I and a host of others who are searching their souls and dreaming the dream might one day, some day—by God's grace—become the "we" of that which follows. The "we" who are poised on the brink of...prayerful...careful... *radical* restoration.

EPILOGUE

Whereas we believe that God has revealed divine patterns of both form and function for our being faithful disciples of Christ, and for working and worshiping together as his children; and

Whereas we desire to rid ourselves of any taint of denominational thinking and practice; and

Whereas we wish to genuinely restore within our own culture and time the faith and practice of the Spirit-led primitive church;

Now therefore, be it hereby resolved ...

That it is our desire to recapture as best we can both the purity and simplicity of apostolic Christianity. To strip ourselves wholly of those things which tend to characterize today's structured church, including elaborate organizations and buildings, staffs and budgets, programs and ministries. To focus, instead, on matters of the heart as well as on matters of faith and doctrine. To seriously equip ourselves in the knowledge of God's Word. To strive earnestly for a vibrant spirituality beyond mere biblical teaching and doctrinal correctness. To assume, as of highest priority, personal, individual responsibility in sharing the gospel with the lost. And to serve our fellow man with greater awareness of needs, both within the church and without, both local and global.

In seeking radical restoration of apostolic worship, we also commit ourselves to radical restoration of the spirit of

Christ within each one of us. We recognize that no mere change in external worship ritual can alone guarantee changed lives. And so we commit to God and to each other a renewal of our covenant relationship with God. We wish not only to be justified by a single past act of faith-prompted immersion, but to be sanctified daily through the working of the Spirit in our lives.

We hereby confess that we are a sinful and rebellious people, having loved this present world and brought shame upon the very cross of Christ by which we have been redeemed. That we have deliberately chosen to participate in acts of immorality unbefitting children of God. That we have tainted our eyes and ears with the ugly images, sounds, and thoughts of an ungodly culture. That, even now, we worship regularly at the shrines of crass consumerism and materialism. That both in our allocation of time and energy and in our financial resources, we have set wrong priorities before God.

We wish, then, not to further exacerbate our rebellion by bringing our love of the world into our worship of God, either to entertain, or to impress, or to take false confidence from congregational attendance, stained glass and steeples, or even frenetic busyness in the pursuit of church-sponsored activities. Rather, we wish to worship in such a way as to be reminded of the only values which are genuine and godly, and to see afresh a spiritual reality that will call us further and further away from the world's allure. Our aim as Christians working and worshiping together is not to be a recognizable religious organization, but rather a spiritual organism visible to each other and to a world in need of a Savior. Claiming no name but Christ's, we shall refer to ourselves simply as Christians. Eschewing the denominational use of any church name, we will studiously avoid any designation which might tempt either ourselves or others to identify us with anything but the Lord's own blood-bought body.

While we welcome the participation of all who have named the name of Christ in obedient faith and immersion and whose lives continue to reflect God's glory, we have no desire to "rob other churches," nor to grow in number by drawing to ourselves those who are already worshiping in other congregations of God's people. True growth will come only from the spread of the gospel to the unsaved. Should our number ever reach a point at which mutual, spontaneous worship and table fellowship is thereby made difficult, it is our predetermined intention to foster the birth of a separate, wholly independent congregation. By the grace of God, it will happen over and over again!

As we therefore launch out in faith wherever this renewed commitment may lead, we seek only to be God's people...radically changed and radically restored...to the glory of Him who has called us higher.

WAS THE "LAST SUPPER" A PASSOVER MEAL?

L et me ask you a question which is pretty much out of the blue. Suppose I were to visit in your home on December 24th. Would you think me mad if I were to say: "It's great to be here for Christmas"? My guess is that you would not think it odd in the least. Even though technically Christmas would not be until the following day, everyone would understand that it's the season generally, not the exact day, to which I was referring.

At least in part, this may help to explain why most people believe that the "Last Supper" (and hence the first Lord's Supper) was a Passover meal. Luke seems to tell us plainly that "then came the day of Unleavened Bread on which the Passover lamb had to be sacrificed. Jesus sent Peter and John, saying, 'Go and make preparations for us to eat the Passover'.... So they prepared the Passover" (Luke 22:7-8; 13). And when the hour came, Jesus said to them, "I have eagerly desired to eat this Passover with you before I suffer" (Luke 22:14-15).

On the evidence of those statements alone, any jury in the world would be justified in finding that the meal in the upper room that night was in fact a Passover meal. Yet, interestingly enough, that eminently reasonable conclusion is put in doubt by a number of other equally compelling facts.

Consider, for example, the fact that the Passover meal in the first century was typically a family affair, including women and children, where the children, in particular, were told the exciting story of God's having brought Israel out of Egypt. It was a time for the older generation to the share the legacy of faith with a younger generation. But there is no mention of anything like that taking place in the upper room; nor does the meal itself have the "feel" of a first-century Passover celebration with all its prescribed ritual.

More important, when (during the meal) Jesus tells Judas, "What you are about to do, do quickly," we read that "some thought Jesus was telling him to buy what was needed for the Feast..." (John 13:27-30). If the Passover were already underway, there is not a chance that any shop in Jerusalem would have been open at that hour; nor the next day when Nicodemus presumably bought the seventy-five pounds of myrrh and aloes with which he and Joseph of Arimathea wrapped Jesus' body before laying it in the tomb.

The clincher, really, is the fact that the Sanhedrin would never have met during the Passover night to put Jesus on trial. Certainly, many procedural rules were broken during the trial, but for the Sanhedrin to have met at all for any purpose would have been a scandal.

It is primarily John who tells us the rest of the story about the events in the upper room—a story which he begins by saying, "It was *just before* the Passover Feast..." and "the *evening meal* was being served..." (13:1-2). It is also John who tells us that, on the morning after that evening meal, "to avoid ceremonial uncleanness the Jews did not enter [Pilate's] palace; they wanted to be able to eat the Passover" (John 18:28).

It is possible, of course, that John was referring to the remainder of the seven-day Feast, but if so, the previously-mentioned problems still remain. Also problematic is John's reference to the day upon which Jesus was crucified: "Now it was the day of Preparation, and the next day was to be a special Sabbath" (John 19:31). Peter and John may have "prepared the Passover," but John himself tells us that the following day (the day upon which Jesus was crucified) was recognized as the actual "day of Preparation."

The emerging picture tends to suggest that we may have misinterpreted the words with which Jesus began the Last Supper. It may well be that Jesus was not expressing his eagerness to eat the *actual* Passover, but his desire to eat the only "Passover" he could share with his disciples *before he suffered*. Which is to say, ahead of time. The day before. On the only evening left before his crucifixion.[12]

Among the many implications which might flow from this understanding of the nature of the Last Supper, perhaps the most poignant is the fact that Jesus did not *eat* a Passover lamb in the upper room, but the following day was *himself the Passover Lamb*, dying for your sins and mine at precisely the hour that the Passover lamb was to be slain!

In terms of the Lord's Supper, certainly, there is nothing to indicate that the early disciples made any connection between their memorial meals and the Passover. Even if for Jewish Christians the liberating themes of the Passover were echoed in the symbolism of the Supper, their regular, weekly observance of the Supper stood in stark contrast to the Passover's hallowed

---

12 See notes for Luke 22:8 in *The Pulpit Commentary* (Eerdmans), where the early "church fathers" accepted that the "Last Supper" was not the Passover meal.

annual observance. It is only we, I believe, who have made a connection which they would never have made.

Apart perhaps from missing out on what might be a fuller appreciation of Jesus' role as the Passover Lamb, it may make little difference if we have wrongly assumed that the Last Supper was a Passover meal—except, perhaps, for its effect on an almost doctrinaire practice in the church today. To disconnect the Lord's Supper from the Passover would be to undermine our usual insistence that only unleavened bread be used for the memorial.

Using unleavened bread, of course, could hardly be considered heretical. After all, Jesus' disciples did *prepare* for the Passover, which would have included removing leaven from the upper room. But insisting that the bread be unleavened does appear to run counter to both the kind of "loaf" which Jesus apparently broke at the Last Supper and to the nature of the memorial meals shared by the early Christians. It wasn't *crackers* they broke in their fellowship meals, but *bread*. The bread of a common meal. Nor was it the "bread of affliction" which they remembered, or the haste of the Israelites in leaving Egypt; but rather the crucified *Bread of Life* who even now nurtures and sustains our every need.[13]

In the end, it's not just that the evidence to support our use of unleavened bread is wafer thin. What's important is to understand that our ritual pinch of unleavened bread bears no resemblance whatsoever to the robust first-century practice of actually eating together in memory of our Lord. You can almost see them holding up a freshly baked loaf of bread during the meal and saying, "As this bread which we are about to eat sustains our bodies, so it is that Christ, the Bread of Life, nurtures our spirits." Or perhaps, "In the same way that grain was gathered from all over the field to be baked together in this one loaf, we too are gathered from every possible background and circumstance into one family in Christ."

Of course, while there is abundant correlative teaching about the significance of "the bread," we are not given the luxury of any similar passages providing a "backup principle" in support of leavened as opposed to unleavened bread. Therefore, especially in light of the unusually-opaque textual record regarding the Last Supper, I wouldn't press either the probable implications regarding the Passover itself or the type of bread which was broken on that occasion. Certainly, the historical argument for leavened bread appears to be unassailable, but whether you agree or disagree with the tex-

13 In their book *The Crux of the Matter* (ACU Press, 2000), Childers, Foster, and Reese observe (at pg. 38) that "from the ninth century, the common bread, leavened bread, was replaced by unleavened bread. Using regular table bread had been the practice of the churches for centuries of Christian worship from very early days."

tual analysis, don't focus there. Concentrate on the bigger picture. Surely, how we observe the memorial established by our Lord himself deserves the closest of scrutiny. In manner and in spirit, is it truly the Lord's Supper that we eat?

WHEN "PATTERN" SEEMS INCONSISTENT

A s one reads the Scriptures looking for the Lord's leading in all matters pertaining to faith and practice, it is almost impossible not to observe principles and precedents which together form the divine pattern we should follow both as individual disciples and as gathered assemblies of God's people. It is this pattern to which we have appealed in the preceding pages as the basis for restoring pure and simple first-century Christianity. However, candor calls us to admit that such a process is imprecise at best and will always leave us less than happy about what appear to be niggling gaps and frustrating inconsistencies.

For example, why (in the previous appendix) do I say, in effect, that we can "agree to disagree" about the use of leavened or unleavened bread, yet remain unremitting in my argument that the scriptural pattern calls for *a cappella* singing? Or again, if the scriptural pattern forbids our use of instruments, then why doesn't that same pattern also demand that we practice footwashing, or take the kind of vows that Paul took, or—to stretch the point—preach until midnight? Are they not all examples of first-century practice?

Indeed, why do we place so much weight on what amounts to little more than circumstantial evidence regarding the *regularity* of the disciples' meeting together on the first day of the week to break bread, when we virtually ignore what appear to be such direct commands as Paul's injunction that women not braid their hair or wear gold or expensive clothes (1 Timothy 2:9-10)? And are we to believe that all possible questions of faith and practice are of equal seriousness in God's eyes?

That last question may be the easiest of all. Jesus himself answered it for us when he referred to "the more important matters" of the Law (Matthew 23:23). Tithing was not to be compared with justice, mercy, and faithfulness. Yet if it is true that not all issues are of equal weight, still, where does that get us? Hear again the Master's words: "You should have practiced the latter, without neglecting the former." If the big stones in a wall happen to carry more weight, it is not to say that smaller stones have no importance.

I will tell you frankly that I believe the issue of musical instruments pales in comparison to the issue of baptism. I say that because of 1) the sheer volume of direct teaching about the crucial role baptism plays in the forgiveness of our sin; 2) baptism's symbolism which associates us with our Savior's death, burial, and resurrection; and 3) the many examples of first-century believers putting on their Lord through faith and immersion.

By comparison, there is no direct teaching against the use of instruments, no similar symbolism which "preaches volumes," and no solid examples in Scripture regarding the mode of singing, whether accompanied or unaccompanied. (As I mentioned in Chapter 8, I believe our traditional use of Ephesians 5:19 and Colossians 3:16 wrests the text from its immediate context.) The case for *a cappella* singing has to be pieced together from implications flowing out of new covenant principles in contrast to old covenant practices, and from secular history which confirms precisely such a change in worship usage.

To contend, as many do today, that *a cappella* singing is not, therefore, a "salvation issue" (as is baptism) is to introduce a false dichotomy. Just because core theological concerns are obviously more crucial to our everlasting salvation does not rule out the possibility that our attitude toward more peripheral matters is nevertheless important to God, and thus potentially relevant to our eternal destiny. Of course, it's always "the big IF," but IF we can legitimately determine that any practice is part of God's divine pattern, then, to that extent, it can never be considered *unimportant*, even if it might not be "more important."

Naturally, this brings us back to the question of how we are to pick and choose among the many "examples" we find in the inspired record of the first-century disciples. Which of them serve as precedent for us today, and which were merely incidental to their own time?

As strange as it may seem, it is precisely the *lack* of example that leads us most directly to *a cappella* singing. Considering that scriptural principles derived from a continuation of old and new covenant worship practices give us our greatest assurance of divine pattern (e.g., prayer, sacrifice, male spiritual leadership, repentance, faith, and obedience), where there is an abrupt break between the two covenants, yellow caution lights immediately start flashing. Take, for example, animal sacrifices, and priests, and ceremonial temple observances. With their cessation, a shift in divine pattern for

Christian worship was obvious. In like fashion, when we see that the use of instruments in conjunction with temple worship was not carried over into first-century Christian worship, we are reminded that whenever pattern for the former covenant is not observed under the second, there is every reason to believe that God no longer calls us to such a practice.

While this is only a superficial look at a single contemporary issue, the flip-side of this line of reasoning helps us immeasurably in sorting through the myriad of examples which have potential impact on the scriptural pattern we are to follow. The greater the coherence between a well-delineated biblical principle and any given example of first-century Christian practice (such as baptism and the Lord's Supper), the greater our assurance that such a practice was more than merely cultural or coincidental. Unfortunately, in less clear cases, this process of analysis is far more challenging than any simple rule of interpretation might accommodate...and certainly more difficult to explain than we have space available in this brief appendix.

For those who wish to pursue this line of inquiry further, I call your attention to Chapters 11-13 in my earlier book, *The Cultural Church* (21st Century Christian). In those chapters, I've attempted to tackle head-on the problem of pattern inconsistency and suggested ways in which we can best minimize the difficulties.

Let me say, finally, that some of my critics for whom I have the greatest respect have challenged what they believe to be a lack of core theology in the present book. While I appreciate their concern that the cross of Jesus is at the heart and soul of biblical interpretation, I am at a loss to see how a more "theologically-based" hermeneutic can avoid the problem of inconsistency any more than a "pattern-based" hermeneutic. (In fact, I don't readily acknowledge a difference between the two, since divine pattern—if we've got it right—is always good theology.)

While the cross vividly reminds us about that which is central, it doesn't really tell us anything more than that everything else is obviously more peripheral. But are we to understand, therefore, that only baptism and the Lord's Supper are "salvation issues" because of their close association with the cross? Even supposing that were the case, just exactly *what* about the Lord's Supper is a matter of salvation? The fact that we observe it? Or that we observe it regularly? Or that we limit our observance to the Lord's Day as opposed to other days of the week? How does core theology help us to answer those thorny questions and so many more on a variety of other issues?

Indeed, how can core theology provide the definitive answers to the very questions that are put to me: What are the consequences when we disagree about the intended implications of a given first-century practice, especially in those instances where there is scant textual foundation available? Is there never a time when such issues are ultimately matters of judgment? What are the eternal consequences if we get one or more of those "close calls" wrong?

What I find most fascinating of all is that those who have lamented the absence in this book of what they would consider to be a robust "theological approach" have agreed with me time and again about what the early disciples actually practiced, and about the importance of our following in their footsteps. What does it say, then, that, regardless of the particular approach we have taken, we have ended up virtually in the same place? What I believe it confirms in a most wonderful way is that, despite all our unanswered questions and the frustrations we feel in the face of our own inconsistencies, God still speaks to us today with such clarity that it is difficult indeed to miss his leading.

As is always the case, surely the greater difficulty is not so much in the knowing, but in the doing.

PART III

RADICAL ROUNDTABLE

As iron sharpens iron, so one man sharpens another.

PROVERBS 27:17

DISSENTING OPINIONS

The first to present his case seems right,
till another comes forward and questions him.

PROVERBS 18:17

A t the heart of Restoration thinking is an eager openness to searching for truth. In that spirit, I would like to share with you some of the comments and observations which I have received both from my initial lectures on radical restoration and from the team of reviewers who read the manuscript prior to publication. These selections represent a wide spectrum of thought, and may well mirror some of your own reactions both positive and negative. Those who contributed most were often those who disagreed the strongest. While I was prompted by their thoughtful criticisms to make a number of changes, there remain significant differences, some of which are reflected in the following views. (To encourage the free exchange of ideas, I have omitted all names and edited where necessary to preserve anonymity.)

"**As you compare the first-century church** with churches of Christ today, it seems to me you are unfair to this century's churches of Christ. As you look at the first-century church, you look at the *perfect ideal* found in apostolic teaching and compare it with our *imperfect practice* of the ideal. Is it possible that the first-century practice of the Lord's Supper in Jerusalem (and especially at Corinth and elsewhere) might have been as defective as our stereotyped prayers, etc.?"

"Regarding the Lord's Supper being part of a larger meal, I would say the following. I have for a long time taught that it was instituted by Christ as a part of a larger meal. I also believe that the Corinthians partook of it as a part of a larger fellowship meal before Paul wrote 1 Corinthians 11. However—and here is our big difference on this point—I believe Paul separated it once for all from the larger meal there in 1 Corinthians 11."

"While I agree that there were many 'house churches' in the first century, I don't think that is the total New Testament picture. Especially at Jerusalem, I do not believe one can establish the 'small house churches' theory in the very first church. There are several passages that seem to indicate one large congregation: Luke 24:53; Acts 2:46; Acts 3:11; and Acts 5:12."

"The question comes down to 'What is to be restored?' We all agree on the 'eternal moral principles.' Name one person among the whole restoration movement who does not agree on these matters. It is when we move beyond those that we hit the snag in the restoration movement that has essentially derailed the movement. Perhaps my objection to this approach comes down to pragmatics, but 200 years of trying to unite on a consensus of the details of the form have led me to opt for the other. 'In matters of faith (eternal spiritual and moral principles): unity; in matters of opinion (anything beyond those moral principles): liberty; in all things love.' 'For the kingdom of God is not eating and drinking, but righteousness, peace and joy in the Holy Spirit' (Romans 14:17). And those who insisted on enforcing their own 'patternist details' on other Christians were to be avoided (16:17). Paul urged that troubled Christian body in

Rome (troubled over this very question) to 'make every effort to do what leads to peace and to mutual edification' (14:19). A good study of Romans 14 and 15 will bring great resolution to this sticky problem. As a 'patternist,' I highly recommend it to other 'patternists.'"

"During the great Restoration of Hezekiah (2 Chronicles 30), three deviations from the 'pattern' of the Passover were instigated by Hezekiah and endorsed by God. They observed the feast in the second month, not the first as prescribed (vs. 2). They ate the Passover in spite of not having purified themselves according to the pattern (vs 18-20). And they kept the feast an additional week (vs. 23). In all of this, form bowed to function, and God blessed their innovations. Any balanced treatment of form and function should take this example into consideration."

"You say that the first-century church provides us 'an imperfectly-modeled model of perfection.' I think this is naive and Pollyannaish. The fact is, there was no ideal church in the first century, nor has there ever been one since. There was no church 'before the onslaught of ruinous innovations and apostasies.' The ruinous innovations existed in the hearts of the people even before they shortly surfaced in the assemblies of the saints. Every church in the first century was an imperfect attempt to replicate the perfect original—Jesus Christ. I used to think that the *composite* of all the apostolic corrective writings would be sufficient to provide us the details of the perfect church. The problem is that people have never been able perfectly to agree on what that is. (And they won't know even after reading *Radical Restoration*.) Jesus is the original we are to pattern ourselves after, then cut some slack for our brothers who read the details in a different way. Otherwise, we'll always be divided."

"**At the same time your raise the bar** back to its first-century level in regard to the Lord's Supper, you express doubt and apprehension regarding the massive logistical overhaul required should we actually restore the first-century form. It comes across as though you are settling for first-century function (i.e., renewal of spirit, etc.). With this I agree, but it compromises, somewhat, your basic thesis. Then, we're back to square one: Who is to decide just which of the forms we are to restore? What present conditions are already so set in concrete (size of congregations, etc.) that we will have to content ourselves with function? Then we are back to subjective judgments; opinions as to when an example is binding, etc. Neither you nor I nor your book will be the standard by which other people judge what is and what is not within the realm of possible restoration. Because of this, I think your book will be an unsettling source of irritation and frustration and discouragement since many of the scores of correctives you suggest are presently outside the realm of possibility."

"**Your generalization regarding youth ministries** may have been shaped by your own experiences with some particular youth ministries. In my experience, some of the finest, most Christ-centered, evangelistic ministries are those of our youth. You paint with too broad a brush."

"**To state that 'Our aim as Christians** working and worshiping together is not to be a recognizable religious organization...' ignores the fact that the net result of implementing the distinguishing patterns recommended in this book will in fact set us apart as a 'recognizable religious organization' rather than a 'spiritual organism visible to us and to a world in need of a Savior.'"

"**I think you go too far** in flatly declaring that we are a denomination. I think your case would be better served if you were to argue that we have adopted too many of the trappings of the denominations, or that we are perilously close to becoming a denomination. One definition of a denomination that I think is fairly good is: 'A group of Christians larger than all the Christians in one locality, but smaller than all the Christians in the world.' Few among us would agree that we fit that description."

"**I think that the house churches** were more likely exceptions rather than the common practice in New Testament times. In fact, I am not sure but what the references are not to the 'called out ones' in the households."

"**I will have to study it further,** but I think that 1 Corinthians 11 describes the degeneration of the Lord's Supper into the common meal, not the opposite. Further, it seems to me that this assembly, wherever it was, was not as informal as you have described it. In fact, it appears to have been the case that a rather structured assembly had degenerated into a bit of confusion (1 Corinthians 12-14)."

"**I seem to sense that you have concluded** that all of 'us' have become part of a denomination. I do not think so. I accept David Lipscomb's dictum that 'someone else's sectarianism does not make me a sectarian.' In much too brief shorthand, I still believe that obeying the gospel makes you a Christian, and that to be a member of a denomination you have to do something else. I realize some of the people I meet with think and talk denominationally about themselves, even while claiming not to be one. However, if someone steadfastly refuses to use 'Church of Christ' with exclusive-name, adjectival significance; and refuses to accept the views of any preacher or editor, or 'what faithful brethren have always believed' as definitive for his or her faith and practice; or whenever he or she speaks of 'the Lord's church' or 'churches of Christ' they consciously include all who have obeyed the gospel, even if they don't know who they are; and several other *et ceteras;* then I think such folks remain truly undenominational."

"Isn't there the distinct possibility that what we read of the church in the New Testament was light years away from what Jesus came to establish (at least in visible practice)? Are we making a major mistake by going back to the New Testament church of the first century with the assumption that among the rubble there is camouflaged the real pattern God wants us to follow? The early church could have started out wrong. Certainly Corinth is a case in point. We need to be getting back to the teachings of Jesus and maybe (just maybe) stay away from the flawed people, the church, as our starting point."

"I find it interesting that you can so easily dismiss *New Testament practices which we do not currently practice as merely cultural and optional,* while practices we have adopted in our tradition are viewed as sacrosanct. On what basis? What discriminates? Why can you upbraid someone for not copying New Testament practices regarding instruments when *you* do not follow practices like footwashing, hair cutting, vow-taking, etc.?"

"Are we sure that the first-century church wouldn't use a building if they had one? Will restoring the bread recipe improve our worship, faith, Christian service or fellowship?"

"I have trouble wrapping my mind around the idea that there is not a place for some of our more gifted pulpit ministers to preach to a large number of people. I know they are blessing many people by being able to preach every week. They are supported so that they can pour themselves into preaching, and many Christians are so thankful that they preach the Word to them at the weekly assembly. It just seems odd to me to think that they would have to quit doing that."

"Theory is always interesting, application can be humorous...and, as the old saying goes, 'The Devil is in the details.'"

"I do meet in 'small groups' whenever possible throughout the week for more 'in-depth' discussion and fellowship. But on the first day of every week, I want as many of us as possible to meet together. When that happens, diversity is a 'given,' and only God could make us 'one accord'...and that is a 'wonder' indeed."

"I have found that when things get 'too deep' in theory, I have to return to Flatland. Even in the precise science of math, where (in base 10) 2 + 2 = 4, a circle exists. Right in the middle of the formula (or pattern) for determining the circumference of this defined object is 'pi,' an irrational, undeterminable number! So, when trying to know how to please God, I will deal with what I *can know*."

"You propose a radical change in the way we conduct our assemblies. Fine, but a small group (30) meeting as a house church can be as dissatisfied with their circumstances and fail in their attempt to be uplifted by the assembly as much as with a large church."

"It seems to me that your suggestions are good, but they are attacking a spiritual problem in a physical way. I believe we need to change the hearts and minds of people, and I believe that we can have that close fellowship and family relationship even in large congregations. There is no doubt that they had house-churches in the early church, but was that more of necessity, and culture, and lack of funds, and opportunity to build other places? We will never know."

"**I am fearful of, and hate,** divisions in Christ's body, and to some extent I believe your emphasis on house-churches may cause just that."

"**I would suggest that you not** emphasize too greatly the minimalist approach to functioning as the church, since that information was influenced more by cultural context than inspired direction."

"**Restoration has focused on the church** as the function, whereas the Bible focuses on being holy as God is holy."

"**Your pattern theology** comes naturally, of course. Thinking theologically—that is, out of the core—has not been taught much in the Restoration Movement. But its absence is telling. For example, there is little mention of the cross in this book. Do all doctrines line up like dominoes? Are some more central than others? How does theology help us discern what is important? What do we do when there is scant evidence in Scripture? Do we all have to agree on each issue? That is why theology precedes the kind of pattern arguments you are making."

"**There is much to commend.** I have argued much of this for years. I guess my greatest concern is how you got there. Pattern theology is the impulse, but it's really hard to be consistent. I agree with your views on unleavened bread (it wasn't used for 1000 years), but there is not a hint one why this is a less important issue than instrumental music, or why commands like women not braiding their hair are unimportant."

"I agree with much of what you say about youth ministries. But what if 'youth ministers' were trained not so much to minister to youth but to equip and encourage parents and the older members to teach and influence the teens? What if someone were calling on teens to love and listen to the older Christians. That is the model many of us are working with."

"One of the issues about house churches is the issue of control. What happens, for example, when a house church studies its way into a Marcionite heresy or reads all of the books by Jim Cymbala and begins praying for a Holy Spirit revival in that house church? Under the present system, what keeps doctrinal deviation from happening is that 'the institution' of the church acts as a conservative check on progressive tendencies."

"The testimony of the New Testament is that the church had all kinds of problems with unity. How does one ensure unity of the body if we return to house churches? Is it imposed by the elders of the city? By some powerful person, like Paul, who threatens a congregation with a demonstration of God's real power when he comes to visit them next?"

"I have been amazed at my response to letters received from churches in foreign countries. They want to build a building because it gives their group some legitimacy in the community. I suspect this has more to do with why we build buildings than having it simply as a vestige of religious evolution. The building not only gives us a place to meet, to plan and to serve, but hopefully stands as a symbol of our permanent commitment to that community."

"Considering the economic challenges facing today's families, should we not admit that culture places limitations of time and effort on what we can expect from everyone, and that preachers and youth ministers may be important because of the cultural demands placed on our families?"

"LaGard, you could not stand three months in the church you have described. The first time some blissed-out college student stood to offer a word of encouragement, beginning every sentence with 'Like' and trying to lead the congregation in 'Jesus, you're my friend, dude!' (with 47 repeats of the chorus), you'd explode."

CONCURRING OPINIONS

And they cried, "Amen, Hallelujah!"

PURLOINED FROM REVELATION 19:4

I'm relieved to say that none of the "dissenting opinions" were wholly negative. (For that matter, even those whose reactions were mostly positive invariably disagreed at points along the way.) The following observations indicate the ideas which seem to have struck the deepest chord with those who have already had an opportunity to think about the concept of radical restoration.

eing with the vast majority of your
it were not so. Your conclusions
roles we preachers routinely fill,
ers and 'directors of the board' in
e gainsaid. I thrilled at your posi-

l to find that I agree with your
alized church, that I am troubled
it minister,' and that I think the
r teaching our youth on the par-
adding a short section on where
e, and suggest that universities

begin offering a specialization in the Bible departments that would equip young men to be evangelists." [Signed: _____, Pulpit Minister, Evangelist Wannabe.]

"**Your view of form versus function** is right on target. I wish you would write an article on this to one of our journals. It is a serious mistake by those who ridicule notions of 'pattern' and clamor for measuring restoration on the basis of Christ being reproduced in the second incarnation, and not seeing that divine- ly appointed forms were chosen to produce that very thing."

"**Your comments on the Lord's Supper** are convicting. I have been pleading for the Supper to be made the focal point of our assemblies, but I had not really scraped off all the abuse and dumbing down we have done to the Supper. Boy! I hope this gets wide review."

"**I fear** _____ with you the possible loss of our rich singing her- itage due to inn___ ___ shall__vations that take away our ability to r__ music; plus, songs so ___ ___ to rob us of the rich the__ the music of days past."

"**I agree wholeheartedly** _ purpose of the assembly. The ass__ evangelism of the lost, but for edi__

"**I have had many conve**r__ church leaders about house chu__ one of the worst things to happ__ version' of Constantine which p__ front of Roman life. Moving f__ nant culture robbed Christiani__ Meeting in auditoriums/sanct__ one of the consequences of th__

CONCURRING OPINIONS

And they cried, "Amen, Hallelujah!"

PURLOINED FROM REVELATION 19:4

I'm relieved to say that none of the "dissenting opinions" were wholly negative. (For that matter, even those whose reactions were mostly positive invariably disagreed at points along the way.) The following observations indicate the ideas which seem to have struck the deepest chord with those who have already had an opportunity to think about the concept of radical restoration.

"I found myself agreeing with the vast majority of your work, and I would to God it were not so. Your conclusions regarding the unscriptural roles we preachers routinely fill, along with the youth ministers and 'directors of the board' in shepherds' clothing, cannot be gainsaid. I thrilled at your position on 'form vs. function.'"

"You may be surprised to find that I agree with your thesis that we are an institutionalized church, that I am troubled by the role I now fill as a 'pulpit minister,' and that I think the Bible places the responsibility for teaching our youth on the parents. I wish you would consider adding a short section on where you think we should go from here, and suggest that universities begin offering a specialization in the Bible departments that would equip young men to be evangelists." [Signed: _____, Pulpit Minister, Evangelist Wannabe.]

"Your view of form versus function is right on target. I wish you would write an article on this to one of our journals. It is a serious mistake by those who ridicule notions of 'pattern' and clamor for measuring restoration on the basis of Christ being reproduced in the second incarnation, and not seeing that divine-ly appointed forms were chosen to produce that very thing."

"Your comments on the Lord's Supper are convicting. I have been pleading for the Supper to be made the focal point of our assemblies, but I had not really scraped off all the abuse and dumbing down we have done to the Supper. Boy! I hope this gets wide review."

"I fear with you the possible loss of our rich singing her-itage due to innovations that take away our ability to read music; plus, songs so shallow as to rob us of the rich theology of the music of days past."

"I agree wholeheartedly with your reflections on the purpose of the assembly. The assembly was not designed for evangelism of the lost, but for edification of the saved."

"I have had many conversations for several years with church leaders about house churches (and cell groups). I think one of the worst things to happen to Christianity was the 'con-version' of Constantine which propelled the church to the fore-front of Roman life. Moving from counterculture to predomi-nant culture robbed Christianity of its essence, in many ways. Meeting in auditoriums/sanctuaries rather than homes is only one of the consequences of that. I think one of the advantages of

America becoming post-Christian is that it will provide an opportunity for the church here to become counter-cultural again. This should have several positive consequences.

"I think we must move to a view of church that is less associated with big, established churches in the suburbs, and more with neighborhood house churches. These are much closer to the biblical model, much more attuned to the needs of Christians, much more flexible in terms of adjusting to changing needs of the community, and allow for the kind of church discipline and accountability that God expects. What we need is a movement of church plantings of radically independent churches aggressively living and spreading the Gospel in every neighborhood. Your advocacy of such will further the dialogue considerably, and I appreciate that."

"**I love your advice:** 'Don't teach them to preach.' AMEN! Teach them to share their study."

"**The more I think about it,** the more I believe that nothing short of a book this direct can possibly create momentum for change."

"**To the biblically-illiterate church goer,** your book will probably read like a foreign language, but this is why I am happy that you used so much scripture, and not *proof-text* but *principle* scripture. It all holds together."

"**I am among those you described as:** 'Others might find that at least some of our discussion has resonated with their own private musings over the years, but remain unconvinced by other parts of the package.' Those things that 'correspond' to my 'musings': Our elders are more likely to think and act as administrators rather than pastors/shepherds; biblical shepherds will feed the flock not just hire others to do it; the preacher sometimes is today (but shouldn't be) the real leader of the congregation; we have elevated style in preaching over substance; we need to develop more men in our congregations who can teach/preach (call it 'mutual ministry' if you wish); parents are abdicating responsibility in the home and leaving that responsibility to the church and especially to youth workers. But at least many of us are not countenancing these changes from the biblical pattern. You seem to think most brethren are accepting these changes rather than trying to correct them. Some of us are not accepting them."

"**Your remarks about the clergy/laity** are right on the mark. So are the ones about being immersed in a cult of youth. I have warned about both these things. And while we deny having a hierarchical arrangement like the Catholics, our spheres of influence are not drastically different; the pressure is just more subtly applied. When we get past local autonomy and personal conscience, we are headed for something other than New Testament Christianity."

"**Thank you for allowing me** to read the manuscript. I believe the book has a place. It may not initiate the radical restoration you would like to see (in fact I doubt that it will), but it will serve to notify all of us that we need to make an introspective examination of not only who we are, but where we are going."

"**I appreciate that the book** was, as you indicated, difficult and disturbing to write. In somewhat the same sense, it was difficult and disturbing to read. But I am glad I read it. It certainly made me think about a lot of things, and I know that is always one of your goals. It is a shame that we have so many non-thinkers among us who will beat you over the head with a sentence or two and ignore the thrust of what you have said."

"**I think you are right** about the big buildings we build, the auditorium arrangement with pews and pulpits, and the ritualistic order of worship style we have adopted. They are major culprits in some of the significant ways our assemblies are different from those of the first century church."

"You may want to mention John Wesley's approach of gathering people in small groups. It was a very effective method."

"I've been attending a home church for some time now. Our Sunday worship normally lasts about three hours, and includes confession of sin, much edification, and encouragement through prayer, reading of the word, and singing, in addition to celebrating the Lord's Supper."

"As a preacher, I was 'evangelistically frustrated' for many of the reasons you brought out ('one-man band' syndrome). Expectations were so high for me and so low for the pew."

"As for youth ministries (as they are often done), I agree that there are some real problems there. The hermeneutical and worship style differences are fed to the youth group and it should surprise no one that they will reject 'older' church worship and hermeneutics."

"I think I'm in TOTAL agreement with your understanding of the role of elders; and you, Dr. Laura, and I agree about the role of parents to children."

"Although I truly do not want a persecution to be brought on the church, I am afraid radical change will not happen without it. We are comfortable and we are complacent. Sometimes I think I'm just crazy because the majority of people don't see why we need to change. I pray the Lord will show me the answer, because eternity is too long a time to play around with. When I get tired and fainthearted, I just keep going over and over in my mind that I know the present checklist denominational system we have cannot be what the Lord wants."

"If pulpit ministers begin to devote their time to community evangelism, many members will move to another church. Brethren are going to have their 'pastor.' The 'pastor system' has its roots in 1 Samuel 8."

"I have often wondered if 'house assemblies' would not give us a clearer picture and deeper understanding of the real nature of the community of the saved (the church). Not an organization, complete with organizational trappings...but a living, breathing organism of close family members devoted to the Lord, to lost souls, and to each other. What a beautiful picture!"

"The issues are provocative. They should at least be considered. I pray God will stir up our churches. Only He has the power to restore us, but we have to surrender to Him."

"I know that this work is going to make a difference. No honest person can deny the clear facts and logic of much of what you have said—things many have seen and been thinking for years. And these are people who love 'the church' and love the Lord and the Scriptures. They are things not 'hard to understand' but hard to swallow and hard to think of in light of all the Herculean efforts of love and patience and courage it will take to go down this radical restoration road."

If you would like to share your own dissenting and concurring opinions, you may do so at:

LaGard@compuserve.com

DISCUSSION QUESTIONS

CHAPTER 1—WHEN FLATLAND IS THE HEARTLAND

1. Have you read Edwin Abbott's *Flatland*? If so, what spiritual parallels, if any, came to mind?
2. In what ways are you challenged by *Flatland's* theme-line: "No, not Northward; upward?"
3. In addition to the account of Nicodemus in John 3, what biblical texts can you think of that echo *Flatland's* theme-line in showing the way to a higher dimension?
4. Do you think that we in the church are spiritual Flatlanders? If so, in what way?
5. In your opinion, are the "Churches of Christ" today a denomination? Would outsiders think we were? Does it matter what they think about us?
6. Would it trouble *you* to think that we were a denomination?
7. Are you bothered by any of the ways in which we use the name "Church of Christ"?
8. Do you think first-century disciples would recognize the way we function as a church today?
9. Does it matter if we express our faith and practice in significantly different ways from the primitive church?
10. For you, personally, how strong is the gravitational pull of your association with the "Churches of Christ"?

CHAPTER 2—"RADICAL" SOUNDS TERRIBLY RADICAL!

1. What experiences of any kind have you had with anything like "radical pruning?"
2. Can you think of examples other than those already given where God employed "radical pruning?"
3. Would you agree to any extent with the statement that the "Churches of Christ" are "fundamentally flawed?"
4. What consequences might there be if, at some deep level, we thought of ourselves more as "Restorationists" than as Christians?
5. What is the difference between the church as an *organism* and the church as an *organization*?
6. Do you see a distinction between thinking of the church as *"we"* and thinking of the church as *"it"*?
7. What do you perceive to be the differences between "exciting innovations" and radical restoration?
8. In what way is personal repentance a parable for radical restoration of the church?
9. Can the church ever be radically restored as long as we think of it apart from a radically-changed people of God?
10. If Jesus walked among us today, do you think he would like what he sees in the "Churches of Christ"? If he were to "cleanse our temple," what might be his most likely targets?

CHAPTER 3—NEITHER CATHOLIC NOR PROTESTANT?

1. Have you ever heard the statement that "We are neither Catholic nor Protestant?" If so, do you agree?
2. Why do you think anyone would insist on making such a statement?
3. How important was the Reformation to our own faith?

4. Is there a difference between being a "reformer" and a "restorationist?" If so, do they have anything in common?

5. What was the unique plea of the Restoration Movement?

6. If Martin Luther were alive today, what do you guess he would think about the "Churches of Christ"?

7. If asked, could you trace your "family tree" of faith over many centuries? Does having such a family tree matter to you?

8. What, if anything, have we inherited from Catholicism?

9. What, if anything, have we inherited from Protestantism?

10. If there is a cycle of "departure, reform, and restoration," where are we in the cycle?

Chapter 4—RESTORATION? THE VERY IDEA!

1. How important to you is history in general, and the history of the church in particular?

2. What is the connection, if any, between history, precedent, and authority?

3. In general, with which of the two "alliances" (Historical or Anti-historical) do you most readily identify?

4. To what extent do you think your age influences your view of precedent and authority?

5. Do you believe there is a "pattern principle" in Scripture? If so, what is it?

6. Assuming we have no divine pattern to follow, to what source of authority might we appeal for what we do religiously? Or does it even matter whether we have authority?

7. Have we concentrated more on the pattern for church organization and ritual than on Christ being our pattern for righteous living? If so, is it wrong to seek a pattern for what we should do when we assemble together as God's people?

8. Does abuse of God-given forms mean that the forms themselves are flawed? How do we know which forms are "God-given" for all times and cultures?

9. Can we agree that function is more important than form, while still maintaining the importance of form?

10. Can an overemphasis on achieving the right forms (even radical restoration) serve to diminish our focus on the functions intended to be cultivated through those correct forms?

Chapter 5—A First-Century Model of Perfection

1. Does the fact that the early church was flawed by human sin preclude viewing the ideal which it represents as the divine model for how we should function as God's people?

2. Are people today drawn to Christ in the same way as in the first century?

3. What difference does it make, if any, that the church in the 21st century is composed largely of people who "grew up in the church" as compared with first-generation Christians?

4. Is there a way to heighten our sense of calling and predestination without taking a Calvinist view that we ultimately have no choice in our salvation?

5. How different might we be as a people of God if we focused more on being God's elect?

6. If we are called to be a holy people, what explains why our lifestyles are often hardly indistinguishable from an unholy world? Or do you even agree with the assumption that one would be hard-pressed to distinguish between us and our morally-good, but unbelieving neighbors?

7. Do we practice *radical* piety in terms of prayer, fasting, benevolence, and hospitality?

8. As we think about our most intimate associations—in particular, our families—can we truly say that we find significant motivation because of our relationship with Christ? If so, what explains the high degree of divorce within the body of Christ?

9. To what extent do you really believe in the world of the supernatural, and what difference does your view of that dimension affect who you are?

10. Does the possibility of Christ's Coming during our lifetime play any role in your faith life? Does the inevitability of your own death have any impact on your thinking?

Chapter 6—THE CHURCH OF...THE SPIRIT!

1. Is it possible that, because we've satisfied ourselves that we have many of the details right about the early church, we've actually missed the heart and soul of what it was all about?

2. What, if any, is the difference between the "tongues" on Pentecost and the kind of "speaking in tongues" done, for example, in the church at Corinth?

3. What is the nature of the "gift of the Holy Spirit" promised to those who were immersed on Pentecost, and is that different from the "gifts of the Spirit?"

4. Did every baptized believer in the primitive church receive one of the spiritual gifts, such as tongues, healing, prophecy, or interpretation?

5. What role did the laying on of hands play in the use of spiritual gifts?

6. To what extent were the spiritual gifts associated with the inaugural age of the apostles?

7. In what way does the Holy Spirit work, or not work, among us today? Have you ever felt that there was some manifestation of the Spirit in your own life?

8. In what way were spiritual gifts a motivating force in the early church?

9. Can the Lord's church today ever function in quite the same way as the early church in the absence of first-century spiritual gifts? If not, are there other compensating factors?

10. Is it possible that, because of our minimalist view of the role of the Holy Spirit, we could actually quench the power of the Spirit, either individually or as the church?

CHAPTER 7—IN AN UNWORTHY MANNER

1. Does our celebration of the Lord's Supper resemble the way the early church would have observed it? If not, what are the differences?

2. What do we know about the "love feasts" of the early church?

3. In what ways did the early Christians "break bread" together?

4. What problem was Paul specifically addressing in 1 Corinthians 11:17-34? Was it that the Corinthian disciples were eating together as a church when they had their own houses to eat in, or eating the memorial meal together in a manner unbefitting Christian brothers and sisters?

5. What, if any, is the difference between the bread and wine being *emblems* and the bread and wine being *symbolic*?

6. Is the focus of the memorial meal to be directed vertically towards God or horizontally towards each other, or somehow both?

7. Does it matter whether the Supper is observed in a solemn, almost funeral-like manner, or as a festive meal of thanksgiving? Is there some way it could be both?

8. How would you feel about observing Christ's memorial as part of a fellowship meal? Could it be done without being abused? Would it bring greater meaning to the occasion?

9. Are there any ways in which our observance of the Lord's Supper could be enhanced short of having a first-century fellowship meal?

10. How would our times of gathered worship be different if we focused on the Supper rather than on the sermon?

CHAPTER 8—AT HOME WITH WORSHIP

1. What do you think we should make of the apparent practice of the early church in meeting for worship in private homes? Was it intentional, or simply a matter of necessity because of persecution or perhaps economic reasons?

2. In the absence of any clear historical rationale, what might you speculate to be the reason purpose-built church buildings were constructed from the third century onwards?

3. Do you think it's possible that the mode and style of worship might have changed with the move from private homes to church buildings?

4. What relationship might there be between meeting in private homes and participating in a weekly memorial meal?

5. Comparing "large" congregations and "small" ones, what are the relative advantages and disadvantages?

6. Do you see any divine hand behind the move from temple, to synagogue, to house churches?

7. What are the relative merits of attempting to evangelize "from house to house" as compared with evangelizing in church buildings?

8. House church or no house church, what is most likely to be the result of *intentionally* meeting as a small group rather than as a much larger congregation?

9. What unique problems might loom for small group fellowships?

10. If intimacy, mutual participation, and spontaneous informality are worthy goals, how could those things best be achieved in your present congregation?

CHAPTER 9—WHEN SHEPHERDS ARE SHEEPISH

1. In terms of elders, do you think there is something unique about the image of a "shepherd" even for urban societies which don't readily relate to shepherds and sheep?
2. With which concept—*organization* or *organism*—should God's shepherds more naturally be associated?
3. What lessons are to be learned from the long history of Israel's elders?
4. Do we have scriptural precedent for elders to be shepherds over a number of "mini-flocks" (small group fellowships) constituting a single, larger congregation? Or for elders in a number of house churches to also constitute the elders for a given town or area?
5. Have we focused too much on the technical *qualifications* for elders and not enough on their *qualities*? And what qualities ought they to have?
6. Why do you think we have such an "elder shortage" these days?
7. How would the church be different today if elders assumed primary responsibility for teaching and preaching to the flock among them?
8. Is there anything wrong with an elder system that is more like a board of directors than a group of teaching pastors?
9. In what way should elders be "gatekeepers" like their ancient Jewish ancestors?
10. What should we learn about elders when we think of Christ being the Good Shepherd?

CHAPTER 10—PULPIT MINISTERS: PATENT PENDING

1. In what way, if any, does the typical role of the pulpit preacher reflect a corporate business approach to church leadership?

2. Was there any role in the early church which resembled today's pulpit ministers—complete with all the responsibilities of a "one-man band?"

3. Whose voice is most often heard when the flock is being led spiritually: the elders' or the preacher's?

4. What are the advantages and disadvantages of having pulpit ministers who have academic degrees in religious studies?

5. What message is being signaled when we demand that pulpit ministers be skilled communicators?

6. In what way has the demand for more professional pulpit ministers led to an undeclared clergy system? Or do you believe we have no such system?

7. What is the difference, if any, between a "pulpit minister" and an "evangelist?"

8. What would be the advantages and disadvantages if preachers left the pulpit and began teaching the gospel from house to house and in public places?

9. How would the departure of pulpit ministers contribute to more of a mutual ministry of all the men? What would likely be the results of fostering a strong mutual ministry?

10. What would it take for all of us to have a greater sense of being evangelists in the spread of the gospel?

CHAPTER 11—A YOUTH-DRIVEN CHURCH

1. What fundamental hierarchy is the subject of *King Lear*, and how does "putting the cart before the horse" relate to it?

2. In what ways, if at all, have we "put the cart before the horse" in terms of the hierarchy of age in the church today?

3. What should the "olders" uniquely possess that those who are younger don't have?

4. What are the comparative advantages and disadvantages of having young people led by youth ministers who are only slightly older than their charges?

5. Do you agree that the current "worship wars" reflect generational differences? Why or why not?

6. In your own experience, have you sensed a literal separation of the young people from the rest of the congregation? If so, to what extent and to what effect?

7. What grade would you give today's young people for biblical knowledge and spiritual depth? For good or for ill, to what extent do you think their biblical and spiritual awareness has been influenced by a youth ministry program?

8. Would you agree or disagree with the proposition that today's church is a youth-driven church?

9. Do you think youth ministries are a desirable *supplement to*, or a questionable *substitute for*, parental guidance of their children?

10 If you are a parent, how much time do you devote to your children's spiritual growth? How does that time compare with the amount of time which is devoted to extra-curricular activities?

Chapter 12—Let's Get Practical

1. Assuming we all began meeting in small group fellowships without the usual sign-posted buildings and Yellow Pages ads, would you feel a loss of identity; or would you, perhaps, have a greater sense of identity?

2. What would it take for us to stop using the name "Church of Christ" in a denominational sense? Or do you believe that we don't, in fact, use the name denominationally?

3. Do you think we could ever function primarily in terms of special contributions rather than the perfunctory contributions we make as part of our worship ritual?

4. Is there an optimum size for a congregation, or is its size immaterial?

5. If you have ever worshiped in a fairly small congregation, did you experience any unique problems? Were there any distinct advantages?

6. How comfortable do you think you would be meeting with a small group fellowship?

7. Do you think it is possible for a number of disciples to separate themselves apart and begin new small group fellowships without causing rancor and division? Looking from all sides (those who leave and those who stay), how could that best be done?

8. What would you say to an elder or a pulpit minister who feels compelled to make a significant change in his traditional role, when there appears to be opposition to that decision?

9. If every "larger" congregation were to down-size into vibrant small group fellowships, what would you miss most? What do you think you might appreciate most?

10. What practical questions do *you* have about implementing radical restoration?

CHAPTER 13—RADICAL TO THE CORE

1. What is your personal reaction to the paradigm shifts listed at the beginning of the chapter? Are you concerned? Relieved? Neutral?

2. Do you think that any of those shifts have had any effect on your life, one way or the other?

3. As you reflect on the congregations of which you have been a part, do you think the ways in which they functioned have had any influence in shaping the kind of person you are?

4. How would you describe yourself in terms of your present congregation: Active, or passive? Involved or detached? Does this affect your personal life?

5. Do you think that being involved in an intimate, mutually-participatory small group fellowship would make you a *better* or *worse* Christian?

6. What might Jesus think of his disciples today? Do you think he would care particularly about how we function as a church, or only how we live as individuals?

7. What does Jesus' own life suggest about how we ought to function together as God's people?

8. (Perhaps more for personal reflection than discussion...) what radical changes do you most need to make in your own life? Do you think how we function as a body of believers might make any difference in your being able to make those changes?

9. Short of being totally radical, can you think of ways in which we might function better as a church within our current parameters?

10. What effect do you think real persecution would have on our being "radical to the core?"

Other Books By F. LaGard Smith

The Narrated Bible

The Daily Bible

Baptism—The Believer's Wedding Ceremony

Male Spiritual Leadership

The Cultural Church

Meeting God In Quiet Places

Who Is My Brother?